THE OTHER SIDE

THE OTHER SIDE

Perspectives on Deviance

Edited by

HOWARD S. BECKER

THE FREE PRESS
A DIVISION OF MACMILLAN PUBLISHING CO., INC.
New York

COLLIER MACMILLAN PUBLISHERS
London

THE FREE PRESS
A DIVISION OF MACMILLAN PUBLISHING CO., INC.
866 Third Avenue, New York, New York   10022

Collier-Macmillan Canada, Ltd., Toronto, Ontario

Library of Congress Catalog Card Number: 64–16953

FIRST FREE PRESS PAPERBACK EDITION 1967

printing number
7   8   9   10

ACKNOWLEDGMENTS

The nucleus of this volume consists of a number of papers on deviance which appeared in the Fall, 1962, issue of *Social Problems,* the official journal of the Society for the Study of Social Problems. Because the material was of more than passing interest and supplies of the issue so soon exhausted, it was decided to reprint the papers and to include with them other papers on deviance that had appeared in *Social Problems* both before and since.

I wish to thank the authors for permission to reprint their papers; the members of the Editorial Board of *Social Problems* for their help in selecting papers and advising on their revision; the officers of the Society for the Study of Social Problems under whose auspices the volume appears; and Lynne Johnson for her help in preparing the manuscript for press.

HOWARD S. BECKER

San Francisco
July 1963

CONTRIBUTORS

DONALD R. CRESSEY, College of Letters and Science, University of California (Santa Barbara)

FRED DAVIS, University of California Medical Center (San Francisco)

LEWIS ANTHONY DEXTER, Belmont, Massachusetts; Consultant, Kate Jackson Anthony Trust (Lewiston, Maine)

KAI T. ERIKSON, Department of Psychiatry, Emory University

HAROLD FINESTONE, Sociologist, Institute for Juvenile Research (Chicago)

EVERETT C. HUGHES, Department of Sociology, Brandeis University

JOHN IRWIN, Department of Sociology, University of California (Berkeley)

JOHN I. KITSUSE, Department of Sociology, Northwestern University

EDWIN M. LEMERT, Department of Sociology, University of California (Davis)

GEORGE J. McCALL, Department of Sociology, University of Iowa

SHELDON L. MESSINGER, Center for the Study of Law and Society, University of California (Berkeley)

MARSH B. RAY, Department of Sociology, Brandeis University

ALBERT J. REISS, JR., Department of Sociology, University of Michigan

HAROLD SAMPSON, Department of Psychiatry, Mt. Zion Hospital and Medical Center (San Francisco)

EDWIN M. SCHUR, Department of Sociology, Tufts University

RICHARD D. SCHWARTZ, Department of Sociology, Northwestern University

JEROME H. SKOLNICK, Department of Sociology, University of California (Berkeley)

CHARLES WINICK, Director of Research, American Social Health Association (New York)

IRVING KENNETH ZOLA, Department of Sociology, Brandeis University

CONTENTS

Contents

THE OTHER SIDE

INTRODUCTION

The sociological study of deviance had an auspicious beginning, rooted in the central concerns of sociological theory. Problems of deviance were problems of general sociology. Durkheim's study of suicide led him to some profound insights into the nature of society; W. I. Thomas' studies of Polish peasants in American cities and of young girls gone wrong during World War I led him to construct important general theories about personal and social disorganization. In these studies, and others like them, the sociologist looked at deviance and learned about society.

Unfortunately, the study of deviance lost its connection with the mainstream of sociological theory and research. It became a practical pursuit, devoted to helping society deal with those it found troublesome. Students of deviance devoted themselves to answering the questions posed by laymen and their elected and appointed officials. Predicting who would violate parole, sorting out youngsters into those who would become delinquent and those who would not, above all inquiring into the sources of deviance and attempting to answer the layman's question, "Why do they do it?"—these were typical concerns in the study of deviance.

In the past several years, however, all this has changed. The connections between the study of deviance and the growth of sociological theory and knowledge have been re-established, as the papers in this volume bear witness. Two things, in particular, give evidence of this trend. One is that the phenomena of deviance are seen in a context of similar phenomena in more conventional settings. For instance, one studies the prison and discovers in it the same phenomena one has discovered in other kinds of formal

Introduction

organizations: in schools, industries, and hospitals. A second sign of the renewed connection between the study of deviance and the rest of sociological thinking can be found in the extended area in which students of deviance find objects of study. They no longer devote themselves simply to delinquents and drug addicts, though these classical kinds of deviance are still kept under observation. Rather, they push on into other areas of society and find that they can increase their knowledge of the processes of deviance by studying physicians, people with physical handicaps, the mentally deficient, and others whose doings were formerly not included in the area. The traffic between the study of deviance and other areas of sociology flows in two directions: In studying even those matters which have conventionally been the focus of research in deviance we discover something about other problems of interest to sociology; at the same time, we find that the phenomena characteristic of deviance are to be found in all areas of society.

The new approach to the phenomena of deviance has some distinguishing characteristics, of which I will discuss two here. One is the focus on deviance as an interactive process involving both deviants and non-deviants. The other is a notable lack of what I shall call sentimentality.

The conventional style of studying deviance has focused on the deviant himself and has asked its questions mainly about him. Who is he? Where did he come from? How did he get that way? Is he likely to keep on being that way? The new approach sees it as always and everywhere a process of interaction between at least two kinds of people: those who commit (or are said to have committed) a deviant act and the rest of society, perhaps divided into several groups itself. The two groups are seen in complementary relationship. One cannot exist without the other; indeed, they are functions of one another in the strict mathematical sense of quantities whose value depends on the value of other quantities. To view deviance in this way has several important consequences.

One consequence is that we become much more interested in the process by which deviants are defined by the rest of society. We do not take for granted, as has sometimes naively been done, that a given action is deviant simply because it is commonly regarded so. Instead, we look to the process by which the common definition arises. This is, with increasing frequency, referred to as the process of labeling. People attach the label "deviant" to others and thereby make deviants of them.

Social groups create deviance by making the rules whose infraction constitutes deviance, and by applying those rules to particular people and labeling them as outsiders. From this point of view, deviance is not a quality of the act the person commits, but rather a consequence of the application by others of rules and sanctions to an "offender." The deviant is one to whom that label has successfully been applied; deviant behavior is behavior that people so label.[1]

In defining the problem this way, we direct our attention in research and theory-building to the questions: Who applies the label of deviant to whom? What consequences does the application of a label have for the person labeled? Under what circumstances is the label of deviant successfully applied? Several of the papers in this volume deal with these problems. Kitsuse, for instance, asks under what circumstances people impute homosexuality to others, and what effect the imputation has on their behavior toward those so labeled. Dexter makes clear the social nature of the labeling process by considering how the people we regard as mentally deficient might under other circumstances escape labeling as deviant, while those who are physically graceless received the label instead.

Another consequence of seeing deviance as an interactive process is that we are able to correct false impressions fostered by earlier theoretical assumptions. For instance, if we assume, as has often been done, that deviance is somehow a quality of the person committing the deviant act, we are likely to suppose without looking any further into the matter that the person who commits the deviant act is somehow compelled to do so and will continue to do so. On the other hand, if we view deviance as something that arises in interaction with others, we realize that changes in interaction may produce significant changes in behavior. One of the lessons of the study reported by Reiss is that juvenile delinquents who "hustle" adult homosexuals are not themselves homosexual. They do engage in homosexual practices, but as part of a delinquent pattern of behavior; their "homosexuality" is strictly governed by the norms of the peer group in which they are primarily involved. When, according to group standards, it is no longer appropriate for them to engage in homosexual activity (because they are old enough and strong enough to make money in other ways) they give it up.

As a third consequence of viewing deviance in a context of interaction, we focus attention on the other people involved in the process. We pay attention to the role of the non-deviant as well as to that of the deviant. Schwartz and Skolnick, for instance, studied people's reactions to someone convicted of a crime. They were not concerned with the criminals themselves; indeed, in one of the studies they report the criminals involved were fictitious characters created for the purpose of studying people's reactions to them. They did not ask why the doctors they studied engaged in malpractice. Rather they asked how patients and others reacted to a malpractice conviction. Similarly, they asked what the consequences of being convicted of a felony are for a person looking for an unskilled job; how will employers react to the knowledge that one has been involved in various ways in the legal process?

Even when we focus on the deviant himself, studies carried on in this style are likely to be exceptionally alive to the effect of the reactions of other people on the behavior of the deviant. Ray's study of the relapse of drug addicts, for instance, points to the crucial role of the behavior of significant others who refuse to validate the addict's conception of himself as cured in explaining the high frequency of relapse.

A lack of sentimentality is a second characteristic of the new approach to deviance. I want to use the term in as precise a way as I can. When I speak of sentimentality in social research, I refer to a disposition on the part of the researcher to leave certain variables in a problem unexamined. He thinks he knows what form they would take and, for reasons that are not scientifically well-founded, would not like it if they took any other form.

I have borrowed this use of the term "sentimental" from Eliot Freidson, and can illustrate it best from his work on the doctor-patient relationship.[2] Most studies of the medical profession take at face value many of the profession's myths about itself. For example, the medical profession publicly contends (although its members of course know it to be false) that all doctors are equally competent and that it is improper for a patient to refuse to accept the contention. Most studies of the doctor-patient relationship accept the contention and assume that if there are any differences in skill and competence between physicians these are too fine and subtle to be properly evaluated by laymen. Freidson found that patients do indeed make discriminations between doctors on the basis of how well they think they have been treated, but he did not make the assumption that patients were therefore being "irrational" by refusing to accept the claims of the profession. Instead, he asked what experiences the patients he studied had with physicians of various kinds and what basis there could be for their discriminations. He assumed that it was at least possible that the patients were making a rational judgment on the basis of objectively discernible differences.[3] Most social scientists either ignore the evidence that led him to this conclusion or, worse, so design their studies that such evidence cannot be gathered. They commit the sentimental fault of refusing to examine the possibility of medical incompetence. It is a *conventional* sentimentality.

Unconventional sentimentality is equally dangerous. The unconventional sentimentalist assumes, and refuses to examine the assumption, that things are in fact "worse" than they might be. He assumes, and does not want to know or learn anything that will challenge the assumption, that all doctors are much worse than they are conventionally thought to be, that they are all incompetent and money-hungry. He assumes, to take a different example, that the underdog is always right and those in authority always wrong. This tendency has been particularly noticeable in studies of race relations, where the possibility that minority groups have some of the faults attributed to them by bigots is systematically slighted. The same kind of sentimentality is sometimes found in studies of deviance, manifesting itself in a tendency to refuse to admit that the deviants under study have done wrong.

Whatever form sentimentality takes, its distinguishing mark is the refusal to consider distasteful possibilities. If the papers in this collection err by being sentimental, it is in the direction of unconventional sentimentality. But this, after all, is the lesser evil. If one outrages certain conventional assumptions by being unconventionally sentimental, a large body of opinion will be sure to tell him about it. But conventional sentimentality is less often attacked, and specious premises stand unchallenged. In any event, the papers in this volume are notable for their willingness to question received opinion.

1. Howard S. Becker, *Outsiders: Studies in the Sociology of Deviance*, New York: The Free Press of Glencoe, 1963, p. 9.

2. Eliot Freidson, *Patients' View of Medical Practice*, New York: Russell Sage Foundation, 1961.

3. *Ibid.*, pp. 171-191.

PART ONE

DEVIANCE AND ITS PLACE IN SOCIETY

NOTES ON THE SOCIOLOGY
OF DEVIANCE

KAI T. ERIKSON

It is common practice in sociology to picture deviant behavior as an alien element in society. Deviance is considered a vagrant form of human activity which has somehow broken away from the more orderly currents of social life and needs to be controlled. And since it is generally understood that this sort of aberration could only occur if something were wrong within the organization of society itself, deviant behavior is described almost as if it were leakage from machinery in poor condition: it is an incidental result of disorder and anomie, a symptom of internal breakdown.

The purpose of the following remarks will be to review this conventional outlook and to argue that it provides too narrow a framework for many kinds of sociological research. Deviation, we will suggest, recalling Durkheim's classic statement on the subject, can often be understood as a normal product of stable institutions, an important resource which is guarded and preserved by forces found in all human organizations.[1]

I

According to current theory, deviant behavior is most likely to occur when the sanctions governing conduct in any given social setting seem to be contradictory[2]—as would be the case, for example, if the work rules posted by a company required one course of action from its employees and the longer-range policies

This is a slightly revised version of a paper that appeared in *Social Problems*, 9 (1962), pp. 307-314.

of the company required quite another. Any situation marked by this kind of ambiguity, of course, can pose a serious dilemma for the individual: if he is careful to observe one set of demands imposed upon him, he runs the immediate risk of violating some other, and thus may find himself caught in a deviant stance no matter how earnestly he tries to avoid it. In this limited sense, deviance can be viewed as a "normal" social response to "abnormal" social circumstances, and we are therefore invited to assume that every act of deviation results from some imbalance within the social order—a condition of strain, anomie, or alienation.

This approach to the study of deviant behavior has generated a good deal of useful research, but it has at least one serious drawback for investigators who share an interest in what is known as "social problems." The "anomie" theory (if we may use that convenient label for a moment) is designed to account for all behavior which varies in some technical way from the norms of the community, whether or not that behavior is considered a problem by anyone else. For example, the bank teller who becomes a slave to routine and the armed bandit who relieves him of the day's receipts both register as deviants according to the logic of this scheme, since each is deviating in his own way from the ideal standards of the culture. Yet the most important difference between these men is one that the "anomie" theory cannot easily take into account: the bank teller, no matter how desperate his private needs, does not ordinarily create any concern in the rest of the community, while the bandit triggers the whole machinery of social control into vigorous action. In short, the "anomie" theory may help us appreciate the various ways in which people respond to conditions of strain, but it does not help us differentiate between those people who infringe the letter of the norm without attracting any notice and those who excite so much alarm that they earn a deviant reputation in society and are committed to special institutions like prisons and hospitals.

II

From a sociological standpoint, deviance can be defined as conduct which is generally thought to require the attention of social control agencies—that is, conduct about which "something should be done." Deviance is not a property *inherent in* certain forms of behavior; it is a property *conferred upon* these forms by the audiences which directly or indirectly witness them. The critical variable in the study of deviance, then, is the social audience rather than the individual actor, since it is the audience which eventually determines whether or not any episode of behavior or any class of episodes is labeled deviant.

This definition may seem a little indirect, but it has the advantage of bringing a neglected sociological issue into proper focus. When a community acts to control the behavior of one of its members, it is engaged in a very intricate process of selection. After all, even the worst miscreant in society conforms most of the time, if only in the sense that he uses the correct spoon at mealtime, takes good care of his mother, or in a thousand other ways respects the ordinary conventions of his group; and if the community elects to bring sanctions against him for the occasions when he does misbehave, it is responding to a few deviant details set within a vast array of entirely acceptable conduct. Thus it happens that a moment of deviation may become the measure of a person's position in society. He may be jailed or hospitalized, certified as a full-time deviant, despite the fact that only a fraction of his behavior was in any way unusual or dangerous. The community has taken note of a few scattered particles of behavior and has decided that they reflect what kind of person he "really" is.

The screening device which sifts these telling details out of the person's over-all performance, then, is a very important instrument of social control. We know very little about the properties of this screen, but we do know that it takes many factors into account which are not directly related to the deviant act itself: it is sensitive to the suspect's social class, his past record as an offender, the amount of remorse he manages to convey, and many similiar concerns which take hold in the shifting moods of the community. This may not be so obvious when the screen is dealing with extreme forms of deviance like serious crimes, but in the day-by-day filtering processes which take place throughout the community this feature is easily observable. Some men who drink too much are called alcoholics and others are not, some men who act oddly are committed to hospitals and others are not, some men who have no visible means of support are hauled into court and others are not—and the difference between those who earn a deviant label and those who go their own way in peace depends almost entirely on the way in which the community sifts out and codes the many details of behavior to which it is witness. In this respect, the community screen may be a more relevant subject for sociological research than the actual behavior which is filtered through it.

Once the problem is phrased in this way we can ask: How does a community decide what forms of conduct should be singled out for this kind of attention? The conventional answer to this question, of course, is that society sets up the machinery of control in order to protect itself against the "harmful" effects of deviation, in much the same way that an organism mobilizes its resources to combat an invasion of germs. Yet this simple view of the matter has not always proven to be a very productive one. In the first place, as Durkheim and Mead pointed out some years ago, it is by no means clear that all acts considered deviant in a culture are in fact (or even in principle) harmful to group life.[3] In the second place, it is gradually becoming more evident to sociologists engaged in this area of research that deviant behavior can play an important part in keeping the social order intact.

This raises a number of interesting questions for sociology.

III

In recent years, sociological theory has become more and more concerned with the concept "social system"—an organization of society's component parts into a form which sustains internal equilibrium, resists change, and is boundary maintaining. In its most abstract form, the "system" concept describes a highly complex network of relations, but the scheme is generally used by sociologists to draw attention to those forces in the social order which promote a high level of uniformity among human actors and a high degree of symmetry within human institutions. The main organizational drift of a system, then, is seen as centripetal: it acts to draw the behavior of actors toward those centers in social space where the core values of the group are figuratively located, bringing them within range of basic norms. Any conduct which is neither attracted toward this nerve center by the rewards of conformity nor compelled toward it by other social pressures is considered "out of control," which is to say, deviant.

This basic model has provided the theme for most contemporary thinking about deviation, and as a result little attention has been given to the notion that systems operate to maintain boundaries. To say that a system maintains boundaries is to say that it controls the fluctuation of its constituent parts so that the whole retains a defined range of activity, a unique pattern of constancy and stability, within the larger environment.[4] Because the range of human behavior is potentially so wide, social groups maintain boundaries in the sense that they try to limit the flow of behavior within their domain so that it circulates within a defined cultural territory. Boundaries, then, are an important point of reference for persons participating in any system. A people may define its boundaries by referring to a geographical location, a set of honored traditions, a particular religious or political viewpoint, an occupational specialty, a common language, or just some local way of doing things; but in any case, members of the group have some idea about the contours of the niche they occupy in social space. They know where the group begins and ends as a special entity; they know what kinds of experience "belong" within these precincts and what kinds do not.

For all its apparent abstractness, a social system is organized around the movements of persons joined together in regular social relations. The only material found in a system for marking boundaries, then, is the behavior of its participants; and the kinds of behavior which best perform this function are often deviant, since they represent the most extreme variety of conduct to be found within the experience of the group. In this sense, transactions taking place between deviant persons on the one side and agencies of control on the other are boundary maintaining mechanisms. They mark the outside limits of the area within which the norm has jurisdiction, and in this way assert how much diversity and variability can be contained within the system before it begins to lose its distinct structure, its cultural integrity.

A social norm is rarely expressed as a firm rule or official code. It is an abstract synthesis of the many separate times a community has stated its sentiments on a given kind of issue. Thus the norm has a history much like that of an article of common law: it is an accumulation of decisions made by the community over a long period of time which gradually gathers enough moral eminence to serve as a precedent for future decisions. And like an article of common law, the norm retains its validity only if it is regularly used as a basis for judgment. Each time the group censures some act of deviation, then, it sharpens the authority of the violated norm and declares again where the boundaries of the group are located.

It is important to notice that these transactions between deviant persons and agents of control have always attracted a good deal of attention in this and other cultures. In our own past, both the trial and punishment of deviant offenders took place in the public market and gave the crowd a chance to participate in a direct, active way. Today we no longer parade deviants in the town square or expose them to the carnival atmosphere of Tyburn, but it is interesting to note that the "reform" which brought about this change in penal policy coincided almost precisely with the development of newspapers as media of public information. Perhaps this is no more than an accident of history, but it is nevertheless true that newspapers (and now radio and television) offer their readers the same kind of entertainment once supplied by public hangings or the use of stocks and pillories. An enormous amount of modern "news" is devoted to reports about deviant behavior and its punishment: indeed the largest circulation newspaper in the United States prints very little else. Yet how do we explain what makes these items "newsworthy" or why they command the great attention they do? Perhaps they satisfy a number of psychological perversities among the mass audience, as commentators sometimes point out, but at the same time they constitute our main source of information about the normative contours of society. In a figurative sense, at least, morality and immorality meet at the public scaffold, and it is during this meeting that the community declares where the line between them should be drawn.

People who gather together into communities need to be able to describe and anticipate those areas of experience which lie outside the immediate compass of the group—the unseen dangers which in any culture and in any age seem to threaten its security. Traditional folklore depicting demons, devils, witches and evil spirits, may be one way to give form to these otherwise formless dangers, but the visible deviant is another kind of reminder. As a trespasser against the group norms, he represents those forces which lie outside the group's boundaries: he informs us, as it were, what evil looks like, what shapes the devil can assume. And in doing so, he shows us the difference between the inside of the group and the outside. It may well be that without this ongoing drama at the outer edges of group space, the community would have no inner sense of identity and cohesion, no sense of the contrasts which set it off as a special place in the larger world.

Thus deviance cannot be dismissed simply as behavior which *disrupts* stability in society, but may itself be, in controlled quantities, an important condition for *preserving* stability.

IV

This raises a delicate theoretical issue. If we grant that deviant forms of behavior are often beneficial to society in general, can we then assume that societies are organized in such a way as to promote this resource? Can we assume, in other words, that forces operate within the social order to recruit deviant actors and commit them to deviant forms of activity? Sociology has not yet developed a conceptual language in which this sort of question can be discussed with any ease, but one observation can be made which gives the question an interesting perspective—namely, that deviant activities often seem to derive support from the very agencies designed to suppress them. Indeed, the institutions devised by society for discouraging deviant behavior are often so poorly equipped for that task that we might well ask why this is considered their "real" function at all.

It is by now a thoroughly familiar argument that many of the institutions built to inhibit deviation actually operate in such a way as to perpetuate it. For one thing, prisons, hospitals, and

similar agencies of control provide aid and shelter to large numbers of deviant persons, sometimes enhancing their survival
chances in the world as a whole. But beyond this, such institutions
gather marginal people into tightly segregated groups, give them
an opportunity to teach one another the skills and attitudes of a
deviant career, and often provoke them into employing these
skills by reinforcing their sense of alienation from the rest of
society.[5] It should be pointed out, furthermore, that this process
is found not only in the institutions which actually confine the
deviant, but throughout the general community as well.

The community's decision to bring deviant sanctions against
an individual is not a simple act of censure. It is a sharp rite of
transition, at once moving him out of his normal position in
society and transferring him into a distinct deviant role.[6] The
ceremonies which accomplish this change of status, ordinarily,
have three related phases. They provide a formal *confrontation*
between the deviant suspect and representatives of his community
(as in the criminal trial or psychiatric case conference); they
announce some *judgment* about the nature of his deviancy (a
verdict or diagnosis, for example); and they perform an act of
social *placement,* assigning him to a special role (like that of
prisoner or patient) which redefines his position in society. These
ceremonies tend to be events of wide public interest and usually
take place in a dramatic, ritualized setting.[7] Perhaps the most
obvious example of a commitment ceremony is the criminal trial,
with its elaborate formality and ritual pageantry, but more modest
equivalents can be found everywhere that procedures are set up to
judge whether someone is deviant or not.

Now an important feature of these ceremonies in our own
culture is that they are almost irreversible. Most provisional roles
conferred by society—like those of the student or conscripted
soldier, for example—include some kind of terminal ceremony to
mark the individual's movement back out of the role once its
temporary advantages have been exhausted. But the roles allotted
to the deviant seldom make allowance for this type of passage.
He is ushered into the deviant position by a decisive and often
dramatic ceremony, yet is retired from it with hardly a word of
public notice. And as a result, the deviant often returns home with

no proper license to resume a normal life in the community. Nothing has happened to cancel out the stigmas imposed upon him by earlier commitment ceremonies; from a formal point of view, the original verdict or diagnosis is still in effect. It should not be surprising, then, that the members of the community seem reluctant to accept the returning deviant on an entirely equal footing. In a very real sense, they do not know who he is.

A circularity is thus set into motion which has all the ear-marks of a "self-fulfilling prophesy," to use Merton's fine phrase. On the one hand, it seems obvious that the community's reluctance to accept the deviant back helps reduce whatever chance he might otherwise have for a successful readjustment. Yet on the other hand, everyday experience seems to show that this reluctance is entirely reasonable, for it is a well-known and highly publicized fact that large numbers of ex-convicts return to criminal activity and that many discharged mental patients suffer later breakdowns. The common assumption that deviants are not often cured or reformed, then, may be based on a faulty premise, but this assumption is stated so frequently and with such conviction that it often creates the facts which later "prove" it to be correct. If the returning deviant has to face the community's apprehensions often enough, it is understandable that he too may begin to wonder whether he has graduated from the deviant role—and respond to the uncertainty by resuming deviant activity. In some respects, this may be the only way for the individual and his community to agree as to what kind of person he really is, for it often happens that the community is only able to perceive his "true colors" when he lapses momentarily into some form of de-viant performance.

Moreover, this prophesy is found in the official policies of even the most advanced agencies of control. Police departments could not operate with any real effectiveness if they did not regard ex-convicts as an almost permanent population of offenders, a pool from which to draw suspects; and psychiatric hospitals could not do a responsible job in the community if they were not alert to the fact that ex-patients are highly susceptible to relapse. Thus the prophesy gains currency at many levels within the social order, not only in the poorly informed opinions of the community at large, but in the best informed theories of most control agencies as well.

In one form or another, this problem has been known in Western culture for many hundreds of years, and the single fact that this is so becomes a highly significant one for sociology. If the culture has supported a steady flow of deviant behavior throughout long periods of historical evolution, then the rules which apply to any form of functionalist thinking would suggest that strong forces must be at work to keep this flow intact—and this because it contributes in some important way to the survival of the system as a whole. This may not be reason enough to assert that deviant behavior is "functional," in any of the many senses of that term, but it should make us wary of the assumption that human communities are organized in such a way as to prevent deviance from occurring.[8]

This in turn might suggest that our present models of society, with their emphasis on the harmony and equilibrium of social life, do a one-sided job of representing the situation. Perhaps two different and often competing currents are found in any well-functioning system: those forces which promote a high over-all degree of conformity among its members, and those forces which encourage some degree of diversity so that actors can be deployed throughout social space to patrol the system's boundaries. These different gravitational pulls in the social system set up a constant tension of opposites, outlining the area within which human life, with all its contradiction and variety, takes place. Perhaps this is what Aldous Huxley had in mind when he wrote:

Now tidiness is undeniably good—but a good of which it is easily possible to have too much and at too high a price. . . . The good life can only be lived in a society in which tidiness is preached and practised, but not too fanatically, and where efficiency is always haloed, as it were, by a tolerated margin of mess.[9]

V

These brief remarks are no more than a prelude to further thinking and research, and in the remaining paragraphs we will try to indicate some of the directions this line of reasoning might take.

In the first place, this paper has indirectly addressed itself to one of the oldest problems in sociology. It is all very well for an investigator to conclude that something called a "system" has certain "requirements" in respect to its participants, but the major problem for research is to ask how these needs are imposed upon the people who eventually satisfy them. Ordinarily, the fact that deviant behavior is not evenly distributed throughout the social structure is explained by declaring that something called "anomie" or "disorganization" prevails at certain sensitive points. Deviance leaks out through defects in the social structure; it occurs when the system *fails* to impose its needs on human actors. But if we consider the possibility that even the best organized collectivity needs to produce occasional episodes of deviation for the sake of its own stability, we are engaged in quite another order of inquiry. Perhaps the coherence of some social groupings is maintained only when a few juvenile offenders are enlisted to balance the conformity of an adult majority; perhaps communities can retain a sense of their own territorial identity only if they keep up an ongoing dialogue with deviants who mark and publicize the outer limits of group space; perhaps some families can remain intact only if one of its members becomes a visible deviant to serve as a focus for the rest.[10] If these suppositions prove useful, we should try to learn how a social system appoints certain of its members to deviant roles and how it encourages them to spend a period of service testing the group's boundaries. This is not to suggest that a system necessarily creates the crises which impel people into deviant activity but that it deploys these resources in a patterned, organized way.

In the second place, it is evident that cultures vary in the way they regulate deviant traffic moving back and forth from their outer boundaries. We might begin with the observation, for example, that many features of the traffic pattern in our own culture seem to have a marked Puritan cast: a defined portion of the population, largely drawn from young adult groups and from the lower economic classes, is stabilized in deviant roles and often expected to remain there indefinitely. The logic which prevails in many of our formal agencies of control and in the public attitudes which sustain them sometimes seems to echo earlier Puritan theories about predestination, reprobation, and the nature of sin. Be this as it may, different traffic patterns are found in other parts of the world which offer an interesting contrast. There are societies in which deviance is considered a natural mode of behavior for the young, a pursuit which they are expected to abandon once they move through defined ceremonies into adulthood. There are societies which give license to large groups of people to engage in deviant behavior during certain seasons or on certain days of the year. And there are societies which form special groups whose stated business is to act in ways contrary to the normal expectations of the culture. Each of these patterns regulates deviant traffic differently, yet each of them provides some institutional means for a person to give up a deviant career without any kind of permanent stigma. In either of these cases, the person's momentary commitment to deviant styles of behavior is easily reversed—when the group promotes him to manhood, declares a period of festival to be over, or permits him to give up the insignia which marked his membership in a band of "contraries." Perhaps the most interesting problem here from the point of view of pure research is to see whether these various patterns are functionally equivalent in any meaningful way. Perhaps the most interesting problem for those of us who lean over into the applied areas of the field, however, is to ask whether we have anything to learn from those cultures which permit re-entry into normal social life for persons who have spent a period of time in the deviant ranks and no longer have any special need to remain there.

1. Emile Durkheim, *The Rules of Sociological Method* (translated by S. A. Solovay and J. H. Meuller), New York: The Free Press of Glencoe, 1958.

2. The best-known statements of this general position, of course, are by Robert K. Merton and Talcott Parsons. Merton, *Social Theory and Social Structure*, Revised Edition, New York: The Free Press of Glencoe, 1957; and Parsons, *The Social System*, New York: The Free Press of Glencoe, 1951.

3. Emile Durkheim, *The Division of Labor in Society* (translated by George Simpson), New York: The Free Press of Glencoe, 1952; and George Herbert

Mead, "The Psychology of Punitive Justice," *American Journal of Sociology*, 23 (1918), 577-602.

4. Cf. Talcott Parsons, *The Social System, op. cit.*

5. For a good description of this process in the modern prison, see Gresham Sykes, *The Society of Captives*, Princeton: Princeton University Press, 1958. For views of two different types of mental hospital settings, see Erving Goffman, "The Characteristics of Total Institutions," *Symposium on Preventive and Social Psychiatry*, Washington, D.C.: Walter Reed Army Institute of Research, 1957; and Kai T. Erikson, "Patient Role and Social Uncertainty: A Dilemma of the Mentally Ill," *Psychiatry*, 20 (1957), 263-274.

6. Parsons, *op. cit.*, has provided the classical description of how this role transfer works in the case of medical patients.

7. Cf. Harold Garfinkel, "Successful Degradation Ceremonies," *American Journal of Sociology*, 61 (1956), 420-424.

8. Albert K. Cohen, for example, speaking for sociologists in general, seems to take the question for granted: "It would seem that the control of deviant behavior is, by definition, a culture goal." In "The Study of Social Disorganization and Deviant Behavior," Merton, *et al.*, editors, *Sociology Today*, New York: Basic Books, 1959, p. 465.

9. Aldous Huxley, *Prisons: The 'Carceri' Etchings by G. B. Piranesi*, London: The Trianon Press, 1949.

10. Cf. Robert A. Dentler and Kai T. Erikson, "The Functions of Deviance in Groups," *Social Problems*, 7 (1959), 98-107.

GOOD PEOPLE AND
DIRTY WORK

EVERETT C. HUGHES

"... une secte est le *noyau* et le *levain* de toute foule. ... Etudier la foule c'est juger un drame d'après ce qu'on voit sur la scène; étudier la secte c'est le juger d'après ce qu'on voit dans les coulisses." Sighele, S. *Psychologie des sectes*. Paris, 1898. Pp. 62, 63, 65.[1]

The National Socialist Government of Germany, with the arm of its fanatical inner sect, the S.S., commonly known as the Black Shirts or Elite Guard, perpetrated and boasted of the most colossal and dramatic piece of social dirty work the world has ever known. Perhaps there are other claimants to the title, but they could not match this one's combination of mass, speed and perverse pride in the deed. Nearly all peoples have plenty of cruelty and death to account for. How many Negro Americans have died by the hands of lynching mobs? How many more from unnecessary disease and lack of food or of knowledge of nutrition? How many Russians died to bring about collectivization of land? And who is to blame if there be starving millions in some parts of the world while wheat molds in the fields of other parts?

I do not revive the case of the Nazi *Endloesung* (final solution) of the Jewish problem in order to condemn the Germans, or make them look worse than other peoples, but to recall to our attention dangers which lurk in our midst always. Most of what follows was written after my first postwar visit to Germany in 1948. The impressions were vivid. The facts have not diminished and disappeared with time, as did the stories of alleged German

23

atrocities in Belgium in the First World War. The fuller the record, the worse it gets.[2]

Several millions of people were delivered to the concentration camps, operated under the leadership of Heinrich Himmler with the help of Adolf Eichmann. A few hundred thousand survived in some fashion. Still fewer came out sound of mind and body. A pair of examples, well attested, will show the extreme of perverse cruelty reached by the S.S. guards in charge of the camps. Prisoners were ordered to climb trees; guards whipped them to make them climb faster. Once they were out of reach, other prisoners, also urged by the whip, were put to shaking the trees. When the victims fell, they were kicked to see whether they could rise to their feet. Those too badly injured to get up were shot to death, as useless for work. A not inconsiderable number of prisoners were drowned in pits full of human excrement. These examples are so horrible that your minds will run away from them. You will not, as when you read a slightly salacious novel, imagine the rest. I therefore thrust these examples upon you and insist that the people who thought them up could, and did, improvise others like them, and even worse, from day to day over several years. Many of the victims of the Camps gave up the ghost (this Biblical phrase is the most apt) from a combination of humiliation, starvation, fatigue and physical abuse. In due time, a policy of mass liquidation in the gas chamber was added to individual virtuosity in cruelty.

This program—for it was a program—of cruelty and murder was carried out in the name of racial superiority and racial purity. It was directed mainly, although by no means exclusively, against Jews, Slavs and Gypsies. It was thorough. There are few Jews in the territories which were under the control of the Third German Reich—the two Germanies, Holland, Czechoslovakia, Poland, Austria, Hungary. Many Jewish Frenchmen were destroyed. There were concentration camps even in Tunisia and Algiers under the German occupation.

When, during my 1948 visit to Germany, I became more aware of the reactions of ordinary Germans to the horrors of the concentration camps, I found myself asking not the usual question, "How did racial hatred rise to such a high level?" but this one,

"How could such dirty work be done among and, in a sense, *by* the millions of ordinary, civilized German people?" Along with this came related questions. How could these millions of ordinary people live in the midst of such cruelty and murder without a general uprising against it and against the people who did it? How, once freed from the regime that did it, could they be apparently so little concerned about it, so toughly silent about it, not only in talking with outsiders—which is easy to understand— but among themselves? How and where could there be found in a modern civilized country the several hundred thousand men and women capable of such work? How were these people so far released from the inhibitions of civilized life as to be able to imagine, let alone perform, the ferocious, obscene and perverse actions which they did imagine and perform? How could they be kept at such a height of fury through years of having to see daily at close range the human wrecks they made and being often literally spattered with the filth produced and accumulated by their own actions?

You will see that there are here two orders of questions. One set concerns the good people who did not themselves do this work. The other concerns those who did do it. But the two sets are not really separate; for the crucial question concerning the good people is their relation to the people who did the dirty work, with a related one which asks under what circumstances good people let the others get away with such actions.

An easy answer concerning the Germans is that they were not so good after all. We can attribute to them some special in-born or ingrained race consciousness, combined with a penchant for sadistic cruelty and unquestioning acceptance of whatever is done by those who happen to be in authority. Pushed to its extreme, this answer simply makes us, rather than the Germans, the superior race. It is the Nazi tune, put to words of our own.

Now there are deep and stubborn differences between peoples. Their history and culture may make the Germans especially susceptible to the doctrine of their own racial superiority and especially acquiescent to the actions of whoever is in power over them. These are matters deserving of the best study that can be given them. But to say that these things could happen in Germany simply because Germans are different—from us—buttresses their own excuses and lets us off too easily from blame for what happened there and from the question whether it could happen here.

Certainly in their daily practice and expression before the Hitler regime, the Germans showed no more, if as much, hatred of other racial or cultural groups than we did and do. Residential segregation was not marked. Intermarriage was common, and the families of such marriages had an easier social existence than they generally have in America. The racially exclusive club, school and hotel were much less in evidence than here. And I well remember an evening in 1933 when a Montreal businessman—a very nice man, too—said in our living room, "Why don't we admit that Hitler is doing to the Jews just what we ought to be doing?" That was not an uncommon sentiment, although it may be said in defense of the people who expressed it, that they probably did not know and would not have believed the full truth about the Nazi program of destroying Jews. The essential underlying sentiments on racial matters in Germany were not different in kind from those prevailing throughout the western, and especially the Anglo-Saxon, countries. But I do not wish to overemphasize this point. I only want to close one easy way out of serious consideration of the problem of good people and dirty work, by demonstrating that the Germans were and are about as good and about as bad as the rest of us on this matter of racial sentiments and, let us add, their notions of decent human behavior.

But what was the reaction of ordinary Germans to the persecution of the Jews and to the concentration camp mass torture and murder? A conversation between a German schoolteacher, a German architect and myself gives the essentials in a vivid form. It was in the studio of the architect, and the occasion was a rather casual visit, in Frankfurt am Main in 1948.

The architect: "I am ashamed for my people whenever I think of it. But we didn't know about it. We only learned about all that later. You must remember the pressure we were under; we had to join the party. We had to keep our mouths shut and do as we were told. It was a terrible pressure. Still, I am ashamed. But you see, we had lost our colonies, and our national honor was hurt. And these Nazis exploited that feeling. And the Jews, they *were* a problem.

They came from the east. You should see them in Poland; the lowest class of people, full of lice, dirty and poor, running about in their Ghettos in filthy caftans. They came here, and got rich by unbelievable methods after the first war. They occupied all the good places. Why, they were in the proportion of ten to one in medicine and law and government posts!"

At this point the architect hesitated and looked confused. He continued: "Where was I? It is the poor food. You see what misery we are in here, Herr Professor. It often happens that I forget what I was talking about. Where was I now? I have completely forgotten."

(His confusion was, I believe, not at all feigned. Many Germans said they suffered losses of memory such as this, and laid it to their lack of food.)

I said firmly: "You were talking about loss of national honor and how the Jews had got hold of everything."

The architect: "Oh, yes! That was it! Well, of course that was no way to settle the Jewish problem. But there *was* a problem and it had to be settled some way."

The schoolteacher: "Of course, they have Palestine now."

I protested that Palestine would hardly hold them.

The architect: "The professor is right. Palestine can't hold all the Jews. And it was a terrible thing to murder people. But we didn't know it at the time. But I am glad I am alive now. It is an interesting time in men's history. You know, when the Americans came it was like a great release. I really want to see a new ideal in Germany. I like the freedom that lets me talk to you like this. But, unfortunately that is not the general opinion. Most of my friends really hang on to the old ideas. They can't see any hope, so they hang on to the old ideas."

This scrap of talk gives, I believe, the essential elements as well as the flavor of the German reaction. It checks well with formal studies which have been made, and it varies only in detail from other conversations which I myself recorded in 1948.

One of the most obvious points in it is unwillingness to think about the dirty work done. In this case—perhaps by chance, perhaps not—the good man suffered an actual lapse of memory in the middle of this statement. This seems a simple point. But the psychiatrists have shown that it is less simple than it looks. They have done a good deal of work on the complicated mechanisms by which the individual mind keeps unpleasant or intolerable knowledge from consciousness, and have shown how great may, in some cases, be the consequent loss of effectiveness of the personality. But we have taken collective unwillingness to know unpleasant facts more or less for granted. That people can and do keep a silence about things whose open discussion would threaten the group's conception of itself, and hence its solidarity, is common knowledge. It is a mechanism that operates in every family and in every group which has a sense of group reputation. To break such a silence is considered an attack against the group; a sort of treason, if it be a member of the group who breaks the silence. This common silence allows group fictions to grow up; such as, that grandpa was less a scoundrel and more romantic than he really was. And I think it demonstrable that it operates especially against any expression, except in ritual, of collective guilt. The remarkable thing in present-day Germany is not that there is so little reference to something about which people do feel deeply guilty, but that it is talked about at all.

In order to understand this phenomenon we would have to find out who talks about the concentration camp atrocities, in what situations, in what mood, and with what stimulus. On these points I know only my own limited experiences. One of the most moving of these was my first postwar meeting with an elderly professor whom I had known before the Nazi time; he is an heroic soul who did not bow his head during the Nazi time and who keeps it erect now. His first words, spoken with tears in his eyes, were: "How hard it is to believe that men will be as bad as they say they will. Hitler and his people said: 'Heads will roll,' but how many of us—even of his bitterest opponents—could really believe that they would do it."

This man could and did speak, in 1948, not only to the likes of me, but to his students, his colleagues and to the public which read his articles, in the most natural way about the Nazi atrocities whenever there was occasion to do it in the course of his tireless effort to reorganize and to bring new life into the German universities. He had neither the compulsion to speak, so that he might excuse and defend himself, nor a conscious or unconscious need to keep silent. Such people were rare; how many there were in Germany I do not know.

Occasions of another kind in which the silence was broken were those where, in class, public lecture or in informal meetings with students, I myself had talked frankly of race relations in other parts of the world, including the lynchings which sometimes occur in my own country and the terrible cruelty visited upon natives in South Africa. This took off the lid of defensiveness, so that a few people would talk quite easily of what happened under the Nazi regime. More common were situations like that with the architect, where I threw in some remark about the atrocities in response to Germans' complaint that the world is abusing them. In such cases, there was usually an expression of shame, accompanied by a variety of excuses (including that of having been kept in ignorance), and followed by a quick turning away from the subject.

Somewhere in consideration of this problem of discussion versus silence we must ask what the good (that is, ordinary) people in Germany did know about these things. It is clear that the S.S. kept the more gory details of the concentration camps a close secret. Even high officials of the government, the army and the Nazi party itself were in some measure held in ignorance, although of course they kept the camps supplied with victims. Stangl The common people of Germany knew that the camps existed; most knew people who had disappeared into them; some saw the victims, walking skeletons in rags, being transported in trucks or trains, or being herded on the road from station to camp or to work in fields or factories near the camps. Many knew people who had been released from concentration camps; such released persons kept their counsel on pain of death. But secrecy was cultivated and supported by fear and terror. In the absence of a determined and heroic will to know and publish the truth, and in the absence of all the instruments of opposition, the degree of knowledge was undoubtedly low, in spite of the fact that all knew that something both stupendous and horrible was going on; and in spite of the fact that Hitler's *Mein Kampf* and the utterances of his aides said that no fate was too horrible for the Jews and other wrong-headed or inferior people. This must make us ask under what conditions the will to know and to discuss is strong, determined and effective; this, like most of the important questions I have raised, I leave unanswered except as answers may be contained in the statement of the case.

But to return to our moderately good man, the architect. He insisted over and over again that he did not know, and we may suppose that he knew as much and as little as most Germans. But he also made it quite clear that he wanted something done to the Jews. I have similar statements from people of whom I knew that they had had close Jewish friends before the Nazi time. This raises the whole problem of the extent to which those pariahs who do the dirty work of society are really acting as agents for the rest of us. To talk of this question one must note that, in building up his case, the architect pushed the Jews firmly into an out-group: they were dirty, lousy and unscrupulous (an odd statement from a resident of Frankfurt, the home of old Jewish merchants and intellectual families long identified with those aspects of culture of which Germans are most proud). Having dissociated himself clearly from these people, and having declared them a problem, he apparently was willing to let someone else do to them the dirty work which he himself would not do, and for which he expressed shame. The case is perhaps analogous to our attitude toward those convicted of crime. From time to time, we get wind of cruelty practiced upon the prisoners in penitentiaries or jails; or, it may be, merely a report that they are ill-fed or that hygienic conditions are not good. Perhaps we do not wish that the prisoners should be cruelly treated or badly fed, but our reaction is probably tempered by a notion that they deserve something, because of some dissociation of them from the in-group of good people. If what they get is worse than what we like to think about, it is a little bit too bad. It is a point on which we are ambivalent. Campaigns for reform of prisons are often followed by countercampaigns against a too high standard of living for prisoners and against having prisons run by softies. Now the people who run prisons are our agents. Just how far they do or could carry out our wishes is hard to say. The minor prison guard, in boastful justification of some of his more questionable practices, says, in effect: "If those reformers and those big shots upstairs had to live with these birds as I do, they would soon change their fool notions about running a prison." He is suggesting that the good people are either naive or hypocritical. Furthermore, he knows quite well that the wishes of his employers, the public, are by no means unmixed. They are quite as likely to put upon him for being too nice as for being too harsh. And if, as sometimes happens, he is a man disposed to cruelty, there may be some justice in his feeling that he is only doing what others would like to do, if they were in his place.

There are plenty of examples in our own world which I might have picked for comparison with the German attitude toward the concentration camps. For instance, a newspaper in Denver made a great scandal out of the allegation that our Japanese compatriots were too well fed in the camps where they were concentrated during the war. I might have mentioned some feature of the sorry history of the people of Japanese background in Canada. Or it might have been lynching, or some aspect of racial discrimination. But I purposely chose prisoners convicted of crime. For convicts are formally set aside for special handling. They constitute an out-group in all countries. This brings the issue clearly before us, since few people cherish the illusion that the problem of treating criminals can be settled by propaganda designed to prove that there aren't any criminals. Almost everyone agrees that something has to be done about them. The question concerns what is done, who does it, and the nature of the mandate given by the rest of us to those who do it. Perhaps we give them an unconscious mandate to go beyond anything we ourselves would care to do or even to acknowledge. I venture to suggest that the higher and more expert functionaries who act in our behalf represent something of a distillation of what we may consider our public wishes, while some of the others show a sort of concentrate of those impulses of which we are or wish to be less aware.

Now the choice of convicted prisoners brings up another crucial point in inter-group relations. All societies of any great size have in-groups and out-groups; in fact, one of the best ways of describing a society is to consider it a network of smaller and larger in-groups and out-groups. And an in-group is one only because there are out-groups. When I refer to *my* children I obviously imply that they are closer to me than other people's children and that I will make greater efforts to buy oranges and cod-liver oil for them than for others' children. In fact, it may mean that I will give them cod-liver oil if I have to choke them to get it down. We do our own dirty work on those closest to us. The very injunction that I love my neighbor as myself starts with me; if I don't love myself and my nearest, the phrase has a very sour meaning.

Each of us is a center of a network of in- and out-groups. Now the distinctions between *in* and *out* may be drawn in various ways, and nothing is more important for both the student of society and the educator than to discover how these lines are made and how they may be redrawn in more just and sensible ways. But to believe that we can do away with the distinction between *in* and *out, us* and *them* in social life is complete nonsense. On the positive side, we generally feel a greater obligation to in-groups; hence less obligation to out-groups; and in the case of such groups as convicted criminals, the out-group is definitely given over to the hands of our agents for punishment. That is the extreme case. But there are other out-groups toward which we may have aggressive feelings and dislike, although we give no formal mandate to anyone to deal with them on our behalf, and although we profess to believe that they should not suffer restrictions or disadvantages. The greater their social distance from us, the more we leave in the hands of others a sort of mandate by default to deal with them on our behalf. Whatever effort we put on reconstructing the lines which divide in- and out-groups, there remains the eternal problem of our treatment, direct or delegated, of whatever groups are considered somewhat outside. And here it is that the whole matter of our professed and possible deeper unprofessed wishes comes up for consideration; and the related problem of what we know, can know and want to know about it. In Germany, the agents got out of hand and created such terror that it was best not to know. It is also clear that it was and is easier to the conscience of many Germans not to know. It is, finally, not unjust to say that the agents were at least working in the direction of the wishes of many people, although they may have gone beyond the wishes of most. The same questions can be asked about our own society, and with reference not only to prisoners but also to many other groups upon whom there is no legal or moral stigma. Again I have not the answers. I leave you to search for them.

In considering the question of dirty work we have eventually to think about the people who do it. In Germany, these were the members of the S.S. and of that inner group of the S.S. who operated the concentration camps. Many reports have been made on the social backgrounds and the personalities of these cruel fanatics. Those who have studied them say that a large proportion were *gescheiterte Existenzen,* men or women with a history of failure, of poor adaptation to the demands of work and of the classes of society in which they had been bred. Germany between wars had large numbers of such people. Their adherence to a movement which proclaimed a doctrine of hatred was natural enough. The movement offered something more. It created an inner group which was to be superior to all others, even Germans, in their emancipation from the usual bourgeois morality; people above and beyond the ordinary morality. I dwell on this, not as a doctrine, but as an organizational device. For, as Eugene Kogon, author of the most penetrating analysis of the S.S. and their camps, has said, the Nazis came to power by creating a state within a state; a body with its own countermorality, and its own counter-law, its courts and its own execution of sentence upon those who did not live up to its orders and standards. Even as a movement, it had inner circles within inner circles; each sworn to secrecy as against the next outer one. The struggle between these inner circles continued after Hitler came to power; Himmler eventually won the day. His S.S. became a state within the Nazi state, just as the Nazi movement had become a state within the Weimar state. One is reminded of the oft quoted but neglected statement of Sighele: "At the center of a crowd look for the sect." He referred, of course, to the political sect; the fanatical inner group of a movement seeking power by revolutionary methods. Once the Nazis were in power, this inner sect, while becoming now the recognized agent of the state and, hence, of the masses of the people, could at the same time dissociate itself more completely from them in action, because of the very fact of having a mandate. It was now beyond all danger of interference and investigation. For it had the instruments of interference and investigation in its own hands. These are also the instruments of secrecy. So the S.S. could and did build up a powerful system in which they had the resources

of the state and of the economy of Germany and the conquered
countries from which to steal all that was needed to carry out
their orgy of cruelty luxuriously as well as with impunity.

Now let us ask, concerning the dirty workers, questions similar
to those concerning the good people. Is there a supply of candi-
dates for such work in other societies? It would be easy to say
that only Germany could produce such a crop. The question is
answered by being put. The problem of people who have run
aground *(gescheiterte Existenzen)* is one of the most serious in our
modern societies. Any psychiatrist will, I believe, testify that we
have a sufficient pool or fund of personalities warped toward perverse punishment and cruelty to do any amount of dirty work
that the good people may be inclined to countenance. It would
not take a very great turn of events to increase the number of
such people, and to bring their discontents to the surface. This
is not to suggest that every movement based on discontent with
the present state of things will be led by such people. That is
obviously untrue; and I emphasize the point lest my remarks give
comfort to those who would damn all who express militant discontent. But I think study of militant social movements does
show that these warped people seek a place in them. Specifically,
they are likely to become the plotting, secret police of the group.
It is one of the problems of militant social movements to keep
such people out. It is of course easier to do this if the spirit of the
movement is positive, its conception of humanity high and in-
clusive, and its aims sound. This was not the case of the Nazi
movement. As Kogon puts it: "The SS were but the arch-type
of the Nazis in general."[3] But such people are sometimes attracted, for want of something better, to movements whose aims
are contrary to the spirit of cruelty and punishment. I would suggest that all of us look well at the leadership and entourage of
movements to which we attach ourselves for signs of a negativistic,
punishing attitude. For once such a spirit develops in a movement,
punishment of the nearest and easiest victim is likely to become
more attractive than striving for the essential goals. And, if the
Nazi movement teaches us anything at all, it is that if any shadow
of a mandate be given to such people, they will—having com-
promised us—make it larger and larger. The processes by which

they do so are the development of the power and inward discipline
of their own group, a progressive dissociation of themselves from
the rules of human decency prevalent in their culture, and an
ever growing contempt for the welfare of the masses of people.

The power and inward discipline of the S.S. became such
that those who once became members could get out only by death;
by suicide, murder or mental breakdown. Orders from the central
offices of the S.S. were couched in equivocal terms as a hedge
against a possible day of judgment. When it became clear that
such a day of judgment would come, the hedging and intrigue
became greater; the urge to murder also became greater, because
every prisoner became a potential witness.

Again we are dealing with a phenomenon common in all societies. Almost every group which has a specialized social function
to perform is in some measure a secret society, with a body of
rules developed and enforced by the members and with some
power to save its members from outside punishment. And here
is one of the paradoxes of social order. A society without smaller,
rule-making and disciplining powers would be no society at all.
There would be nothing but law and police; and this is what the
Nazis strove for, at the expense of family, church, professional
groups, parties and other such nuclei of spontaneous control. But
apparently the only way to do this, for good as well as for evil
ends, is to give power into the hands of some fanatical small
group which will have a far greater power of self-discipline and
a far greater immunity from outside control than the traditional
groups. The problem is, then, not of trying to get rid of all the
self-disciplining, protecting groups within society, but one of
keeping them integrated with one another and as sensitive as can
be to a public opinion which transcends them all. It is a matter
of checks and balances, of what we might call the social and
moral constitution of society.

Those who are especially devoted to efforts to eradicate from
good people, as individuals, all those sentiments which seem to
bring about the great and small dirty work of the world, may
think that my remarks are something of an attack on their
methods. They are right to this extent; that I am insisting that we
give a share of our effort to the social mechanisms involved as

well as to the individual and those of his sentiments which concern
people of other kinds.

1. ". . . a sect is the nucleus and the yeast of every crowd. . . . To study a
crowd is to judge by what one sees on the stage; to study the sect is to judge
by what one sees backstage." These are among the many passages underlined
by Robert E. Park in his copy, now in my possession, of Sighele's classic work
on political sects. There are a number of references to this work in Park and
Burgess, *Introduction to the Science of Sociology*, Chicago, 1921. In fact, there
is more attention paid to fanatical political and religious behavior in Park and
Burgess than in any later sociological work in this country. Sighele's discussion
relates chiefly to the anarchist movement of his time. There have been fanatical
movements since. The Secret Army Organization in Algeria is but the latest.

2. The best source easily available at that time was Eugen Kogon's *Der SS-
Staat. Das System der Deutschen Konzentrationslager*, Berlin, 1946. Many of my
data are from his book. Some years later H. G. Adler, after several years of
research, wrote *Theresianstadt, 1941-1945. Das Antlitz einer Zwangsgemeinschaft*
(Tuebingen, 1955), and still later published *Die Verheimlichte Wahrheit, There-
sienstaedter Dokumente* (Tuebingen, 1958), a book of documents concerning
that camp in which Czech and other Jews were concentrated, demoralized and
destroyed. Kogon, a Catholic intellectual, and Adler, a Bohemian Jew, both
wrote out of personal experience in the Concentration Camps. Both considered
it their duty to present the phenomenon objectively to the public. None of their
statements has ever been challenged.

3. *Op. cit.*, p. 316.

ON THE POLITICS AND
SOCIOLOGY OF STUPIDITY
IN OUR SOCIETY

LEWIS ANTHONY DEXTER

Why are the high grade retarded—and more generally the "dull" and stupid, slow learners of all sorts—regarded as one of the great problem groups of our society? Why is a special association devoted to mental deficiency and another set up chiefly for parents of retarded children? This inquiry is part of an effort[1] to determine whether application of a prevailing point of view in the study of social problems may be useful in thinking about stupidity. Our concern here is with what Josiah Royce[2] has described as "regulative principles of research [which may] provide the larger ideas of guidance [to] empirical investigation [but which are not in themselves subject to] precise, empirical tests; which, if they happen to prove coherent and illuminating, may provide the basis for more specific hypotheses which can be empirically tested." This prevailing point of view about social problems is based on the postulate that "social problems" are not properly or adequately defined in terms of the obvious and manifest rationalizations or explanations of them by those who experience them. Thus, Myrdal,[3] for instance, demonstrated that the

Financial aid was provided in the preparation of this paper by the Kate Jackson Anthony Trust of Lewiston, Maine; I also am grateful to Michael Begab (U.S. Children's Bureau), Chairman of the Section of the American Association for Mental Deficiency at which the original version of the paper was read (in 1960).

problem of "race," so-called, could best be understood by analysis of *conflicting* moral values; while Wirth[4] similarly was able to show that the common-sense "explanation" of the housing dilemma in the United States in the 1930s omitted the significant *social* factors; and Davis[5] that the stigma imposed upon illegitimacy in most Western societies is subtly interrelated to neglected social institutions.

Generally, problems, ideas, and institutions are taken as given and their consequences seen as self-evident facts of nature. For decades, as is well known, many people, white *and* Negro, saw the issues of "race relations" as self-evident. Similarly, for a century or more, statesmen and thinkers alike adopted a version of laissez-faire economics which made mass unemployment seem absolutely natural in an industrial society. Ultimately, within the last generation, Keynesian economics clarified the conception that the 1929 type of depression is a consequence of systems and institutions, rather than a necessary product of the nature of man in industrial society. This revision of economic thought forced those of us whose economic ideas were learned before 1935 to *un*learn a good deal. A similar effort at rethinking the problems of mental deficiency may be worth while.

An Analogy: Gawkiness as a Cardinal Social Defect

An easy way to indicate how we might reinterpret mental deficiency along these lines is by means of an analogy. Let us imagine a society in which the major target group of social discrimination is composed of the clumsy people, the so-called "gawkies." Let us assume that this is because such a society stresses grace and style in movement *as* we stress intellectual skill. Let us assume that people are taught to abhor clumsiness as many people in our society are taught to abhor stupidity. Let us suppose, to put the analogy on all fours, that there has been invented a system of writing in that society which can only be mastered by those who are graceful; and that the technology of the society is such that a high degree of grace and skill are necessary to run its machines. This will be so, *not* because of the inherent necessities of industrial processes, but because the engineers and businessmen of the society arrange to have things done in a way which takes grace—as a matter of course.

The schools in such a social system would stress movement, dancing, rhythmics, etc. The psychometric institutes of the society would develop an elaborate vocabulary and even more elaborate testing mechanisms for distinguishing between *manifest* grace and inherent *potentiality* for grace of movement. A considerable literature would develop about the "pseudo-clumsy"—and in many cases, parents and schools would be so embarrassed and bothered by the presence of gawky children that they would send them to special custodial institutions where they would not be a constant reminder of parental or pedagogical inadequacy.

Naturally, under such circumstances, the marginally clumsy, permitted to remain at large in the community, would always be conscious of having two strikes already called against them. They would be liable to be institutionalized if they did anything unusual. Naturally, too, clumsy children would become social rejects and isolates, and instead of the moron jokes, beloved in this country,[6] there would probably develop pantomime jokes, directed against the gawky.

Some academic iconoclast might raise considerable doubts as to his own accuracy and academic probity by reporting that, in fact, once out of school and in those economic activities where grace of movement was not really imperative, many persons with a subnormal grace quotient (G.Q.) could earn their own living and even make an economic contribution. There would be great surprise when it was reported that some superficially or evidently clumsy persons could hunt effectively, walk competently, even play games successfully; those reporting such findings would be under considerable pressure to "explain them away." And a scholar, giving a paper with such findings at the National Association on Clumsiness, would find that the news report on her paper made her the target of many scurrilous letters, much as though she had written a Kinsey-type book.[7]

Nevertheless, under the circumstances just described, clumsiness would be regarded as pathological. And these circumstances are analogous to Western European and American attitudes toward stupidity. In making such an assertion, there is no intention to deny the reality of the social problem created by mental deficiency. In the first place, mental deficiency is a problem, or creates problems, because, in fact, there are many activities in our society which *demand* a substantial degree of verbal intelligence. As our analogy suggests, it is probable that some of these activities could be reorganized so as to lessen the problems attendant upon mental deficiency. Nevertheless, mental deficiency would still remain a problem.

But even more significantly in terms of our hypothesis, and going back to the analogy for the moment, clumsiness in our imaginary society would be a real social problem with real social consequences, for as W. I. Thomas[8] has pointed out, the way situations are defined by the society as a whole is for the people in that society the realest of realities. The mother of twins in a society which regards twin-bearing as wicked and repulsive, cannot escape from that "reality" (nor can the mother of twins in a society which regards twin-bearing as a noble act escape from that reality either!)[9] In our imaginary society, clumsiness would be a real social problem with real consequences. It is necessary to emphasize this because it sometimes happens that if we raise questions about the one-factor strictly physiological explanation of a social problem, we are interpreted as denying its reality.

But Are the Stupid Really Discriminated Against and Despised?

Articles by Strickland[10] and by Johnson and Kirk[11] and such studies as that by Wolfenstein[12] seem to the writer to demonstrate that indeed they are. There is also the experience which may be observed over and over again of the denial of employment, of legal rights, of a fair hearing, of an opportunity, to the stupid because they are stupid (e.g., have a low IQ or show poor academic performance), *and not because the stupidity is relevant to the task, or claim, or situation.* A comment by one student of social problems[13] suggests that because discrimination against stupidity *per se* rarely comes to the attention of middle-class people, they ordinarily are quite unaware of it.

This objectively demonstrable, gross discrimination is of great significance. Within the actual life of most readers of these pages, however, the more subtle forms of "discrimination" against stupidity are more likely to be experienced; by analogy, few U.S. sociologists are likely to observe the type of crude anti-Semitism which occurred in medieval Europe or modern Germany: but most of them have seen gestures of withdrawal, listened to anti-Semitic jokes, etc. Unfortunately, no systematic, empirical study of attitudes toward cleverness or dullness is known to exist. As hypothesis, it is suggested that many influential people in our society —including particularly classroom teachers (the carriers par excellence of public, middle-class culture)—show more repugnance (e.g., frown and scold more often) toward stupidity than toward anything else except dirtiness.

A change appears to have taken place in these attitudes toward "stupidity" in recent years. At one time, the stupid were simply objects of derision or scorn: "Simple Simon met a pieman. . . ." Then, in the first two decades of the twentieth century, in the United States and Great Britain at least (concurrently with the growth of mass education), the stupid were regarded with genuine fear and apprehension; "moron" became a synonym for rapist. Both attitudes closely resemble feelings which people have displayed toward foreigners: foreigners are either ridiculous *or* frightening and wicked. But nowadays, in the era of foreign aid and Point IV programs, we believe in teaching foreigners "democracy," modern technology, and other aspects of "our way of life." And, just as some of us are willing to spend a good deal of money on foreign aid, we are willing to do so on teaching the stupid *not* to be stupid.

But the one thing we often find it hard to tolerate about the foreigner is his remaining *fundamentally* alien *and wishing to do so;* and so, similarly, many with a deep interest in mental defectives, are concerned *only* to make them less defective, less stupid. This is a truism which is so obvious as to "go without saying," but since hardly anybody says it we do not perhaps fully realize its consequences.

Clearly, the hypotheses just advanced could be better tested by study of verbal expression, of gesture, of manner, than by analyses of overt ideology. The sophisticated modern, familiar with cultural differentiation, may not *express* his distaste for foreign ways of doing things, but he will manifest in withdrawal or frown exactly the distaste he is trying to conceal, and perhaps *is* concealing from himself.[14]

The analogy with reactions to stupidity is apparent. What needs to be determined is the degree to which the stupid are aware of the slights, contempt, and scolding to which they are exposed and how far they are affected by them in developing a self-image. On the basis of available knowledge, the most plausible hypothesis seems to be that intellectual skill—skill at handling abstract conceptions—is not related to ability to perceive that one is the object to contempt; stupid people are quite as likely to suffer psychologically from contempt as are the more intelligent.[15]

The School, the Democratic Dogma, and the Glorification of Intellectual Aptitudes

But, in most societies, the stupid are not victims of the same overt discrimination as in our society. For in other societies, race, clan-membership, ancestry, religion, status, physical prowess, and probably appearance, play more of a part in determining what rewards one gets and what values one is deprived of than in ours. A stupid person with the right ancestry, for instance, can "get by" better than with us. A society which increasingly focuses on "excellence," meaning thereby intellectual excellence,[16] as does ours, tends more and more to discriminate against stupidity. This is not logically defensible. Because intellectual excellence is required of atomic physicists or for students of sociology is no reason to require intellectual prowess from people in most occupations and activities. In athletics, we admire skilled performance; but we do not[17] discriminate much more against the very incompetent athlete than against the merely mediocre performer. It seems probable that the attitude and response toward stupidity, characteristic of our society, is a function of the common school and of two interrelated ideologies which affect that school. These ideologies are: (1) the post-Renaissance emphasis upon achievement in certain lines of activity as a justification of one's righteousness, The Protestant Ethic, and (2) the radical aspect of democratic thought, identified particularly with the French Revolution and, later, with Jacksonian democracy, with its emphasis on the rights and obligations of equality.

For our present purposes, it is needless to recapitulate the extensive literature on The Protestant Ethic, and its secular variants, as expressed for instance in "Poor Richard's Almanac."[18] It is sufficient to point out that the impact of that ethic upon those affected by it was to lead them to regard stupidity as a sin, rather than as a common human failing. For, it led to failure; and failure was a manifestation of Heavenly displeasure.

The French Revolutionary notion of equality, as it spread to the American frontier and, later, to Soviet Russia, involved not only the *opportunity* to be equal, but the *obligation* to take advantage of the opportunity to be equal. Equal opportunity for education tended to result in compulsory education; and this notion of compulsory equality was embedded in the institution of the public or common school. As Sarason and Gladwin[19] make clear, the school and its demands and instruments—the intelligence test, for instance—play a substantial part in making the high-grade retarded a problem to themselves and to society. The public school has become, under the inspiration of egalitarian democracy, the central sacred institution of the community to a good many people in our society—more in the suburbs than in the slums, more among the tepidly religious than among the fundamentalists, more for some occupations and temperaments than others.

The high-grade retarded become, in such an intepretation of the school, heretics—unwilling heretics, heretics despite themselves, but heretics nevertheless. By merely being what they are, they challenge and cast doubt upon the system through which most people have gone. If, as many of them do, they succeed in earning their own living and getting along well in the community, they are even more puzzlingly unorthodox than those who accommodate to the system by cheating their way through. For the cheat, like the medieval penitent, admits the rightness of the system by his short-cut method of conforming to it. But the stupid who get along well cast doubt on the alleged secular justification of the system—that it helps people succeed. It is repulsive for some to believe that mental defectives can support themselves, no matter how much evidence is amassed to this effect, because, if so, how can we justify the discomforts and sacrifices and anguish of schooling? And when a scholar reported that some mental defectives have been more successful than non-defective counterparts, it is not surprising that she received fifty or so scurrilous attacks; she was denying the sacred.[20]

Community Reorganization and the Social Problem Status of the Retarded and Stupid: A Wholesaler's Approach to Vocational Placement of the Retarded

It follows from what has just been said that if "society" were reorganized, the social problem and the individual problems of the retarded would be much less serious. Clearly, "society" taken as a whole, is not going to be reorganized. But it may help to clarify the sociological nature of the problem of retardation by making the following conceivable assumption. Suppose that a community were to be planned on the assumption that approximately 25 per cent of its adults would be "feeble-minded." How should it differ from the towns and cities we actually know?

First: we would underline the point that there is no evidence that such a community would have any great economic difficulty. Verbal intelligence is necessary for administrators, accountants, attorneys, and engineers, for instance; but this intelligence is not necessary for all employees in manufacturing and service occupations *as such*. (It is, of course, necessary for these individuals as citizens, and as consumers, in the *modern* world, but it is precisely these peripheral necessities we wish to reconsider.)

The widespread use of secondary symbols—for purposes of legal contract and for borrowing money, even for such mechanical activities as reading road signs—is the heart of the problem of the stupid in our world. Accordingly, we would attempt to reorganize matters so that such symbols become less significant.[21]

In such a society, we would, necessarily, abandon our present pattern of education and even compulsory literacy. We would have to change patterns of voting and limit seriously the right to borrow and to lend on credit for consumer purchases. We would probably reorganize certain activities so that they would be conducted more on a group basis and less by individuals than is currently the case;

a stupid woman, as one nursemaid among several caring for children, may do an excellent job, but she lacks the adaptability and initiative to care for them *by herself*. In many old-fashioned villages, mothers, aunts, and cousins, on the whole, cared for children as a joint enterprise, so one particularly stupid woman did not necessarily cause too much trouble. Day-care centers could make it possible for our imaginary community to make similar good use of stupid, good-hearted, affectionate women to care for young children.[22]

The proposal is not purely speculative. If constitutional barriers could be overcome,[23] the organization of such a town or city (ideally on some isolatable spot, such as St. Croix or Martha's Vineyard) would permit us to find out how much of a handicap mental retardation really is (and vice versa, where verbal intelligence is essential). But even if the idea remains in the realm of speculation, it would be extremely valuable if specialists on retardation and backwardness worked out in detail what it would involve if put into practice, because this would permit us to "think out" the social meaning of these conditions in a way which has never been done.

Directions of Research

Usually, when research is started on social problems, it is based upon common-sense assumptions. The history of knowledge suggests, however, that common-sense assumptions are frequently inadequate or erroneous. Until fundamental assumptions have been critically examined, and alternatives postulated and explored, much talent and ingenuity may be wasted. The entire argument of the present paper rests on the assertion that perhaps the common-sense assumptions about mental deficiency need more criticism than they have received. One way to criticize them is to suggest alternative ways of looking at the issues as in the examples of the "gawkies" above, or the proposal in the last section for setting up a community with 25 per cent retarded adults. It is very likely that the last approach is unworkable; but this is not the major point. So long as effort is devoted to formulating alternative constructions[24] and alternative formulations of the issues, there is a better prospect of resolving our problems successfully than there is if we simply stick to elementary common-sense.[25] In other words, the greatest current need in mental deficiency research is the search for new, unorthodox perspectives; they can help to test the value and appropriateness of the prevailing doctrines.

Postscript (1963)

The comments on this article indicate that I should have elaborated the reason why I used the word "Politics" in the title. Perhaps I should have instead used the words "Political Ideology. . ." In any case, I was suggesting or trying to suggest that the whole set of values focusing upon equality, tracing back or often attributed to the French Revolution, help to make the high-grade retardate a problem. In our society, particularly in the United States and in Russia, but to a considerable degree throughout "modern" nations, emphasis upon education as a means of equality is considerable. But in the case of the high-grade retardate (and probably of other "exceptional" persons) the distinction between an opportunity and a compulsion becomes seriously blurred. This is characteristic of the Rousseauian emphasis upon the general will and universal democracy, and poses one of the traditional dilemmas of political philosophy: To emphasize equality means penalizing individuals (loss of liberty) but to stress liberty (for high-grade retardates, for example) means that they ought not to be compelled to be equal. Empirically it is quite probable (the experiments by Moore, Sarason, and Blatt may modify the statement) that compulsory equality cannot in fact produce the results it is supposed to; which is to say merely that human differences in ability are real.

I stated some other aspects of the relationship of political theory to the problem of retardation elsewhere:

Research (in this field) demands an initial philosophical willingness to consider the possibility that traditional values are contradictory and dysfunctional; without a willingness to consider the possibility that the fundamental sources of the problem of high-grade retardation lie in the conflict between the insistence upon forcing everybody to be academically equal, or at least to expose themselves to the opportunity for intellectual equality, and the facts of personality difference, we are not going to get any great benefit out of sociological research on high-grade retardation. To be sure, we will get *comfortable* studies labelled "sociological" in the periphery of the problem, or dealing with the treatment of the severely retarded, but they will be largely irrelevant to the central issue of "adaptation" to retardation.

The point is: sociological research is often *by itself* of little use; to solve problems demands, also, a willingness to reconsider deeply-felt values. The reverse may also be true. The willingness to reconsider values may be useless without implementing research. Remembering Immanuel Kant's famous remark: "The percept without the concept is blind: the concept without the percept is empty," let us say: "Research-based knowledge without the flexible-mindedness to realize that it may imply reconsideration of basic values is blind: the flexible-mindedness which would permit the reconsideration of basic values without any supporting research data is empty."

But following what has just been said, the final point is that in the seemingly practical field of mental retardation, we need to subsidize and underwrite and encourage and listen to political and social philosophy, just as much as we need to develop field research studies. The two should go together; but in view of the greater likelihood that government will finance empirical field studies, it would perhaps be appropriate for private associations and foundations to concentrate on financing the opportunity for political and social reflection—bearing in mind in both cases that the wider the perspective, the broader the framework, the greater the likelihood of valuable results.[26]

1. Other articles in the series include: Lewis A. Dexter, "Research on Problems of Mental Subnormality," *American Journal of Mental Deficiency*, 64 (1960), 835-838. Lewis A. Dexter, "A Social Theory of Mental Deficiency," *ibid.*, 62 (1958), 920-928 (bibliog.). Lewis A. Dexter, "Towards a Sociology of Mental Deficiency," *ibid.*, 61 (1956), 10-16. Lewis A. Dexter, "The Sociology of Adjudication: Who Defines Mental Deficiency?" *American Behavioral Scientist*, 4 (October, 1960, 13-15. Lewis A. Dexter, "Heredity and Environment Re-explored," *Eugenics Quarterly*, 3 (1956), 88-93. Lewis A. Dexter, "A Note on Selective Inattention in Social Science," *Social Problems*, 6 (1958), 176-182.

2. Josiah Royce, "Introduction" to Henri Poincaré, *The Foundations of Science*, New York: Science Press, 1921, pp. xiv-xxi.

3. G. Myrdal, *American Dilemma*, New York: Harper's, 1944.

4. L. Wirth, *Contemporary Social Problems*, Second Edition, Chicago: University of Chicago Press, 1940.

5. K. Davis, "Illegitimacy and the Social Structure," *American Journal of Sociology*, 45 (1939), 215-233.

6. M. Wolfenstein, *Children's Humor, a Psychological Analysis* (esp. the chapter on the moron joke), New York: The Free Press of Glencoe, 1954.

7. This actually happened in the field of mental deficiency.

8. W. I. Thomas and F. Znaniecki, *Polish Peasant in Europe and America*, New York: Knopf, 1927.

9. W. I. Thomas, *Primitive Behavior*, New York: McGraw-Hill, 1937, 9-18. (The three articles by Dexter, cited in footnote 1, which were published in *American Journal of Mental Deficiency*, expand the relevance of Thomas' theory of "definition of the situation" to the social role of the retarded.)

10. C. Strickland, "The Social Competence of the Feeble-Minded," *American Journal of Mental Deficiency*, 53 (1949), 504-515.

11. G. O. Johnson and S. Kirk, "Are Mentally Handicapped Children Segregated in The Regular Grades?" *Journal of Exceptional Children*, 17 (1950), 65-68.

12. *Op. cit.*

13. On my article dealing with the judicial treatment of alleged mental defectives, *American Behavioral Scientist, op. cit.*

14. Edward T. Hall, *The Silent Language*, Garden City: Doubleday, 1959, shows how unspoken Latin-American and Anglo-American reactions to the *embrazo*, for instance, and the degree of physical distance it is appropriate to maintain, color many transcultural relationships. The type of analysis which underlies Hall's entire argument could most profitably be applied to the sphere of disapproval.

15. A particularly perceptive social scientist who has had some contact with retardates, was much surprised at this hypothesis: he had assumed that sensitiveness to slight *and* intelligence go together. No doubt, the definition or recognition of slights depends upon intelligence: a stupid person may notice the praise and not the damnation in being "damned with faint praise," but this and similar facts do not in all probability permit the stupid to live according to the widely accepted stereotype of "the happy moron . . . who does not give a damn."

16. Many stupid would be better off if we attached more weight to *moral* excellence: "Be good, sweet child, let who will be clever."

17. Some groups of young males may, in fact, make such a distinction; but it is not a norm for the society as a whole.

18. M. Weber, *Protestant Ethic and the Spirit of Capitalism*, New York: Scribner's, 1948.

19. S. Sarason and T. Gladwin, "Psychological and Biological Problems in Mental Subnormality: A Review of Research," *American Journal of Mental Deficiency*, 63 (1958), 1115-1307 (reprinted from *Genetic Psychology Monographs*, 1958, and in S. Sarason, *Psychological Problems of Mental Deficiency*, Third Edition, New York: Harper's, 1959).

20. Fortunately for the stupid, the eccentric and the unorthodox, we are not consistent in our acceptance of the sacredness of schooling. There are reservations and ambiguities which permit loopholes for escape and accommodation. This is presumably always true of attitudes toward the sacred.

21. See Lewis A. Dexter, *American Journal of Mental Deficiency*, 1958, *op. cit.*

22. Another example: in the nineteenth century, in a large house with several servants, one *stupid* maid might be very useful. Nowadays, most large houses have only one maid, and she is expected to write down telephone messages, cope with door-to-door salesmen, and otherwise manifest verbal intellligence.

23. Real barriers *are* constitutional, and for the idea to become practical, a very careful study of constitutional law as it affects proposals of this sort would have to be made. This fact is extremely ironic, because in reality, as I have pointed out in my article in *American Behavioral Scientist, op. cit.* (and as the National Council for Civil Liberties has demonstrated in great detail in Great Britain), under present circumstances, retardates do not receive the benefits of due process. Nevertheless, we can be reasonably certain that a formal proposal of the sort here made would, in the present temper of the Courts and especially of the U.S. Supreme Court, be regarded as depriving stupid citizens of essential rights (even though these citizens do not, in practice, get the opportunity to exercise many of these rights).

24. The ideas in the present paper were in part stimulated by the theory of postulation, by the theory of naming and by the transactional approach of the late Arthur F. Bentley in his *An Inquiry into Inquiries,* Boston: Beacon Press, 1954, and also *Behavior . . . Knowledge . . . Fact,* Bloomington: Principia Press, 1935. Mr. Bentley in correspondence with me indicated that he thought the present effort a satisfactory application of his approach.

25. It may very well be that there is a brain damage affecting all mental defectives, not otherwise physiologically abnormal, and that this will ultimately be ascertained. Even supposing this to be so, the brain damage is not necessarily the important point. To the medieval leper, the sociology of leprosy was often more important than its pathology; to the contemporary homosexual, employed by a Federal agency, the sociology of attitudes toward homosexuality is far more significant than the physiological basis (if any) of his deviation; and so, to the "garden variety" mental defective, attitudes toward his affliction may matter more than its genesis. It might, indeed, also be literally true that the exceptionally clumsy or awkward also suffer from some form of brain damage; but, in our imaginary society, postulated above, the social psychology affecting clumsiness would be far more vital to them than the physiology of their situation.

26. Lewis A. Dexter, "The Sociology of the Exceptional Person," *Indian Journal of Social Research,* IV: 1 (January 1963), 35-36.

SYMBIOSIS: THE CASE
OF HOODOO AND THE
NUMBERS RACKET

GEORGE J. McCALL

Everett Hughes has recently called for a systematic re-examination of certain of the seminal concepts of Robert E. Park, singling out for special attention the concept of *"symbiotic* or survival relationships without social interaction—that is, of relationships without any mutual sensitivity or interpenetration of attitudes and sentiments."[1]

The present paper represents only an oblique response to Hughes' challenge, in that the notion of "symbiosis" is here treated in relative isolation from the remainder of Park's theory and attention is focused on the intricacies of a single empirical case—that of hoodoo[2] and the numbers racket.[3]

For Park, interaction was the basic sociological phenomenon, and his theory undertook to explain it in its various *levels*—the level of the senses, of gestures, of symbols, of norms. In fact, his conception of interaction was so broad that he gave serious attention to the competition of men for the very air they breathe. One can abstract from his manifold writings a conception of interaction as something like "the implications of the actions of

This paper is heavily indebted to Albert J. Reiss, Jr., and to J. L. Simmons, who contributed helpful advice throughout the study. I am also grateful to Everett C. Hughes and Talcott Parsons for their comments on an earlier draft and to Martin U. Martel for many insights regarding Park's theoretical framework.

an organism (or set of organisms) for the life-process of other organisms, one upon the other."[4]

To encompass this huge range of social influences, Park proposed a fundamental polar typology of principles of collective organization: (1) *symbiosis,* and (2) conscious coaction (*"socialization"*). The centrality of this distinction within his theory is manifest in the title of one of his last papers: "Symbiosis and Socialization: A Frame of Reference for the Study of Society."[5]

Symbiosis and Socialization

The concept of "symbiosis," like so many of those introduced into the sociological literature by Park, was borrowed from the field of animal ecology and modified to capture the essence of one important form of human relations. And, in fact, Park considered that of the two fundamental principles of organization, symbiosis is the earlier and more basic:

. . . there are many forms of human association in which there is cooperation sufficient to maintain a common economy, but no communication and no consensus sufficient to insure anything like effective collective action. Any association in which widely scattered individuals unconsciously compete and cooperate, or by exchange of goods and services constitute themselves an economic unit, may be described as an entity that is symbiotic rather than social . . . there are forms of associations in which human beings live upon society as predators or parasites upon a host; *or they live together in a relation in which they perform, directly or indirectly, some obscure function of mutual benefit but of which neither they nor their symbionts are conscious.* All these varied forms of association may be described as examples of symbiosis. . . .[6]

There is, however, or there presently emerges in both animal and human societies, the necessity for a more stable form of association . . . [Such] is likely to occur when the interaction of the competing organisms, by adaptation to the habitat or in any other fashion, achieves a relatively stable equilibrium. In such a situation, with the gradual rise in the animal species of a capacity for and means of communication . . . a new and more intimate type of solidarity is made possible; a solidarity which enables societies to coordinate and direct the acts of their individual components in accordance with the interests and purposes of the society as a whole, . . . a more intimate form of association based on communication, consensus, and custom.[7]

This formulation, so basic to the classical period of Chicago sociology, came under heavy fire in the great ecological controversy of the 1940s and seems never to have recovered from the rash of interpretations, reinterpretations, and misinterpretations placed upon it then.[8] Park's published phrasings of it certainly left much to be desired from the standpoint of clarity, consistency, and dimensional analysis, and it was these inadequacies which did much to foster the controversy. Various critics were able to recast Park's polar typology of principles of grouping into those of biotic vs. cultural, ecological vs. social, natural vs. human, subsocial vs. social, impersonal vs. personal, economic vs. moral, competitive vs. cooperative, and a number of other such dichotomies. All these reformulations have some grounds in the writings of Park and his associates, but it seems to this author that all of them miss the central core of the concepts, which receive perhaps their fullest (albeit implicit) application in Long's important paper on the community as an ecology of games.[9]

Long seems to imply that Park was getting at a distinction which Merton was later to make explicit—a distinction between manifest and latent consequences of action. What Park called "socialization" might be regarded as those actions of organisms the social consequences of which are largely *manifest* (i.e., both intended and recognized) to the actors, whereas "symbiosis" represents actions whose social consequences are, to the actors, *latent* (i.e., unintended and unrecognized).[10] The former is most closely approximated in rational and conscious human cooperation, based upon consensus; the latter is found most clearly among animals but can also be seen in human behavior, especially in its organismic, economic, and political aspects.

No amount of scholarly exegesis can serve to establish conclusively that it was indeed this distinction that Park was chiefly working toward, but I submit that it has at least as much support as any of the alternative interpretations. In any case, it is a useful and compatible distinction and will form the basis of the analysis which follows.

There remains, however, one other confusing connotation to be confronted. In general parlance, "symbiosis" means a mutually beneficial interdependence, and this usage has sometimes turned up in the technical literature of general ecology. In the main, however, animal and plant ecologists employ the term to refer to any co-occurrence of diverse species, one or both of which condition the life-process of the other. The special case of a mutually beneficial relationship is termed *mutualism*. Other types of symbiotic relationships include *parasitism* and *predation,* cases in which any benefits are decidedly unilateral.

Of course, there is no compelling reason why sociologists should carry over directly the exact usages of borrowed terms, but Park certainly attempted to do so. To preserve continuity, therefore, we too shall adopt the general ecological usage, substituting for the word "species" the phrase "socially differentiated unit" (e.g., social category, group, association, institution, and the like). Thus, *symbiosis* will refer to the existence of unintended and unrecognized consequences of the action of one socially differentiated unit for the continued functioning of another, and/or vice versa. The term *mutualism* will be reserved for symbiotic relations in which the consequences are mutually eufunctional at some level. *Parasitism* and *predation* are symbiotic relations in which the consequences are eufunctional for one symbiont and in varying degree dysfunctional for the other. (No consensual term exists for mutually dysfunctional symbiosis.)[11]

Examples of each of these types would not be hard to find, but it is not our purpose here to spin out taxonomies of social relations, important as such an endeavor might be in its own right. Rather, our purpose has been to clarify some concepts for the concrete analysis of the relation between two pervasive institutions of the underworld—hoodoo and the numbers racket.

Carlson, in his otherwise incisive analysis of the numbers racket,[12] interprets the relation as one of what he calls "parasitism" but in the usage adopted here might better be termed "exploitation," in that he sees hoodoo as *manifestly* profiting from association with the numbers racket without important consequences for the latter.

It is the thesis of the present paper that the relation is rather one of mutualism, in that it is latently eufunctional for both institutions. In support of this interpretation, we turn now to an examination of data culled from the writer's field observations in

Harlem, from police reports, and from other documentary sources of various kinds.

Hoodoo and Its Charms

"Hoodoo" represents the syncretistic blend of Christian and Nigritic[13] religious traditions in the United States, corresponding to *vodun* ("voodoo") and *obeah* in Haiti, *shango* in Trinidad, *candomble* and *macumba* in Brazil, *santeria* in Cuba, and *cumina* in Jamaica. In twentieth-century hoodoo, however, Catholic elements are less prominent than in the other variants, and Nigritic collective rituals have largely disappeared.[14] Instead, hoodoo has been assimilated to the bewildering variety of store-front spiritualist churches in its truly religious aspects,[15] leaving a heavy residue of sorcery and fetishism as the remaining native elements.

As with sorcery among other peoples, the major foci of hoodoo sorcery lie in the realms of health, love, economic success, and interpersonal power. In all these cases, hoodoo doctors—after careful spiritual "reading" of the client—prescribe courses of action (which always include some hoodoo ritual) and gladly sell him the charms, potions, and amulets the ritual requires.[16]

And lest such piney-woods practices be thought beneath the sophistication of the urban Negro, consider that the writer has visited some 25 of these full-service establishments in Harlem alone.[17] In addition, the colorful window-signs of innumerable "readers" (who carry no line of religious goods) cry out from their store-front or walk-up locations. Marvel Cooke, writing in the *New York Amsterdam-News* of May 25, 1940, declares that "it is a conservative estimate that these people reap nearly $1,000,000 from approximately 50,000 or more Harlemites passing through their door annually." Similar takes are recorded in Chicago, Detroit, Philadelphia, and the other Negro centers of the North. Moreover, many other "doctors" and "readers" carry on thriving businesses by mail, advertising their goods and services in Negro newspapers and popular magazines.

Of the many hoodoo charms prescribed by these agents for securing good luck in gambling, perhaps the most popular is the fabled John the Conqueror Root, with its associated oils and incenses. One possible reason for the pre-eminence of this charm is its greater scope, as indicated in the enthusiastic pitch of a Lenox Avenue "doctor":

Y'know, the women and the numbers, they's both jus' alike. Ain't neither of 'em can hold out long when yuh got Big Johnny workin' fo' yuh.

Other widely sold items include pairs of lodestones (male and female, which must be carefully nourished with iron filings) and minature bone hands (the increasing substitution of plastic in the manufacture of these hands is uniformly deplored by the older "doctors," and a few have refused to handle any but the genuine article). Goldstones, snake vertebrae, and the well-known rabbit's foot are further examples of such gambling charms and are not infrequently encountered.

Among the magical perfumes recommended for gamblers' use, Lucky Dog is widely reputed to be the most powerful, although some experts hold out for Essence of Van Van, Three Jacks and a King, or Has-no-harra. Then too, sachets of Fast Luck or Money Drawing Powders are available for those who prefer a more subtle fragrance.

Turning to a few of the remaining Christian elements of hoodoo, we may note that certain of the Psalms have been credited with magical efficacy as symbols of prayer (e.g., for gambling, Psalms 4, 57, and 114), and these are sold in the form of medals or on parchment, in blood-red ink. The power of these Psalms is thought to be more fully realized if incorporated in a meticulous prayer ritual involving the burning of specially prescribed candles dressed with Prosperity Oil and supplemented by Lady Luck Incense. Experts hold that the ritual must be conducted on a special altar cloth, decked out with Bible and a lithograph or statue of the appropriate saint (Saint Anthony, in the case of gambling rituals).

All of these artifacts (among others) are associated with attempts to secure simple good luck in gambling. Another set is employed in the more interesting and important process of *divination*—specifically, in the attempt to supernaturally divine the specific three-digit number that will prove to be the winning combination on a given day.

Among the more ingenious devices for this purpose are the so-called Psalm Prayer Candles. When lit, these candles reveal a three-digit "Psalm number" as the wax melts away. Needless to say, these numbers are taken to be a revelation of the winning number, despite the fact that most candles are advertised in advance as containing 12 different numbers, one for each day.

Chief among the divining artifacts, however, are the ubiquitous "dream books," in which thousands of objects, events, or themes which might occur in a dream or unusual experience are assigned three-digit numbers.[18] Of those books now used in Harlem, the most popular include Rajah Rabo's Dream Book, the Three Witches Dream Book, Aunt Sally's Dream Book, The Harlem Pete Dream Book, and The Black Cat Dream Book. In some, the numbers are assigned in keeping with well-known hoodoo symbolisms, such as 769 for death or 369 for fecal matter, while in others the assignment seems essentially random. When questioned about the inconsistency between books, not all informants were able to explain as cleverly as one young "reader," who turned the potentially embarrassing situation to her own advantage:

> Well, honey, some books works good fo' some people, 'n others works good fo' other ones. You jus' needs advice about which one'll work fo' you.

Some widely known readers have specialized exclusively in numbers divination and operate largely by telephone and telegraph, advertising in the Negro press. By telegraphing "donations" of $10 to $20 to these big-time readers, one can obtain by return telegram the "blessing" of a certain Psalm—of three digits, of course. In the February 24, 1962, issue of *The New York Courier*, no fewer than 14 such specialists advertised their "hot money blessings," many of them openly mentioning the numbers game.

In fine, then, it is clear that a considerable proportion of the multimillion-dollar "take" of the hoodoo complex stems from its accommodation to the urban Negro's dedicated interest in "playing the numbers."[19] Up to this point, of course, the argument—though considerably more detailed—is in substantial agreement with Carlson's, to the effect that the hoodoo complex profits enormously from its association with the numbers racket.

Beliefs, Bets, and Bankers

What Carlson fails to bring out is the fact that the benefit is *reciprocated,* in that the hoodoo belief system bolsters the profits of the numbers racket in at least two important respects.

First of all, hoodoo *increases the volume of business* in numbers gambling, through evoking greater confidence in the bets by attaching supernatural significance to the numbers played. And then, should a bet still miss, there is almost always available a supernatural explanation of the failure.[20] The player may have used the wrong dream book or placed his bet with the wrong numbers "bank," or, most significantly, he may have failed to play separately all the permutations of his three lucky digits.

In such cases, the player will often stick by a particular hunch for long periods of time, even years, hopping from book to book, bank to bank, and betting the full "combination" (set of permutations). As a less extreme example of this perseverance, one inveterate player had, at the time of interview, played regularly for some months a number listed for his birthday in a particular dream book, explaining that:

God give me that number when I was born, so it must be lucky for me. My birthday ain't gonna change, so I reckon it'll always be lucky. . . . 'Course it don't hit every time, but I reckon it'll hit more often than any other one for me. So why mess around guessin' all the time?

Then too, should a player have a number revealed to him and fail to play it, yet see it win—the most tragic of all fates in the lore of the numbers game—he will curse his stupidity loudly and attempt to make up for it by playing that number long and hard thereafter.[21]

All these mechanisms, deriving from the hoodoo belief system, can be seen to yield the same result: a greater number of bets being placed, even in the face of failure to win.

Secondly, the hoodoo beliefs actually *increase the already overwhelming odds in favor of the "bank,"* by causing bets to cluster on certain numbers corresponding to commonly occurring hoodoo symbols, such as dreams of phalluses or of treading in feces. The utility of this clustering can be manifested in a number of ways. For example, in one variant of the numbers game in which a drawing is made from balls numbered 1 to 78, the "puller" may actually surreptitiously remove any ball on which bets have clustered heavily, then slip it back into the bag after the winner has been drawn, thus dramatically reducing the probability of having to pay off big.[22] In the "night number" variant in which the winning number is determined by rolling three ten-sided dice, the bankers often reserve the right to roll them again if they do not "like" the first number to come up (i.e., if the bets on it are too heavy).[23] Even in those variants in which the bank has no control over the winning number, such clustering naturally decreases the probability of anyone hitting the winner by sheer chance.

However, such clustering can also backfire, if a popular number actually turns up as the winner, for the bank must then pay off all the holders of that number at something like 500 to 1. Maisel relates an ironic instance of such a backfiring when a leading Cleveland numbers banker was sentenced to 6-60 years in prison. Bettors in great numbers immediately bought 660—the eventual winner—and the bank was forced to pay off heavily.[24] Such occasional catastrophes have led the smaller banks to establish "lay-off" systems similar to those in bookmaking, whereby bankers can insure themselves against heavy loss on a popular number through placing part of the bets with other banks (called "spreading the action").[25]

In addition, some banks have instituted "cut number" systems, in which the payoff rate on certain of the most popular numbers is reduced to 300 or 250 to 1. Thus a player who wishes to bet a dollar on one of these importantly symbolic (and hence well-played) numbers must give away as much as 70 cents for the privilege of making his bet at the unreduced odds of 1000 to 1 against him.[26]

The Mutualism of Games

In summary, then, we have seen that the association of hoodoo and the numbers racket is a mutually beneficial one.[27] The numbers bankers profit from the hoodoo beliefs that one can supernaturally manipulate one's fate in gambling, which beliefs serve to increase both the volume of betting and the odds against paying off heavily. In turn, the manufacturers and distributors of hoodoo goods and services receive the benefits of increased sales due to widespread interest in numbers gambling.

Is it, however, a case of true mutualism, as we have so laboriously defined that concept above? Clearly, the criterion of mutual benefit is met, but are the requirements that the consequences be unintended and unrecognized by the actors similarly met?

Generally speaking, the hoodoo practitioners and the numbers bankers do not actively *intend* that their clients should divert any of their limited cash resources to the other; that is, it is a genuinely competitive relationship. (On the other hand, there seem to be some exceptions to this rule, in that a few individuals are said to occupy positions of power in both complexes, cashing in at both ends, as it were.)[28] Nonetheless, many of the personnel of each institution recognize that they do indirectly give business to, and receive it from, the other complex. Thus, on this level of conceptualization, the criteria for mutualism are not met, as Long seems to have realized in his own work:

> A great deal of the communities' activities consist of undirected co-operation of particular social structures, each seeking particular goals and, in doing so, meshing with others. While much of this might be explained in Adam Smith's terms, much of it could not be explained with a rational atomistic model of calculating individuals. . . . The behavior of X is not some disembodied rationality but, rather, behavior within an organized group activity that has goals, norms, strategies, and roles that give the very field and ground for rationality. . . .

It is the contention of this paper that the structured group activities that co-exist in a particular territorial system can be looked at as games. . . . Within each game there is a well-established set of goals whose achievement indicates success or failure for the participants, a set of socialized roles making participant behavior highly predictable, a set of strategies and tactics handed down through experience and occasionally subject to improvement and change, an elite public whose approbation is appreciated, and, finally, a general public which has some appreciation for the standing of the players.[29]

Long suggests, then, that the relevant symbionts are *games,* not categories, groups, or associations. To what extent do hoodoo and the numbers racket qualify as "games" in this sense?

Clearly, such an interpretation of the numbers racket is strictly correct, for its central activity is literally a game—a game of chance, which dictates goals, roles, and strategies and often commands the entire community as an interested and informed public. As has happened with so many play-forms of games (e.g., baseball, boxing, football, racing, etc.), it has become a "multi-situated game,"[30] requiring a vast proliferation of goals, roles, and strategies beyond those of the "gaming encounter" itself. Many of these extrinsic game-elements are oriented toward the ecological struggle with the other games of the community—the law enforcement game, the ecclesiastical game, the hoodoo game, etc.

Although the game-character of hoodoo is perhaps less obvious than that of the numbers racket, it is no less essential. Hoodoo is basically a game of men against the supernatural powers (rather than against chance), in which certain moves—in the form of rituals—are calculated to pay off in very specific valued outcomes. In some instances, the game can become an interpersonal one, as when two enemies bring to bear upon one another their most horrible "tricks" and counter-tricks. And because this is a game which depends so heavily on esoteric knowledge and ritual expertise (rather than chance), a whole body of supporting specialists has arisen to function as coaches and elite public.

This characterization of the game-structure of hoodoo and the numbers racket is, of course, much too brief and is intended only to suggest the applicability of Long's concepts to the present case. If this much be granted, we must note that the two games are truly distinct entities, so that the assertion of a relationship between them does not become tautological. As we have seen, one of the games involves man against chance for cash payoffs, with other men involved in holding the pot, recording bets, and allocating the money. The other game pits man—aided by expert human counsel—against the supernatural, for a wide variety of payoffs. Thus, the games differ in roles, goals, strategies, and publics, and neither involves any essential consideration of the continued playing of the other. Furthermore, they are historically independent, hoodoo originating among the Negro slaves of the South, and the numbers game being introduced to this country by the early Italian immigrants to New York City.

How, then, do these games come to have latent, eufunctional consequences for one another? And whose actions are generating these consequences?

Sharing a common territorial field and collaborating for different and particular ends in the achievement of over-all social functions, the players in one game make use of the players in another and are, in turn, made use of by them. . . . Each is a piece in the chess game of the other, sometimes a willing piece, but, *to the extent that the games are different, with a different end in view.*[31]

It is in this framework that Park's conception of symbiosis can most clearly be seen to operate in human society, in that the game-actions of the players in one game latently affect the outcome-structure of another game—and in the present case, these effects are mutual and beneficial, constituting an instance of true mutualism.

The Future of the Relation

In looking back at the mechanisms of the mutualism between the two illicit games, it should be clear that without substantial overlap in players, none of these mechanisms can operate effectively.[32] If hoodoo clients do not play the numbers on the basis of divination, hoodoo is of no more consequence to the numbers racket than is a political party or a social lodge. If numbers players do not buy gambling charms and divination artifacts, the numbers racket is likewise of no special importance to hoodoo.

Consequently, if a separation of clientele could be effected, both operations might be substantially weakened, possibly result-

ing in considerable saving of ill-spent cash for many Negro families. However, such a facile "solution" to this social problem
seems unlikely to occur, for at least three important reasons.

First, the lore of each of the games contains references to how
the other can be played for personal ends. Therefore, participation
in one game has implications for the individual's "learning structure" *vis-à-vis* the other.[33] The more he learns about hoodoo,
the more likely he is to learn about the numbers racket, and vice
versa. Given the fact that in the Negro sections of the larger
cities the "opportunity structure" for participation in each is
approximately the same, the learning structure probably accounts
for most of the variance in predicting participation. On the other
hand, because there is and has been such an extensive overlap
in clientele, the learning structures available to the individual
before participation in either are also roughly comparable; hence,
it is "overdetermined" that a great many individuals will learn
about (and probably play) both games.

Second, the two games, in their intersection, seem to have a
certain integrative function for the Negro community, furnishing
much of the content of casual conversation, imparting temporal
structure to the day, and offering a sense of participation in a
community-wide institution.[34]

Third, the proceeds from the numbers racket constitute a vital
source of capital for other criminal activities.[35] Consequently,
given the beneficial relationship of hoodoo to the numbers game,
organized crime as a whole has a not inconsiderable stake in
hoodoo, as do large numbers of politicians and law enforcement
agents receiving bribes in return for their protection of numbers
gambling.[36]

In light of this interdependence of powerful interests and the
continuing influx of Negroes from the rural South—the heartland
of hoodoo—it seems safe to conclude that the mutualism of hoodoo
and the numbers racket will persist in the ghettos of the metropolitan North for some time to come.

1. Everett C. Hughes, "What Other?" in Arnold M. Rose, editor, *Human
Behavior and Social Processes,* Boston: Houghton Mifflin, 1962, pp. 119-127.
Quotation from p. 120, italics added.

64   *Deviance and Its Place in Society*

2. "Hoodoo," a term explained in some detail in subsequent sections, is one of several sometimes used to refer to the syncretistic blend of Christianity and African fetishism which still exerts considerable influence on the Negro in America. See, for example, Zora Neale Hurston, "Hoodoo in America," *Journal of American Folklore*, 44 (1931), 317-418; and Norman E. Whitten, Jr., "Contemporary Patterns of Malign Occultism Among Negroes in North Carolina," *Journal of American Folklore*, 75 (1962), 311-325.

3. By the "numbers racket" is meant here the illicit institution organized around those forms of gambling in which players bet on numbers within a specified range, one of which is later selected in a "random" fashion as the winner. The most popular variant currently is "mutuel racehorse policy," in which a three-digit number is derived from the published odds figures of the race-result chart of some given track. A most intensive analysis of the institution is found in Gustav G. Carlson, *Numbers Gambling: A Study of a Culture Complex*, unpublished Ph.D. dissertation, University of Michigan, 1940. Also useful are Capt. Frederick W. Egen, *Plainclothesman: A Handbook of Vice and Gambling Investigation*, New York: Arco Publishing Co., 1959, 60-82; and *An Investigation of Law Enforcement in Buffalo*, New York: New York State Commission of Investigation, January, 1961, 31-39.

4. See, for example, his endorsement of Georg Simmel's usage: "That which constitutes 'society' is evidently types of reciprocal influencing. . . . Only when an influence is exerted, whether immediately or through a third party, from one upon the other has society come into existence in place of a mere spatial juxtaposition or temporal contemporaneousness or succession of individuals. If, therefore, there is to be a science, the object of which is to be 'society' and nothing else, it can investigate only these reciprocal influences. . . ." Quoted in Robert E. Park and Ernest W. Burgess, *Introduction to the Science of Sociology* (2nd ed.), Chicago: University of Chicago Press, 1924, 341, 349.

5. *American Journal of Sociology*, 45 (1939) 1-25.

6. *Ibid.*, p. 4, italics added.

7. *Ibid.*, p. 21. It is illuminating to note that Talcott Parsons makes a distinction strikingly similar to Park's polar typology but explicitly chooses to restrict his theory to the second mode of association. See Talcott Parsons and Edward A. Shils, with James Olds, "The Social System," in Parsons and Shils, editors, *Toward a General Theory of Action*, Cambridge: Harvard University Press, 1951, 190-233, especially p. 193.

8. The controversy, precipitated by Milla A. Alihan's withering critique of ecology (see her *Social Ecology*, New York: Columbia University Press, 1938), is amply documented in George A. Theodorson, editor, *Studies in Human Ecology*, Evanston, Ill.: Row, Peterson and Co., 1961, especially pp. 5-7 and 77-154.

9. Norton E. Long, "The Local Community as an Ecology of Games," *American Journal of Sociology*, 64 (1958), 251-261.

10. Robert K. Merton, "The Unanticipated Consequences of Purposive Social Action," *American Sociological Review*, 1 (1936), 894-904.

11. A similar taxonomy can be constructed for manifest consequences and for mixed cases such as those in which the consequences are unintended but recognized. All these types (as well as many others) can be derived from three taxonomic parameters: (1) which party or parties *intended* the particular consequences of its actions? (2) which *recognized* these consequences? and (3) for which are they *eu*- or *dysfunctional*? Cf. Robert K. Merton, "Manifest and Latent Functions," in Merton, *Social Theory and Social Structure* (revised ed.), New York: The Free Press of Glencoe, 1957, 19-84, especially pp. 50-54.

12. Carlson, *op cit.*, 4-5, 89, 114-126.

13. Following the usage of George Peter Murdock, in his *Africa: Its Peoples and Their Culture History*, New York: McGraw-Hill, 1959, 14-16.

14. Zora Neale Hurston, *Mules and Men,* Philadelphia: Lippincott, 1935, 221-235; and Newell N. Puckett, *Folklore Beliefs of the Southern Negro,* Chapel Hill, N.C.: University of North Carolina Press, 1926, 520-582.

15. St. Clair Drake and Horace R. Cayton, *Black Metropolis: A Study of Negro Life in a Northern City,* New York: Harcourt, Brace, 1945, 641-653; and Arthur Huff Fauset, *Black Gods of the Metropolis: Negro Religious Cults of the Urban North,* Philadelphia: University of Pennsylvania Press, 1944.

16. Hurston, "Hoodoo in America," *op. cit.;* Robert Tallant, *Voodoo in New Orleans,* New York: Macmillan, 1946; and Whitten, *op. cit.*

17. Ronald Sullivan, writing in *The New York Times Magazine* of November 11, 1962, 136-137, estimates that there are approximately 100 such shops in the whole of New York City.

18. Harry B. Weiss, "Oneirocritica Americana: The Story of American Dream Books," *Bulletin of the New York Public Library,* 1944, 519-541, 642-653.

19. Drake and Cayton, *op. cit.,* 470-494; Dan Wakefield, "Harlem's Magic Numbers," *The Reporter,* February 4, 1960, 25-26; Julian Mayfield, *The Hit,* New York: Vanguard Press, 1956.

20. In the metaphysical tradition of numerology, it is held that "The 'number field' is merely the normal location of the nine digits, and the naught or cipher. This formation, as applied to dreams, is not entirely stationary. In fact numbers are constantly on the move. That is the real safeguard to the [numbers] game, otherwise it would be a simple thing to 'hit,' day after day. Remember, the figures change positions each time a play is checked into the day's 'totals.' " *The Lucky Red Devil Combination Dream Book,* 1961 edition, McKees Rocks, Pa.: Caro Book Co., 1961, p. 14.

21. Mayfield, *op. cit.,* 190-191; Egen, *op. cit.* p. 77; and Paul Oliver, *Blues Fell This Morning: The Meaning of the Blues,* New York: Horizon Press, 1960, p. 148.

22. Albert Q. Maisel, "Return of the Numbers Racket," *Collier's,* January 19, 1949, p. 22.

23. *An Investigation of Law Enforcement in Buffalo, op. cit.,* 36-37.

24. Maisel, *op. cit.,* p. 73.

25. *An Investigation of Law Enforcement in Buffalo, op. cit.,* 37-38.

26. *Ibid.,* p. 35.

27. One of the persistent difficulties in functional analysis is specification of the desideratum in terms of which eu- or dysfunctionality are to be judged. In the present paper, the cash income of the institutions has served as the primary index of their relative well-being. Other indicators—such as the number of participants, the ratio of staff to clients, the areal coverage of their services, the rate of cultural innovations within each complex, etc.—might also have been chosen, with essentially similar results, but none of these reveal the actual *mechanisms* of benefit so cleanly and directly as do the cash transactions themselves.

28. Oliver, *op. cit.,* 147-150; Maisel, *op. cit.,* p. 71; and Carlson, *op. cit.,* 112-113.

29. Long, *op. cit.,* 252-253.

30. The concepts of "multi-situated game" and "gaming encounter" have been borrowed from Erving Goffman's analysis of game-structure in his "Fun in Games," in Goffman, *Encounters,* Indianapolis: Bobbs-Merrill, 1961, 15-81, especially 34-44.

31. Long, *op. cit.,* p. 253. Italics added.

32. As Long notes, "the simultaneous playing of roles in two or more games is an important manner of linking separate games." *Ibid.,* p. 253.

33. The use of "learning structure" and "opportunity structure" in this paragraph stems from Cloward's analysis of illegitimate means for securing legitimate ends, e.g., in this case, personal gain. See Richard A. Cloward, "Ille-

gitimate Means, Anomie, and Deviant Behavior," *American Sociological Review*, 24 (1959) 164-176.

34. Mayfield, *op. cit.*, 144-146; Julian Mayfield, "Numbers Writer: A Portrait," *The Nation*, May 14, 1960, 424-425; and Wakefield, *op. cit.*

35. Estes Kefauver, *et al.*, *The Kefauver Committee Report on Organized Crime*, New York: Didier, 1951, p. 175. The racket is estimated to gross something between two and six billion dollars annually, largely in the Negro sections of Northern cities. See Maisel, *op. cit.*, and Harry C. Barnes and Negley Teeters, *New Horizons in Criminology* (3rd edition), Englewood Cliffs, N.J.: Prentice-Hall, 1959, p. 30.

36. Fred J. Cook, *A Two-Dollar Bet Means Murder*, New York: Dial Press, 1961, 130-139.

DRUG ADDICTION
UNDER BRITISH POLICY

EDWIN M. SCHUR

As Lindesmith recently pointed out,[1] most research on opiate addiction has tended to neglect crucial policy questions. There has, for example, been little research into the social consequences of different laws regarding addiction. This is unfortunate for not only may such research facilitate evaluation of policy alternatives, but also it may permit the drawing of an important distinction—between primary and secondary aspects of addict behavior.[2] Because major features of the American drug situation—especially illicit trafficking and addict-crime—have been attributed largely to prevailing American policies toward addiction,[3] it would seem vital to examine the conditions which prevail where alternative policies are in force. The operation of British narcotics policy offers an interesting basis for comparison.

While it is not possible here to spell out in detail the British policies,[4] these may be summarized briefly as follows. British drug laws strictly regulate the possession and supplying of opiates (and other dangerous drugs). Authorized drug-handlers are required to keep full records of all drug transactions, such records being subject to periodic inspection. Doctors who violate the drug laws are subject to fine or imprisonment, and further may lose the right to possess and prescribe such drugs. The basic approach to the addict, however, is nonpunitive. Although doctors are warned against supplying drugs for "the mere gratification of addiction," the doctor has the basic responsibility of deciding when an addict is in medical need of drugs. Prevailing policy directives permit prescription of drugs to addicts in connection with gradual withdrawal treatment; also where severe withdrawal symptoms make a "cure" medically inadvisable or where regular small doses afford the addict a fairly normal existence which he could not otherwise achieve. (In practice, most doctors apparently attempt to limit or reduce the dosage given to addict-patients.) While there is no official registration of addicts, doctors are requested to inform the Home Office of addicts they are treating, and there is reason to believe that a high proportion of addicts is reported. Medical and law-enforcement authorities appear to be in general agreement that this medically-oriented approach to addiction is desirable. And in fact this approach seems to have been eminently successful in controlling addiction. The number of addicts in Britain is believed not greatly to exceed 500, and even this represents a long-term decrease, from an estimate of 700 addicts made in 1935.

Sources of Data

Available data do not permit one to generalize with assurance about all aspects of the British narcotics situation. There is, for example, no way in which one can obtain a representative sample of British addicts. (The Home Office file of known addicts, established through assurances of complete anonymity, is not accessible for research purposes.) Nonetheless, if one recognizes at the outset that definite quantitative findings are unlikely, collection of various types of data can give us a fairly clear picture of the British approach in operation. The present writer has relied[5] on the following sources of information: government reports and personal interviews by the writer with narcotics officials from the Home Office; further interviews with several physicians and psychiatrists specializing in the treatment of addiction; questionnaire responses of thirteen British medical specialists reporting a collective experience with over 400 addiction cases encountered in a variety of medical settings;[6] more detailed information about twenty-one "representative" addict-patients, also provided by these specialists; brief descriptions of all recent addict-customers of one of the two large London chemists which are believed to supply drugs to a good many of London's "legal" addicts;[7] information provided to the writer by five narcotic addicts, four in lengthy personal interviews (together with some written materials) and the fifth in writing (with comments by the referring social worker); a sample survey of 147 twenty-one-year-olds in

Table 1
Characteristics of Reported British Addicts
(1951-1959)

	1951	1954	1955	1957	1959
Total number of addicts	301	317	335	359	454
Male	153	148	159	174	196
Female	148	169	176	185	258
Total in medical and allied occupations	77	72	86	88	68*
Doctors	75	69	70	70	
Dentists	1	2	2	2	
Pharmacists	1	1	—	1	
Nurses	—	—	14	15	

Age: Majority of Known Addicts Over Thirty Years of Age†

* For 1959 no breakdown by specific professions was provided.

† In 1959 further statistics regarding age were presented: no addicts under 20; 50 (11%) 20-34; 92 (20%) 35-49; 278 (61%) 50 and over; 34 (8%) unknown.

Source: Adapted from Home Office, *Reports to the United Nations* on the Working of the International Treaties on Narcotic Drugs, 1951, 1954, 1955, 1957, 1959.

one borough of Greater London, inquiring into contact with drug use, knowledge of drug laws, and attitudes toward addiction. The data presented here are those which it is thought bear most directly on the issue of "primary" and "secondary" aspects of addiction.

Social Characteristics of Addicts

Occupation and Social Class. All available evidence supports the contention that a large proportion of British addicts is found in medical and related occupations. The official figures are given in Table 1. In 1959, 68 of 454 known addicts (15 per cent) were in this occupational category. Table 2 shows the occupations of addict-patients admitted to one large British mental hospital from 1950 to 1957. This hospital, under the National Health Service, treats patients from a large area of Great Britain. While there is

Table 2
Occupations of Addicts in Large British Mental Hospital, 1950-1957 (N 73)

Occupation	Number of Patients
Doctor	42
Housewife	9
Nurse	7
Doctor's wife	2
Chemist	1
Radiographer	1
Physiotherapist	1
Soldier	1
Sailor	1
Sheep farmer	1
Housemaid	1
Clerk	1
Laborer	1
Teacher	1
Wine merchant	1
Engineer	1
Banker	1

Source: Personal communication to the writer.

no assurance that admissions to this hospital were fully representative of British addicts generally, data based on such a large number of addicts (for this country) and covering all admissions during an eight-year period, merit attention. Of 73 addicts admitted, 54 (74 per cent) were in medical or allied occupations (this includes two listed as "doctor's wife"). "Housewife" was the only nonmedical category with more than one case. Among the remaining cases there was, it may be noted, no preponderance of working-class persons, or persons who would seem especially exposed to underworld influences. A somewhat similar distribution of occupations was found among the twenty-one "representative" addict-patients reported by specialists. Seven of these addicts were physicians and three nurses; three had "independent means" and two were musicians. Remaining cases included a secretary, a housewife, a journalist, and a designer of film sets; one addict had no occupation and in one case no information was reported.

A pharmacist's description of addict-customers suggests the social class background found in a group of addicts not so heavily dominated by the medical profession. Although the descriptions were incomplete, a large proportion seemed to come from the middle and upper-middle classes (indeed "aristocracy" was mentioned in two cases). Similarly, specialists who provided general information about their experience with addiction cases reported that most of the addicts they had observed belong to the middle class. No respondent specified only the working class. One indicated both the working and middle classes, but nine of the thirteen specialists mentioned only the middle class and two others indicated that addicts belong to the middle and upper classes. It has been suggested that in America "the disproportionate number of addicts who originate in the lower class can undoubtedly be attributed to the greater availability of drugs in slum areas. . . ."[8] Such greater availability does not seem to exist in Britain (see below) and this difference is reflected in the apparently differing social class distribution of British addicts.

Age and Sex. Such data on age as the writer has been able to collect bear out official statements that most British addicts are over thirty years of age. Of the addicts reported on in detail by specialists, eighteen were over thirty; only three were in the 20-29 age group, and none was under twenty. Similarly most of the addict-customers described by the pharmacist appeared to be over thirty and no case of an addict under twenty was specifically indicated. An unpublished study of Borstal boys and wayward girls[9]—in which virtually no addiction was encountered—strongly suggests that addiction is not a major pattern of behavior among disturbed adolescents in Britain. And this writer's survey of a sample of twenty-one-year-olds (see below) uncovered little contact with addictive drugs—at least in one section of Greater London. Clearly the age of addicts is related to the differential exposure to drugs of various class and occupational groups. If many or most British addicts are doctors (and this would strongly suggest professional access to drugs as a major circumstance in the introduction to drug use), it can easily be seen why the onset of addiction typically would not occur before the age of thirty. Where (as in the United States) initiation into drug use appears to be due to association with other users, or to the efforts of a "pusher," it is more likely that young people will be drawn to the narcotic habit.

As Table 1 indicates, there is in Britain a high proportion of female addicts. This sex distribution is also indicated in the twenty-one addicts described by specialists; eleven were female and ten male. In the series of cases reported by the pharmacist there were sixteen female addicts and only seven males (doctors are underrepresented in this group of addicts). The fact that probably there are in Britain at least as many female addicts as male ones is interesting. This is in sharp contrast to America—where male addicts greatly outnumber female addicts, even if one makes allowance for unrecorded cases. Furthermore, the addict sex ratio in Britain is quite unlike the familiar sex ratio (in Britain as well as in the U.S.) for "criminal" activities.[10] We may at least wonder whether the fact that "criminal" is a typical male role in both countries, coupled with the differing legal definitions of addiction, has not itself affected the addict sex ratios.

Race. The writer knows of no evidence indicating a sizeable number of colored addicts in Great Britain. It is true that in recent years the majority of persons convicted for unlawful possession of marihuana have been colored. But the same has not been true of the small number of opiate addicts who come into conflict with the law. For example, in 1959 twenty-six persons were convicted of offenses involving manufactured drugs; most of these persons were addicts who forged prescriptions or obtained drugs from two doctors at once. "Those convicted were mostly British subjects of European origin."[11] Very likely few of the doctor-addicts in Britain are colored persons. And there is no reason to assume a high proportion of colored addicts among the remaining cases. In the series reported by the pharmacist—which seems to include a good variety of nonphysician addict types—there was only one colored person, a West Indian jazz drummer. Eighteen of the twenty-three addicts were native Britons, there were two Americans and for two cases this information was not provided. A strikingly similar distribution was found among the twenty-one "representative" cases reported by specialists: eighteen were British, one Indian, one West Indian, and one American.

Many colored persons in Britain have arrived there relatively recently, and such persons have not been subjected to such systematic discrimination as have the American Negroes. One would not expect, for instance, to find among them any organized "expressive social movement" involving the use of addictive drugs, of the sort described by Finestone.[12] Furthermore, while some colored people in Britain have come from countries where marihuana use is widespread, they may well be totally unfamiliar with the use of truly addictive drugs. Finally, to the extent that minorities may be especially exposed to underworld influences, the fact that apparently there is in Britain no strong link between narcotics and the underworld (this point is developed below) reduces the likelihood of colored addiction. The British experience seems to make quite clear (though perhaps nobody has contested this point) that racial characteristics, *as such,* in no way directly affect susceptibility to addiction.

Addict Behavior

Sex and Marriage. It is well recognized that addiction to opiates almost always decreases sexual appetite and activity. This factor, together with other aspects of the addict's situation, has been said to "corrode marriage and family relationships."[13] There is little information available regarding the sexual and marital adjustment of British addicas. Data collected by the writer suggest that addiction does interfere with normal sexual functioning, even where (as in Great Britain) the addict is relatively free from persecution. Several British addicts told me that they could get along reasonably well with regular doses of low-cost drugs—except for normal sexual relations. Most of the specialists who supplied information about addiction stated that few or no addicts seem able to function satisfactorily in sexual or family relationships, even if regularly supplied with drugs. In two of the twenty-one specific cases reported, addiction "completely" prevented satisfactory functioning in this realm, in ten cases such functioning was "very much" prevented and in five cases it was "somewhat" prevented. However, two addicts (a doctor and a nurse—both reported by the same psychiatrist) were said to be "not at all" affected in this way. For two cases, this information was not available. This same series provides the only information the writer has obtained concerning the marital status of British addicts:

of these patients, nine were married, eight single, two widowed, one divorced and one separated.

Occupational Adjustment. Even American studies have recognized that some addicts are able to maintain work efficiency provided they regularly obtain the necessary drugs. Nonetheless, as these same studies stress, usually there are formidable obstacles to the addict's holding down a job.[14] In Britain at least a few of the difficulties are lessened. The addict is relieved of the time-consuming and money-eroding task of procuring illicit drugs. But he is still in need of frequent injections (often a difficult thing to reconcile with normal job demands) and he still is subject to such soporific effects as opiates may have on him. As might be expected, then, even British addicts appear to have considerable job difficulties. None of the specialists completing the writer's questionnaire felt that "practically all" addicts can function satisfactorily in an occupation when regularly provided with drugs; only one respondent thought that "many" addicts can get along in a job. Of the twenty-one "representative" patients, one was said to be "completely" prevented from satisfactorily functioning in a job, eleven were held to have been "very much" prevented from doing so, and four were reported to have been "somewhat" prevented from doing so. Only one was "very little" prevented, and two (the same two whose sexual behavior was said to be unaffected) were "not at all" impaired in this way. (No answer was provided in two cases.) Many of the addicts in the dispensary-customer series were not holding down full-time jobs; apparently quite a few either had independent means or were being supported temporarily by their families. Available evidence, in short, suggests that even under a medically-oriented approach, most addicts probably will remain social liabilities of sorts.

Criminality. There is wide agreement among American researchers that most addict-crime is undertaken to provide funds for the purchase of illicit drugs.[15] This conclusion seems to be supported by the British evidence. British addicts crave their drugs every bit as much as addicts elsewhere.

It is the lack of drugs, says R, not the influence of them, which leads to crime. He pointed out to the writer that if an addict didn't have drugs he would do almost anything to get them: "Say I knew you had some on you, and I asked you to lend me a tablet, sell me one or give me one. There's no limit to what I could do to get it. If I had a gun in that closet [pointing to a closet near the writer], man, you'd be as good as dead. I might regret it later, but you could commit murder without hardly thinking, if you needed the drug" (from personal interview by writer).

But legal provision of narcotics largely obviates the need to commit crimes in order to support one's habit. Very few addicts are imprisoned for any kind of offense.[16] As already noted, the few addicts who are convicted of drug offenses have obtained drugs from chemists by forged prescriptions or obtained supplies from more than one doctor.[17] Most of the writer's medical respondents felt that few or none of the addicts they had observed were "likely to have close friends in the criminal underworld" or to identify themselves with a criminal role or way of life. Similarly, they reported knowledge of few criminal violations (no violent crimes) on the part of the addicts; such slight criminal activity as was reported was believed to have begun largely after the onset of addiction. Likewise, little criminality was reported for the twenty-one detailed cases; in fact, only about half of these patients were believed to have committed violations of the narcotics laws. (Only six of the seventy-three addict patients in the mental hospital were reported to have violated the drug laws, and none was known to have committed any other sort of crime.)

Proselytism. It is well known that in the United States many addicts have introduced other persons to the drug habit. Often addicts sell drugs in order to finance their own habits, though the psychological need to recruit fellow-addicts also has been cited.[18] It is possible that this latter factor may be operative, to a certain extent, even in Britain. However, the overriding point would seem to be that given the British practice, "there is little or no economic incentive to spread the habit to others."[19] In the United States most addicts can hardly afford not to "push" drugs, but in Britain a statement such as the following could well be a truthful one:

S feels that there is some psychological pressure on the addict to get someone else "turned on," but he says that since becoming "hooked" he has never encouraged anyone to take up drugs (although he has sold some pills to fellow-addicts who needed drugs). He states that to get someone else hooked, "would give me the terrible horrors, make me jump, I couldn't live with myself. There *are* things that matter to me *before* the fix. Some things I wouldn't do; very few, but there are some" (from personal interview by writer).

Thus one British medical observer writes: "Generally speaking, I feel that to say 'addicts make addicts' is untrue. Very few addicts influence others to start the habit. Their reaction to a request for a taste of the drug is usually to warn of its dangers and to point out what harm it had done to them."[20] Most of the present writer's medical respondents felt that none or only a few of the addicts they had seen would be likely to induce friends to take up drugs. (One doctor answered that many addicts would be likely to do this, adding "Very important, that is how it spreads." But a number of this respondent's replies differed sharply from those of other specialists, and there is reason to believe his experience is somewhat unusual.)[21] This writer knows of no evidence seriously contradicting the Government's assertion that "The addict who is also a 'pusher' is seldom encountered in the United Kingdom."[22]

Not only can the British addict avoid personal involvement in the sale of illicit drugs, but actually there is very little illicit trafficking at all, on anyone's part. Table 3 shows that in recent years most drug convictions have involved hemp (marihuana) while very few have involved manufactured drugs (opiates, etc.). Clearly these statistics reflect variations in the nature and extent of enforcement efforts (note for example the interesting fluctuations

Table 3
Convictions for Violations of Dangerous Drugs Act, 1951-1959

CONVICTIONS FOR OFFENSES INVOLVING

Year	Hemp	Opium	Manufactured Drugs	Total
1951	127	62	43	232
1954	144	28	47	219
1955	115	17	37	169
1957	51	9	30	90
1959	185	18	26	229

Source: Same as Table 1.

in hemp and opium convictions in 1955-57-59). But variations
in enforcement alone cannot account for the fact that the authorities hardly ever encounter opiate traffickers; one official told the
writer he could not even recall a case involving heroin trafficking
in recent years.[23] Even addicts who have had contact with such
black market as does exist agree that these illicit operations are
very small-scale.

According to R, there is very little illicit trafficking in drugs.
"Archer Street [London] is about the only place. You can't get it
anywhere else. Leave Archer Street, you leave it all behind. Hang
around Archer Street, you're in trouble. The more you see people
use it, the more you need it all the time." Such drug traffic as does
exist is kept up mostly for (and by) "joy poppers" or "jazz junkies"
who aren't hooked yet and can't show a doctor they need it." (And
also for those who, like himself in the early days, are afraid of
getting involved with the law.) Those persons who are really addicted
invariably end up in hospital, then "if they can't do anything for you,
you probably go to a doctor—maybe with a letter from the hospital
saying that you need it."
    . . . While R has had his difficulties "stretching" the drugs given
him by the doctor, he writes of the legal prescription of drugs for
addicts: "I think it's a great ideal. Because it help people like me
who has to have it, and prevent the underworld dope-peddlers starting
that bussness [sic] in G. Britain" (interview and personal correspondence).

Addict Subculture. As might be expected from the above
data, there has been no pronounced development of an addict
subculture in Britain. Cohen has noted that the prerequisite for the
emergence of a subculture is "the existence in effective interaction
with one another, of a number of actors with similar problems of
adjustment."[24] For many British addicts, there need be little interaction with other addicted persons; furthermore, their typical
problems of adjustment (some of which are noted above) tend
to call for individual rather than group solutions. We are familiar
with American findings showing a high degree of geographical
concentration of addicts.[25] There is no evidence of any such concentration in Britain, and the Home Office informed this writer
that addresses of known addicts indicate a widespread geographical
distribution. Unlike his American counterpart, the British addict
need not seek out special areas where it is "easier to obtain an

in-group solidarity and maintain contacts with other addicts and 'dope' peddlers."[26]

The fact that addict argot probably is used by only a minority of British addicts also points to the incomplete subcultural development. It may be noted that both S and R (whose cases are referred to above) use addict-jazz argot fairly regularly; apparently the familiar American usage is now spreading to small groups of jazz-connected drug users in Britain.[27] But while Lindesmith's earlier assertion that in England "there is apparently no argot in existence"[28] may no longer hold true, there is no evidence that the use of such argot is widespread. Doctors, nurses and pharmacists who become addicted are not *ipso facto* members of an addict subculture.

Dr. M presents an appearance which is entirely at odds with all stereotyped notions about the "typical" drug addict. A tall and somewhat portly middle-aged man, rather distinguished looking with gray hair and a neat moustache, he was meticulously dressed for the interview in a sombre pin-stripe suit. Although he did give signs of possible nervousness, other that Dr. M in no way seemed anything other than a quiet, polite and ordinary medical doctor.

. . . M clearly does not in any way think of himself as a "criminal," and although he probably accepts the fact that for some time he definitely has been an "addict," almost certainly he would dissociate himself from "junkies." At no time during the interview did M use any term of addict argot; furthermore he stated that he did not know any other persons who were addicted. In general, the writer felt that the likelihood of Dr. M ever having had contact with an addict subculture was extremely slim. He had no knowledge of, or interest in, any of the nonmedical literature about addiction. And indeed, despite his condition, he showed no strong interest in addiction as a general topic of discussion . . . (from personal interview by writer).

Of course we know that addicts of this type exist even in America, but the significant thing is that as far as can be determined M probably represents the prevailing type of British addict, rather than the exception.

Public Contact and Attitudes

Further light was thrown on the British addiction situation by the writer's attitude survey (during the summer of 1958) of a sample of 147 twenty-one-year-olds in the Greater London Borough of Willesden—only fragmentary results of which can be included in this brief article. Findings there substantiated the hypothesis that there would be (for all socioeconomic categories) very little personal contact with narcotics. This was so despite the fact that general attitude responses (anomie, attitudes toward police, etc.) indicated, particularly among the working-class respondents, a climate of opinion which might well have been conducive to experimentation with drugs. Of the 147 respondents seven reported seeing someone using a "reefer," one of these persons had also tried to obtain a reefer for himself, and three persons (including one of those who had seen a reefer) reported possibly having seen someone taking heroin.[29]

Also interesting was the relatively low rate of elementary knowledge of these drugs. Seventy-six per cent knew (given four choices) that a reefer looks like a cigarette, and 52 per cent correctly indicated that heroin usually is taken by injection; "don't know" responses on these items were 21 per cent and 38 per cent, respectively. Only 47 per cent answered both items correctly. Correct knowledge of the drugs was not concentrated in the deteriorated areas of the borough; in fact such knowledge was significantly greater in the "better" areas. Similarly, while the obtained differences were not statistically significant, there was an evident tendency for knowledge of drugs to vary directly (rather than inversely) with social class. Furthermore, while somewhat higher percentages of those reporting attendance at jazz clubs than of those not attending correctly identified the drugs, none of these differences was statistically significant. Both for those correctly identifying the drugs, and for the sample as a whole, the most frequently cited sources of information about drugs were the mass media; interpersonal communication (friends, school, jazz club, youth club) was cited only infrequently. While the Willesden sample may not be fully representative (colored persons were somewhat underrepresented among these respondents), at the very least the findings indicate that knowledge and use of these drugs has not become at all widespread among the white majority at this age level.

Although these respondents were considerably misinformed

about the British laws regarding addicts, their attitudes toward addicts coincided with the tenor of British policies. Asked whether the drug addict is primarily a sick person or primarily a bad person, 2 per cent answered bad, 80 per cent said sick, 12 per cent said both, and 6 per cent answered "don't know." Respondents were also asked, "What should be done with drug addicts? Should they be sent to prison, put in hospital, or merely be left alone?" Not a single respondent said that addicts should be sent to prison; 93 per cent suggested hospital, 2 per cent said addicts should be left alone, and 5 per cent answered "don't know." (This result is interesting when compared with the response to another item, "Prison is too good for sex criminals; they should be publicly whipped or worse." 50 per cent of the sample agreed with this statement, yet not one of these same persons prescribed prison for the addict.)

Interpretation

Admittedly it is a big question whether differences between the American and British addiction situations can be attributed to the contrast in policies. Even prior to the enactment of current laws, there was in Britain little feeling that a really pressing addiction problem existed. And various other cultural and historical differences between the two countries also may relate to the current differences. Such factors, however, seem inadequate to explain fully the persistence in Britain of such a slight drug "problem." While one might attribute the absence of antisocial behavior among British addicts to "the kind of person" who becomes an addict there, the question remains why such persons, and not others, become addicts. It may well be that for our kind of society certain doctors represent an "irreducible minimum" addiction problem. Britain has fairly well prevented addiction from spreading to other persons typically believed to be susceptible to addiction. It can hardly be maintained that there is a paucity of such persons in Britain.[30] The well-recognized connection between supply-and-demand mechanisms and underworld operations[31] lies at the heart of the matter. This writer knows of no evidence, or common-sense argument, refuting the assertion that low-cost and legal provision of drugs (as in Britain) inevitably curtails illicit traffic. Conversely, it is clear that current American policy cannot achieve its stated aims. A close analogy may be seen in the continuing ineffectiveness of efforts to eradicate illegal abortion facilities.[32]

The British data seem to indicate that certain aspects of addict behavior (notably addict-crime, involvement in trafficking, development of addict-subculture) cannot directly be attributed either to the effects of the drugs or to psychological characteristics of the individuals involved. Rather the presence or absence of such behavior appears to be determined largely by the nature of the societal reaction to the addict. As such, these features of a country's addiction "problem" are subject to intentional modification through changes in public policy. Other aspects of addict behavior (such as impairment of sexual and occupational functioning) seem to be primary and hence would almost always be incident to a state of addiction. The likelihood of nonproductivity by the addict does not, however, imply any overtly antisocial behavior. Recognizing this fact is crucial, both for the understanding of addiction as a social problem, and for the development of adequate policies toward that problem.

1. Alfred R. Lindesmith, "Social Problems and Sociological Theory," *Social Problems*, 8 (Fall, 1960), 98-102.

2. "When a person begins to employ his deviant behavior or a role based upon it as a means of defense, attack, or adjustment to the overt and covert problems created by the consequent societal reaction to him, his deviation is secondary." Edwin M. Lemert, *Social Pathology*, New York: McGraw-Hill, 1951, p. 76.

3. Rufus King, "The Narcotics Bureau and the Harrison Act: Jailing the Healers and the Sick," *Yale Law Journal*, 62 (April, 1953), 736-749, and "Narcotic Drug Laws and Enforcement Policies," *Law and Contemporary Problems*, 22 (Winter, 1957), 113-131; various writings of Alfred Lindesmith, including "Federal Law and Drug Addiction," *Social Problems*, 7 (Summer, 1959), 48-57; E. M. Schur, "Drug Addiction in America and England," *Commentary*, 30 (September, 1960), 241-248.

4. See Jeffery Bishop, "A Commentary on the Management and Treatment of Drug Addicts in the United Kingdom," in Marie Nyswander, *The Drug Addict as a Patient*, New York: Grune and Stratton, 1956, 148-161; Alfred Lindesmith, "The British System of Narcotics Control," *Law and Contemporary Problems*, 22 (Winter, 1957), 138-154; and E. M. Schur, "British Narcotics Policies," *Journal of Criminal Law, Criminology and Police Science*, 51 (March-April, 1961), 619-629.

5. E. Schur, "Drug Addiction in Britain and America: A Sociological Study

of Legal and Social Policies," doctoral thesis, London School of Economics, University of London, 1959.

6. Questionnaires were sent to the 100 active members of the Society for the Study of Addiction residing in Britain. Sixty-three replies were received. Many of the respondents had retired from medical practice, had merely an academic interest in addiction, or were concerned only with alcoholism—a major interest of the Society. While only thirteen supplied data on addict-patients, it should be recognized that experience with addiction, for the country as a whole, probably is very limited. These specialists collectively did encounter a large number of cases. (There is the possibility of some slight duplication in the cases on which general responses were based. There was no duplication in the twenty-one detailed cases, referred to below.)

7. There are two all-night chemists in Central London, and many addicts (anxious to know that a new supply of drugs is in their possession at the earliest possible moment) will seek to have their prescriptions filled just after midnight on the date listed. These two pharmacies have large dispensing departments, and keep large supplies of narcotics on hand. (The second firm refused to cooperate in this study.)

8. D. P. Ausubel, *Drug Addiction: Physiological, Psychological and Sociological Aspects*, New York: Random House, 1958, p. 64.

9. I am grateful to Dr. T. C. N. Gibbens, of the Institute of Psychiatry, University of London, for providing this information. His study covered one hundred boys sent to Borstal in 1953 and another hundred in 1955, and about 700 wayward girls seen in a London remand home between 1951 and 1958.

10. Howard Jones, *Crime and the Penal System*, London: University Tutorial Press, 1956, 110-112.

11. Home Office, *Report to the United Nations on the Working of the International Treaties on Narcotic Drugs for 1959*, London, 1960, p. 8.

12. Harold Finestone, "Cats, Kicks, and Color," *Social Problems*, 5 (July, 1957), 3-13 (reprinted in this volume).

13. Charles Winick, "Narcotic Addiction and its Treatment," *Law and Contemporary Problems*, 22 (Winter, 1957), 18.

14. *Ibid.*, 14-15.

15. For discussion of this question see Harold Finestone, "Narcotics and Criminality," *Law and Contemporary Problems*, 22 (Winter, 1957), 69-85. For the view that the addict is basically a criminal, and that his deviance antedates his addiction, see H. J. Anslinger and W. F. Tompkins, *The Traffic in Narcotics*, New York: Funk and Wagnalls, 1953.

16. Lindesmith cites unofficial figures given him by a British official: "in 1952, there were six; in 1953, sixteen; in 1954, eleven; and up to July 1956, eleven." Lindesmith, "The British System of Narcotics Control," *op. cit.*, 141-142. More recent inquiries by the present writer corroborated this assertion that there is only a very small number of addicts in prison.

17. See note 11, *supra*. Since most doctors attempt to reduce the addict's dosage, a point may be reached at which the addict feels he can "stretch" his drugs no further and must obtain a somewhat increased dosage (preferably from another doctor). The situation of addicts "between doctors" may lead to drug violations, but the low rate of addict-crime and the limited nature of illicit traffic (discussed further below) indicate that this is not a major problem.

18. Winick, *op. cit.*, p. 17.

19. Lindesmith, "The British System of Narcotics Control," *op. cit.*, p. 148.

20. Bishop, *op. cit.*, p. 159.

21. For example, he referred specifically to two addicts who acquired the habit abroad and later came to England; one of these cases also involved extensive underworld connections and activities—which had begun in the original country of residence. These hardly seem typical British cases.

22. Home Office, *Report to the United Nations for 1957*, p. 6. Similarly, in its 1959 Report (p. 5), the Government notes with regard to occupations of reported addicts that there was no known case of an "illicit trafficker" among them.

23. A recent report stated: "No evidence of organised illicit traffic in manufactured drugs in the United Kingdom has come to light, nor has there been any case in which a person addicted to such drugs has been found to have obtained regular supplies from illicit sources." Home Office, *Report to the United Nations, for 1954*, p. 2. Similarly, the 1959 Report (p. 6) asserts: "there was no evidence to suggest that manufactured drugs were illicitly imported into or illicitly produced in the United Kingdom."

24. Albert K. Cohen, *Delinquent Boys*, New York: The Free Press of Glencoe, 1955, p. 59.

25. See the summary of recent findings in John A. Clausen, "Social Patterns, Personality and Adolescent Drug Use," in Alexander Leighton, J. Clausen, and R. Wilson, eds., *Explorations in Social Psychiatry*, New York: Basic Books, 1957, 230-277, esp. 237-239.

26. R. Faris and H. W. Dunham, *Mental Disorders in Urban Areas*, New York: Hafner Publishing Co., 1960, p. 122.

27. A popular writer claiming to have had considerable personal experience in the British underworld has written that addict jargon "comes to us from America," and that it "is not used very much over here as yet. . . ." Frank Norman, "A Bit About Slang," *Encounter* (October, 1958), 41-42.

28. Alfred Lindesmith, "The Argot of the Underworld Drug Addict," *Journal of Criminal Law and Criminology*, 29 (July-August, 1938), 263.

29. It should be noted that in Britain marihuana is taken in the form of cigarettes and that the term "reefer" is in use there. Similarly, while it may be difficult to distinguish the taking of heroin from other injections (and morphine and pethidine are often used by British addicts, rather than heroin) it was assumed that any respondent seeing a person thought to be a drug addict taking an injection would give at least a qualified affirmative answer. The questions regarding marihuana were included because of claims by critics of the British approach (U.S. officials) that British policy has given rise to a serious marihuana menace.

30. One study of personality development in an English slum, revealed the prevalence of just the sort of psychological traits American researchers associate with addiction-proneness. Betty Spinley, *The Deprived and the Privileged*, London: Routledge and Kegan Paul, 1953. As Clausen has noted (pointing to this finding), "the prevalence of such characteristics, coupled with the availability of narcotics and the laxness of local social controls, would constitute important predisposing influences to drug use and addiction." John Clausen, "Social and Psychological Factors in Narcotics Addiction," *Law and Contemporary Problems*, 22 (Winter, 1957), 46.

31. E. R. Hawkins and W. Waller, "Critical Notes on the Cost of Crime," *Journal of Criminal Law and Criminology*, 26 (Jan.-Feb., 1936), 679-694; Alfred Lindesmith, "Organized Crime," *Annals*, 217 (September, 1941), 119-127; Robert K. Merton, *Social Theory and Social Structure*, Revised Edition, New York: The Free Press of Glencoe, 1957, 78-80.

32. As one early study succinctly observed: "the stakes were so large that an effective technique was developed to make abortion available to all those who wished it and who had the price to pay, and at the same time, to escape the penalties that the law provided." Abraham Rongy, *Abortion: Legal or Illegal?* New York: Vanguard Press, 1933, 118-119.

PART TWO

DEVIANCE AND THE
RESPONSE OF OTHERS

SOCIETAL REACTION TO DEVIANT BEHAVIOR: PROBLEMS OF THEORY AND METHOD

JOHN I. KITSUSE

Sociological theory and research in the area traditionally known as "social pathology" have been concerned primarily with the classification and analysis of *deviant forms of behavior* and relatively little attention has been given to societal reactions to deviance.[1]

In a recent paper, Merton has noted this lack of a "systematic *classification* of the responses of the conventional or conforming members of a group to deviant behavior."[2] Similarly, Cohen has observed that "a sociology of deviant behavior-conformity will have to devise ways of conceptualizing responses to deviant behavior from the standpoint of their relevance to the production or extinction of deviant behavior."[3] In this paper, I shall discuss some of the theoretical and methodological issues posed by the problem of societal reactions to deviant behavior and report on a preliminary attempt to formulate a research design which specifically takes them into account.

I propose to shift the focus of theory and research from the forms of deviant behavior to the *processes by which persons come*

An earlier form of this paper was read at the meetings of the American Sociological Association, 1960. I have profited from the critical comments and suggestions of Herbert R. Barringer, Aaron V. Cicourel, Sheldon L. Messinger, and H. Jay Shaffer. Troy S. Duster's valuable assistance in the analysis of the data is gratefully acknowledged.

to be defined as deviant by others. Such a shift requires that the sociologist view as problematic what he generally assumes as given—namely, that certain forms of behavior are *per se* deviant and are so defined by the "conventional or conforming members of a group." This assumption is frequently called into question on empirical grounds when the societal reaction to behaviors defined as deviant by the sociologist is nonexistent, indifferent, or at most mildly disapproving. For example, in his discussion of "ritualism" as a form of deviant behavior, Merton states that it is not that such behavior is treated by others as deviant which identifies it as deviant "since the overt behavior is institutionally permitted, though not culturally prescribed."[4] Rather, the behavior is deviant because it "clearly represents a departure from the cultural model in which men are obliged to move onward and upward in the social hierarchy."[5] The discrepancy between the theoretically hypothesized and empirically observable societal reaction is also noted by Lemert: "It is fairly easy to think of situations in which serious offenses against laws commanding public respect have only mild penalty or have gone entirely unpunished. Conversely, cases are easily discovered in which a somewhat minor violation of legal rules has provoked surprisingly stringent penalties."[6]

Clearly, the forms of behavior *per se* do not activate the processes of societal reaction which sociologically differentiate deviants from non-deviants. Thus, a central problem for theory and research in the sociology of deviance may be stated as follows: What are the behaviors which are defined by members of the group, community, or society as deviant, and how do those definitions organize and activate the societal reactions by which persons come to be differentiated and treated as deviants? In formulating the problem in this way, the point of view of those who interpret and define behavior as deviant must explicitly be incorporated into a sociological definition of deviance. Accordingly, deviance may be conceived as a process by which the members of a group, community, or society (1) interpret behavior as deviant, (2) define persons who so behave as a certain kind of deviant, and (3) accord them the treatment considered appropriate to such deviants. In the following pages, this con-

ception of deviance and societal reaction will be applied to the
processes by which persons come to be defined and treated as
homosexuals.

Societal Reactions to "Homosexual Behavior"

As a form of deviant behavior, homosexuality presents a
strategically important theoretical and empirical problem for the
study of deviance. In the sociological and anthropological literature[7] homosexual behavior and the societal reactions to it are
conceptualized within the framework of ascribed sex statuses and
the socialization of individuals to those statuses. The ascription
of sex statuses is presumed to provide a complex of culturally
prescribed roles and behaviors which individuals are expected to
learn and perform. Homosexual roles and behaviors are conceived
to be "inappropriate" to the individual's ascribed sex status, and
thus theoretically they are defined as deviant.

With reference to American society, Allison Davis states:
"Sex-typing of behavior and privileges is even more rigid and
lasting in our society than is age-typing. Indeed, sexual status and
color-caste status are the only life-long forms of rank. In our
society, one can escape them in approved fashion only by death.
Whereas sexual mobility is somewhat less rare today than formerly, sex-inappropriate behavior, social or physical, is still one of
the most severely punished infractions of our social code."[8] In
Lemert's terminology, norms concerning sex-appropriate behavior
have a high degree of "compulsiveness" and social disapproval of
violations is stringent and effective.[9] Homosexuals themselves
appear to share this conception of the societal reaction to their
behavior, activities, and subculture.[10]

Such a view of homosexuality would lead one to hypothesize
that "sex-appropriate" (and conversely "sex-inappropriate") behaviors are unambiguously prescribed, deviations from those
prescriptions are invariably interpreted as immoral, and the reactions of the conventional and conforming members of the society
to such deviations are uniformly severe and effective. The evidence
which apparently supports this hypothesis is not difficult to find,
particularly with reference to the definition and treatment of male

homosexuals. Individuals who are publicly identified as homosexuals are frequently denied the social, economic, and legal rights of "normal" males. Socially they may be treated as objects of amusement, ridicule, scorn, and often fear; economically they may be summarily dismissed from employment; legally they are frequently subject to interrogation and harassment by police.

In citing such evidence, however, it is important to note that the societal reaction to and the differentiation of homosexuals from the "normal" population is a consequence of the fact that the former are "known" to be homosexuals by some individuals, groups or agencies. Thus, within the framework of the present formulation of homosexuality as a form of deviant behavior, the processes by which individuals come to be "known" and treated as sexually deviant will be viewed as problematic and a problem for empirical investigation. I shall not be concerned here with the so-called "latent homosexual" unless he is so defined by others and differentially treated as a consequence of that definition. Nor will I be concerned with the variety of "internal" conflicts which may form the "clinical" picture of the homosexual except insofar as such conflicts are manifested in behavior leading others to conceive of him as a homosexual. In short, I shall proceed on the principle that it is only when individuals are defined and identified by others as homosexuals and accorded the treatment considered "appropriate" for individuals so defined that a homosexual "population" is produced for sociological investigation.[11] With reference to homosexuality, then, the empirical questions are: What forms of behavior do persons in the social system consider to be "sex-inappropriate," how do they interpret such behaviors, and what are the consequences of those interpretations for their reactions to individuals who are perceived to manifest such behaviors?

In a preliminary attempt to investigate these questions, an interview schedule was constructed[12] and administered to approximately seven hundred individuals, most of whom were college undergraduates. The sample was neither random nor representative of any specified population, and the generalizability of the interview materials is limited except insofar as they are relevant to the previously noted hypothesis that homosexual behavior is uniformly defined, interpreted, and negatively sanctioned. The interview materials will therefore be used for the purpose of illustrating the theory and method of the present conception of deviance and societal reaction.

The objectives of the interview were threefold: It attempted to document (1) the behavior forms which are interpreted as deviant, (2) the processes by which persons who manifest such behaviors are defined and (3) treated as deviant. Thus, in the construction of the interview schedule, what the interviewees considered to be "deviant" behavior, the interpretations of such behavior, and the actions of subjects toward those perceived as deviant were addressed as empirical questions. Labels such as alcoholic, illiterate, illegitimate child, and ex-convict were assumed to be categories employed by persons in everyday life to classify deviants, but the behavioral forms by which they identify individuals as deviants were treated as problematic. "Sexual deviant" was one of ten categories of deviants about which subjects were questioned in the interview. Among the more than seven hundred subjects interviewed, seventy-five stated they had "known" a homosexual and responded to questions concerning their experiences with such individuals. The data presented below are drawn from the protocols of interviews with this group of subjects.

The interview proceeded as follows: The subject was asked, "Have you ever known anyone who was a sexual deviant?" If he questioned the meaning of "deviant," the subject was asked to consider the question using his own meaning of "sexual deviant."

When the subject stated he had known a sexual deviant—a homosexual in this case—as he defined the term, he was asked to think about the most recent incident involving him in an encounter with such a person. He was then asked, "When was the first time you noticed (found out) that this person was a homosexual?" followed by "What was the situation? What did you notice about him? How did he behave?" This line of questioning was focused on the interaction between the subject and the alleged deviant to obtain a detailed description of the situation which led the subject to define the person as homosexual. The subject's description of the person's behavior was systematically probed to clarify the terms of his description, particularly those which were interpretive rather than descriptive.

Evidence of Homosexuality

Responses to the question, "When was the first time you noticed (found out) that this person was homosexual?" and the related probes suggest that an individual's sexual "normality" may be called into question with reference to two broad categories of evidence. (a) *Indirect evidence* in the form of a rumor, an acquaintance's experience with the individual in question subsequently communicated to the subject, or general reputational information concerning the individual's behavior, associates, and sexual predilections may be the occasion for suspecting him to be "different." Many subjects reported that they first "found out" or "knew" that the individuals in question were homosexuals through the reports of others or by "reputation." Such information was generally accepted by the subjects without independent verification. Indeed, the information provided a new perspective for their retrospective as well as prospective observations and interpretations of the individuals' behaviors. An example of how hearsay organizes observation and interpretation is the following statement by a thirty-five-year-old male (a draftsman):

I: Then this lieutenant was a homosexual?
S: Yes.
I: How did you find out about it?
S: The guy he approached told me. After that, I watched him. Our company was small and we had a bar for both enlisted men and officers. He would come in and try to be friendly with one or two of the guys.
I: Weren't the other officers friendly?
S: Sure, they would come in for an occasional drink; some of them had been with the company for three years and they would sometimes slap you on the back, but he tried to get over friendly.
I: What do you mean "over friendly"?
S: He had only been there a week. He would try to push himself on a couple of guys—he spent more time with the enlisted personnel than is expected from an officer.

(b) *Direct observation* by the subject of the individual's behavior may be the basis for calling the latter's sexual "normality" into question. The descriptions of behavior which subjects took to be indicative of homosexuality varied widely and were often vague. Most frequently the behaviors cited were those *"which everyone knows"* are indications of homosexuality. For example, a twenty-year-old male subject reports an encounter with a stranger at a bar:

I: What happened during your conversation?
S: He asked me if I went to college and I said I did. Then he asked me what I was studying. When I told him psychology he appeared very interested.
I: What do you mean "interested"?
S: Well, you know queers really go for this psychology stuff.
I: Then what happened?
S: Ah, let's see. I'm not exactly sure, but somehow we got into an argument about psychology and to prove my point I told him to pick an area of study. Well, he appeared to be very pensive and after a great thought he said, "Okay, let's take homosexuality."
I: What did you make of that?
S: Well, by now I figured the guy was queer so I got the hell outta there.

The responses of other subjects suggest that an individual is particularly suspect when he is observed to behave in a manner which deviates from the *behaviors-held-in-common* among members of the group to which he belongs. For example, a behavior which is presumed to be held-in-common among sailors in the U.S. Navy is intense and active sexual activity. When a sailor does not affirm, at least verbally, his interest in such activity, his competence as a "male" may be called into question. A twenty-two-year-old engineer, recently discharged from the Navy, responds to the "how did you first know" question as follows:

All of a sudden you just get suspicious of something. I began to wonder about him. He didn't go in for leave activities that most sailors go for. You know, girls and high times. He just never was interested and when you have been out at sea for a month or two, you're interested. That just wasn't Navy, and he was a career man.

Although the responses of our subjects indicate there are many behavioral gestures which "everyone knows" are indicators of homosexuality in males, there are relatively few such gestures that lead persons to suspect females of homosexuality. Following is an

excerpt from a twenty-one-year-old college co-ed whose remarks
illustrate this lack of define indicators *prior* to her labeling of an
acquaintance as a homosexual:

I: When was the first time you noticed she was a deviant?
S: I didn't notice it. I thought she had a masculine appearance
when I first saw her anyway.
I: What do you mean?
S: Oh, her haircut, her heavy eyebrows. She had a rather husky
build.
I: Exactly when did you think she had a masculine appearance?
S: It was long after [the first meeting] that I found out that she
was "one."
I: How do you define it?
S: Well, a lesbian. I don't know too much about them. It was
_____ who told me about her.
I: Did you notice anything else about her [at the first meeting]?
S: No, because you really don't know unless you're looking for
those things.

Unlike "effeminate" appearance and gestures in males, "masculine" appearance in females is apparently less likely to be immediately linked to the suspicion or imputation of homosexuality. The
statements of the subject quoted above indicate that although
"masculine appearance" is an important element in her conception
of a lesbian, its significance did not become apparent to her until
a third person told her the girl was homosexual. The remarks of
other subjects in our sample who state they have "known" female
homosexuals reveal a similar ambiguity in their interpretations of
what they describe as indicators of sexual deviance.

A third form of evidence by direct observation is behaviors
which the subjects interpreted to be *overt sexual propositions*.
Descriptions of such propositions ranged from what the subjects
considered to be unmistakable evidence of the person's sexual
deviance to ambiguous gestures which they did not attempt to
question in the situation. The following is an excerpt from an
interview with a twenty-four-year-old male school teacher who
recounts an experience in a Korean Army barrack:

I: What questions did he [the alleged homosexual] ask?
S: "How long have you been in Korea?" I told him. "What do
you think of these Korean girls?" which I answered, "Not

too much because they are dirty." I thought he was probably homesick and wanted someone to talk to. I do not remember what he said then until he said, "How much do you have?" I answered him by saying, "I don't know, about average I guess." Then he said, "Can I feel it just once?" To this I responded with, "Get the hell out of here," and I gave him a shove when he reached for me as he asked the question.

In a number of interviews, the subjects' statements indicate that they interpreted the sequence of the alleged deviants' behavior as progressively inappropriate or peculiar in the course of their interaction with them. The link between such behavior and their judgment that a sexual proposition was being made was frequently established by the subjects' growing realization of its deviant character. A twenty-one-year-old male subject recalls the following experience involving his high school tennis coach who had invited him to dinner:

S: Anyway, when I get there he served dinner, and as I think back on it—I didn't notice it at the time—but I remember that he did act sort of effeminate. Finally he got up to change a record and picked up some of my English themes. Then he brought them over and sat down beside me. He began to explain some of my mistakes in my themes, and in the meantime he slipped his arms around me.

I: Would you say that this was done in a friendly manner or with an intent of hugging you or something?

S: Well, no, it was just a friendly gesture of putting his arm around my shoulder. At that time, I didn't think anything of it, but as he continued to explain my mistakes, he started to rub my back. Then he asked me if I wanted a back rub. So I said, "No! I don't need one." At this time, I began thinking something was funny anyway. So I said that I had to go. . . .

The Imputation of Homosexuality

When a detailed description of the subject's evidence concerning the alleged homosexual was obtained, he was asked, "What did you make of that?" to elicit information about how he interpreted the person's observed or reported behavior. This line of questioning yielded data on the inferential process by which the subject linked his information about the individual to the deviant category "homosexual."

A general pattern revealed by the subjects' responses to this section of the interview schedule is that when an individual's sexual "normality" is called into question, by whatever form of evidence, the imputation of homosexuality is documented by *retrospective interpretations* of the deviant's behavior, a process by which the subject reinterprets the individual's past behavior in the light of the new information concerning his sexual deviance. This process is particularly evident in cases where the prior relationship between the subject and the alleged homosexual was more than a chance encounter or casual acquaintanceship. The subjects indicate that they reviewed their past interactions with the individuals in question, searching for subtle cues and nuances of behavior which might give further evidence of the alleged deviance. This retrospective reading generally provided the subjects with just such evidence to support the conclusion that "this is what was going on all the time."

Some of the subjects who were interviewed were themselves aware of their retrospective interpretations in defining individuals as sexually deviant. For example, a twenty-three-year-old female graduate student states:

I: Will you tell me more about the situation?

S: Well, their relationship was a continuous one, although I think that it is a friendship now as I don't see them together as I used to; I don't think it is still homosexual. When I see them together, they don't seem to be displaying the affection openly as they did when I first realized the situation.

I: How do you mean "openly"?

S: Well, they would hold each other's hand in public places.

I: And what did you make of this?

S: Well, I really don't know, because I like to hold people's hands, too! I guess I actually didn't see this as directly connected with the situation. What I mean is that, if I hadn't seen that other incident [she had observed the two girls in bed together] I probably wouldn't have thought of it [i.e., hand-holding] very much. . . . Well, actually, there were a few things that I questioned later on that I hadn't thought really very much about. . . . I can remember her being quite affectionate toward me several times when we were in our room together, like putting her arm around my shoulder. Or I remember one time specifically when she asked me for a kiss. I was shocked at the time, but I laughed it off jokingly.

The Interactional Contexts of Societal Reactions

When the description of the alleged deviant's behavior and the subject's interpretations of that behavior were recorded, the subject was asked "What did you do then?" This question was directed toward documenting societal reactions to deviant behavior. Forms of behavior *per se* do not differentiate deviants from non-deviants; it is the responses of the conventional and conforming members of the society who identify and interpret behavior as deviant which sociologically transform persons into deviants. Thus, in the formulation of deviance proposed here, if the subject observes an individual's behavior and defines it as deviant but does not accord him differential treatment as a consequence of that definition, the individual is not sociologically deviant.

The reactions of the subjects to individuals they defined as homosexuals ranged from immediate withdrawal from the scene of interaction and avoidance of further encounters with the alleged deviants to the maintenance of the prior relationship virtually unaltered by the imputation of deviance. The following responses to the question, "What did you do then?" illustrate the variation in sanctions directed toward persons defined as homosexuals.

Explicit disapproval and immediate withdrawal. The most negatively toned and clearly articulated reaction reported by our subjects is that of the previously quoted Korean War veteran. It is interesting to note that extreme physical punishment as a reaction to persons defined as homosexuals, a reaction which is commonly verbalized by "normal" males as proper treatment of "queers," is not reported by any of the subjects. When physical force is used, it is invariably in response to the deviant's direct physical overtures, and even then it is relatively mild, e.g., "I gave him a shove when he reached for me."

Explicit disapproval and subsequent withdrawal. In the following excerpt, a twenty-year-old male college student describes an encounter with a man whom he met in a coffee shop. In the course of their conversation, the man admitted his homosexuality to the subject. The two left the coffee shop and walked together to the subway station.

> I: What happened then?
> S: We got to the subway whereupon he suggested that he hail a cab and take me up to Times Square—a distance of almost 40 blocks.
> I: Did you agree, and what did you think?
> S: Yes, I thought he was just being very nice and I had no qualms about getting in a cab with a homosexual since I was quite sure I could protect myself against any advances in a cab.
> I: What happened then?
> S: When we had ridden a little distance, he put his hand on my knee, and I promptly removed it saying that it just wasn't right and that I wanted nothing of it. However, after a while, he put his hand back. This time I didn't take it away for a while because I was interested in what he would do. It was the funniest thing—he rubbed and caressed my knee the same way in which I would have done this to a girl. This time I took his hand and hit him across the chest with it, telling him to "cut it out." Finally, we got to Times Square, and I got out.

This example and that provided by the Korean War veteran's reaction to behavior interpreted as overt sexual propositions suggest the possibility that responses to persons suspected of homosexuality or defined as homosexuals on the basis of more indirect evidence of appearance, "confessions," hearsay, reputation, or association will vary within an even wider range of applied sanctions. Indeed, the statements of subjects concerning their responses to persons alleged to be deviant on such evidence indicate that the modal reaction is disapproval, implicitly rather than explicitly communicated, and a restriction of interaction through partial withdrawal and avoidance. It should be noted further that although the subject's silent withdrawal from an established relationship with an alleged deviant may represent a stronger disapproval than an explicitly communicated, physically enforced sanction against a stranger, moral indignation or revulsion is not necessarily communicated to the deviant. The subject's prior relationship with the alleged deviant and the demands of propriety in subsequent interactions with him qualify the form and intensity of the sanctions which are applied. Thus, when the organization of the subject's day-to-day activities "forces" him into interaction with the deviant, expressions of disapproval are frequently constrained and diffused by the rules of deference and demeanor.[13] The following excerpts provide illustrations:

Implicit dissapproval and partial withdrawal. A twenty-year-old co-ed's reaction to a girl she concluded was a homosexual was expressed as follows:

> Well, I didn't want to be alone with X [the homosexual] because the four of us had two connecting rooms and I was in the room with X. As much as I liked the girl and felt sorry for her, I knew she could really wring me through the wringer. So the rest decided that I should tell her that if she and Y wanted to be homos, to do it somewhere else and not in the room.

No disapproval and relationship sustained. The "live and let live" response to homosexuals, which is implied in the preceding reaction, was not uncommon among the subjects. Some subjects not only affirmed the right of the homosexual to "live his own life" but also reported that their knowledge of the deviance has had little or no effect upon their subsequent relationships with the deviants. In this regard, the mildest reaction, so mild that it might be considered no reaction at all, was that of a nineteen-year-old male college student:

> I: What was your reaction to him?
> S: My reactions to him have always been friendly because he seems like a very friendly person. Uh, and he has a very nice sense of humor and I've never been repelled by anything he's said. For one thing, I think he's tremendously interesting because he seems to have such a wide range for background. . . .
> I: When was the last time you saw this person?
> S: Last night. . . . I was sitting in a restaurant and he walked in with some friends . . . he just stopped in and said hello, and was his usual friendly self.
> I: What in particular happened after that?
> S: Actually, nothing. He sat down with his friends and we exchanged a few words about the records that were playing on the juke box. But nothing, actually. . . .

The theoretical significance of these data for the conception of deviance and societal reaction presented here is not that the subjects' information is of dubious accuracy or questionable relevance as evidence of homosexuality. Nor is it that the subjects' interpretations of them are unreasonable, unjustifiable, or spurious. They suggest rather that the conceptions of persons in everyday life concerning "sex-appropriate" or "sex-inappropriate" behavior may lead them to interpret a variety of behavioral forms as indications of the same deviation, and the "same" behavioral forms as indications of a variety of deviant as well as "normal" behavior. An individual's sexual "normality" may be made problematic by the interpretations and reinterpretations of his behavior by others, and the interpretive process may be activated by a wide range of situational behaviors which lend new significance to the individual's past and present behavior. His behavior with respect to speech, interests, dress, dating, or relations with other males are not *per se* significant in the deviant-defining process. The data suggest that the critical feature of the deviant-defining process is not the behavior of individuals who are defined as deviant, but rather the interpretations others make of their behaviors, whatever those behaviors may be.

With specific reference to homosexuality as a form of deviant behavior, the interview materials suggest that while reactions toward persons defined as homosexuals tend to be negatively toned, they are far from homogeneous as to the forms or intensity of the sanctions invoked and applied. Indeed, reactions which may appear to the sociological observer or to the deviant himself as negative sanctions, such as withdrawal or avoidance, may be expressions of embarrassment, a reluctance to share the burden of the deviant's problems, fear of the deviant, etc., as well as moral indignation or revulsion. In none of the interviews does the subject react with extreme violence, explicitly define or directly accuse the deviant of being a "queer," "fairy," or other terms of opprobrium, nor did any of them initiate legal actions against the deviant. In view of the extreme negative sanctions against homosexuality which are posited on theoretical grounds, the generally mild reactions of our subjects are striking.

The relative absence of extreme and overtly expressed negative sanctions against homosexuals among our subjects may, of course, reflect the higher than average educational level of the sample. A sample of subjects less biased toward the highly educated, middle-class segment of the population than was interviewed in this preliminary study may be expected to reflect a more definite pattern with reference to such negative reactions. We must, therefore, be cautious in generalizing the range of reactions among our subjects to the general population. It is equally important to note, however, that these data do indicate that reactions to homosexuals in American society are not *societal* in the sense of being uniform within a narrow range; rather, they are significantly conditioned by subcultural as well as situational factors. Thus, not only are the processes by which persons come to be defined as homosexuals contingent upon the interpretations of their behavior by others, but also the sanctions imposed and the treatment they are accorded as a consequence of that definition vary widely among conventional members of various subcultural groups.

The larger implications of these data are that a sociological theory of deviance must explicitly take into account the variety and range of conceptions held by persons, groups, and agencies within the society concerning any form of behavior. The increasing differentiation of groups, institutions, and subcultures in modern society generates a continually changing range of alternatives and tolerance for the expression of sexual as well as other forms of behavior. Consequently, it is difficult if not impossible to derive theoretically a set of *specific behavioral prescriptions* which will in fact be normatively supported, uniformly practiced, and socially enforced by more than a segment of the total population. Under such conditions, it is not the fact that individuals engage in behaviors which diverge from some theoretically posited "institutionalized expectations" or even that such behaviors are defined as deviant by the conventional and conforming members of the society which is of primary significance for the study of deviance. A sociological theory of deviance must focus specifically upon the interactions which not only define behaviors as deviant but also organize and activiate the application of sanctions by individuals, groups, or agencies. For in modern society, the socially significant differentiation of deviants from the non-deviant population is increasingly contingent upon circumstances of situation, place, social and personal biography, and the bureaucratically organized activities of agencies of control.[14]

1. A notable exception is the work of Edwin M. Lemert who systematically incorporates the concept of societal reaction in his theory of sociopathic behavior. See *Social Pathology*, New York: McGraw-Hill, 1951.

2. Robert K. Merton, "Social Conformity, Deviation, and Opportunity-Structures: A Comment on the Contributions of Dubin and Cloward," *American Sociological Review*, 24 (1959), 177-189.

3. Albert K. Cohen, "The Study of Social Disorganization and Deviant Behavior," in *Sociology Today*, R. Merton, L. Broom, and L. Cottrell, eds., New York, Basic Books: 1959, 465-466.

4. Robert K. Merton, *Social Theory and Social Structure*, revised edition, New York: The Free Press of Glencoe, 1957, p. 150.

5. *Ibid.*, p. 150.

6. *Op. cit.*, p. 55.

7. For examples, see Talcott Parsons and Robert F. Bales, *Family Socialization and Interaction Process*. New York: The Free Press of Glencoe, 1955, 103-105; Ruth Benedict, "Continuities and Discontinuities in Cultural Conditioning," *Psychiatry*, 1 (1938), 161-167; Abram Kardiner and Associates, *Psychological Frontiers of Society*, New York: Columbia University Press, 1945, 57, 88, etc.; Clifford Kirkpatrick, *The Family*, New York: Ronald Press, 1955, 57-58; Margaret Mead, *Sex and Temperament*, New York: William Morrow, 1955.

8. Allison Davis, "American Status Systems and the Socialization of the Child," *American Sociological Review*, 6 (1941), p. 350.

9. *Op. cit.*, Chapter 4.

10. Evelyn Hooker, "Sequences in Homosexual Identification," read at the meetings of the American Sociological Association, 1960; Donald Webster Cory, *The Homosexual in America*, New York: Greenburg, 1951, esp. Part I.

11. This principle has been suggested by Harold Garfinkel. See "Some Sociological Concepts and Methods for Psychiatrists," *Psychiatric Research Reports*, 6 (1956), 181-195.

12 The interview schedule and methods were conceived and constructed in consultation with Aaron V. Cicourel.

13. Erving Goffman, "The Nature of Deference and Demeanor," *American Anthropologist*, 58 (1956), 473-502.

14. For a discussion of such contingencies, see Edwin M. Lemert, *op. cit.*, Chapter 4, and Erving Goffman, "The Moral Career of the Mental Patient," *Psychiatry*, 22 (1959), 123-142.

TWO STUDIES OF
LEGAL STIGMA

RICHARD D. SCHWARTZ and JEROME H. SKOLNICK

Legal thinking has moved increasingly toward a sociologically meaningful view of the legal system. Sanctions, in particular, have come to be regarded in functional terms.[1] In criminal law, for instance, sanctions are said to be designed to prevent recidivism by rehabilitating, restraining, or executing the offender. They are also said to be intended to deter others from the performance of similar acts and, sometimes, to provide a channel for the expression of retaliatory motives. In such civil actions as tort or contract, monetary awards may be intended as retributive and deterrent, as in the use of punitive damages, or may be regarded as a *quid pro quo* to compensate the plaintiff for his wrongful loss.

While these goals comprise an integral part of the rationale of law, little is known about the extent to which they are fulfilled in practice. Lawmen do not as a rule make such studies, because their traditions and techniques are not designed for a systematic examination of the operation of the legal system in action, especially outside the courtroom. Thus, when extra-legal consequences—e.g., the social stigma of a prison sentence—are taken into account at all, it is through the discretionary actions of police, prosecutor, judge, and jury. Systematic information on a variety of unantici-

This is a revised version of a paper read at the Annual Meeting of the American Sociological Association, August, 1960. This paper draws upon materials prepared by students of the Law and Behavioral Science Division of the Yale Law School. We wish to acknowledge the contributions of Michael Meltzner, who assisted in the experiment, and especially that of Dr. Robert Wyckoff, who surveyed medical practitioners. We are indebted to Donald T. Campbell and Hanan Selvin for valuable comments and suggestions.

pated outcomes, those which benefit the accused as well as those which hurt him, might help to inform these decision makers and perhaps lead to changes in substantive law as well. The present paper is an attempt to study the consequences of stigma associated with legal accusation.

From a sociological viewpoint, there are several types of indirect consequences of legal sanctions which can be distinguished. These include differential deterrence, effects on the sanctionee's associates, and variations in the degree of deprivation which sanction imposes on the recipient himself.

First, the imposition of sanction, while intended as a matter of overt policy to deter the public at large, probably will vary in its effectiveness as a deterrent, depending upon the extent to which potential offenders perceive themselves as similar to the sanctionee. Such "differential deterrence" would occur if white-collar antitrust violators were restrained by the conviction of General Electric executives, but not by invocation of the Sherman Act against union leaders.

The imposition of a sanction may even provide an unintended incentive to violate the law. A study of factors affecting compliance with federal income tax laws provides some evidence of this effect.[2] Some respondents reported that they began to cheat on their tax returns only *after* convictions for tax evasion had been obtained against others in their jurisdiction. They explained this suprising behavior by noting that the prosecutions had always been conducted against blatant violators and not against the kind of moderate offenders which they then became. These respondents were, therefore, unintentionally educated to the possibility of supposedly "safe" violations.

Second, deprivations or benefits may accrue to nonsanctioned individuals by virtue of the web of affiliations that joint them to the defendant. The wife and family of a convicted man may, for instance, suffer from his arrest as much as the man himself. On the other hand, they may be relieved by his absence if the family relationship has been an unhappy one. Similarly, whole groups of persons may be affected by sanctions to an individual, as when discriminatory practices increase because of a highly publicized crime attributed to a member of a given minority group.

Finally, the social position of the defendant himself will serve to aggravate or alleviate the effects of any given sanction. Although all three indirect consequences may be interrelated, it is the third with which this paper will be primarily concerned.

Findings

The subjects studied to examine the effects of legal accusation on occupational positions represented two extremes: lower-class unskilled workers charged with assault, and medical doctors accused of malpractice. The first project lent itself to a field experiment, while the second required a survey design. Because of differences in method and substance, the studies cannot be used as formal controls for each other. Taken together, however, they do suggest that the indirect effects of sanctions can be powerful, that they can produce unintended harm or unexpected benefit, and that the results are related to officially unemphasized aspects of the social context in which the sanctions are administered. Accordingly, the two studies will be discussed together, as bearing on one another. Strictly speaking, however, each can, and properly should, stand alone as a separate examination of the unanticipated consequences of legal sanctions.

Study I. The Effects of a Criminal Court Record on the Employment Opportunities of Unskilled Workers. In the field experiment, four employment folders were prepared, the same in all respects except for the criminal court record of the applicant. In all of the folders he was described as a thirty-two-year-old single male of unspecified race, with a high school training in mechanical trades, and a record of successive short-term jobs as a kitchen helper, maintenance worker, and handyman. These characteristics are roughly typical of applicants for unskilled hotel jobs in the Catskill resort area of New York State where employment opportunities were tested.[3]

The four folders differed only in the applicant's reported record of criminal court involvement. The first folder indicated that the applicant had been convicted and sentenced for assault; the second, that he had been tried for assault and acquitted; the third, also tried for assault and acquitted, but with a letter from the judge certifying the finding of not guilty and reaffirming the legal presumption of innocence. The fourth holder made no mention of any criminal record.

A sample of one hundred employers was utilized. Each employer was assigned to one of four "treatment" groups.[4] To each employer only one folder was shown; this folder was one of the four kinds mentioned above, the selection of the folder being determined by the treatment group to which the potential employer was assigned. The employer was asked whether he could "use" the man described in the folder. To preserve the reality of the situation and make it a true field experiment, employers were never given any indication that they were participating in an experiment. So far as they knew, a legitimate offer to work was being made in each showing of the folder by the "employment agent."

The experiment was designed to determine what employers would do in fact if confronted with an employment applicant with a criminal record. The questionnaire approach used in earlier studies[5] seemed ill-adapted to the problem, since respondents confronted with hypothetical situations might be particularly prone to answer in what they considered a socially acceptable manner. The second alternative—studying job opportunities of individuals who had been involved with the law—would have made it very difficult to find comparable groups of applicants and potential employers. For these reasons, the field experiment reported here was utilized.

Some deception was involved in the study. The "employment agent"—the same individual in all hundred cases—was in fact a law student who was working in the Catskills during the summer of 1959 as an insurance adjuster. In representing himself as being both an adjuster and an employment agent, he was assuming a combination of roles which is not uncommon there. The adjuster role gave him an opportunity to introduce a single application for employment casually and naturally. To the extent that the experiment worked, however, it was inevitable that some employers should be led to believe that they had immediate prospects of filling a job opening. In those instances where an offer to hire was made, the "agent" called a few hours later to say that the applicant had taken another job. The field experimenter attempted in such instances to locate a satisfactory replacement by contacting an employment agency in the area. Because this procedure was used and since the jobs involved were of relatively minor consequence, we believe that the deception caused little economic harm.

As mentioned, each treatment group of twenty-five employers was approached with one type of folder. Responses were dichotomized: those who expressed a willingness to consider the applicant in any way were termed positive; those who made no response or who explicitly refused to consider the candidate were termed negative. Our results consist of comparisons between positive and negative responses, thus defined, for the treatment groups.

Of the twenty-five employers shown the "no record" folder, nine gave positive responses. Subject to reservations arising from chance variations in sampling, we take this as indicative of the "ceiling" of jobs available for this kind of applicant under the given field conditions. Positive responses by these employers may be compared with those in the other treatment groups to obtain an indication of job opportunities lost because of the various legal records.

Of the twenty-five employers approached with the "convict" folder, only one expressed interest in the applicant. This is a rather graphic indication of the effect which a criminal record may have on job opportunities. Care must be exercised, of course, in generalizing the conclusions to other settings. In this context, however, the criminal record made a major difference.

From a theoretical point of view, the finding leads toward the conclusion that conviction constitutes a powerful form of "status degradation"[6] which continues to operate after the time when, according to the generalized theory of justice underlying punishment in our society, the individual's "debt" has been paid. A record of conviction produces a durable if not permanent loss of status. For purposes of effective social control, this state of affairs may heighten the deterrent effect of conviction—though that remains to be established. Any such contribution to social control, however, must be balanced against the barriers imposed upon rehabilitation of the convict. If the ex-prisoner finds difficulty in securing menial kinds of legitimate work, further crime may become an increasingly attractive alternative.[7]

Another important finding of this study concerns the small number of positive responses elicited by the "accused but acquitted" applicant. Of the twenty-five employers approached with this folder, three offered jobs. Thus, the individual accused but acquitted of assault has almost as much trouble finding even an unskilled job as the one who was not only accused of the same offense, but also convicted.

From a theoretical point of view, this result indicates that permanent lowering of status is not limited to those explicitly singled out by being convicted of a crime. As an ideal outcome of American justice, criminal procedure is supposed to distinguish between the "guilty" and those who have been acquitted. Legally controlled consequences which follow the judgment are consistent with this purpose. Thus, the "guilty" are subject to fine and imprisonment, while those who are acquitted are immune from these sanctions. But deprivations may be imposed on the acquitted, both before and after victory in court. Before trial, legal rules either permit or require arrest and detention. The suspect may be faced with the expense of an attorney and a bail bond if he is to mitigate these limitations on his privacy and freedom. In addition, some pretrial deprivations are imposed without formal legal permission. These may include coercive questioning, use of violence, and stigmatization. And, as this study indicates, some deprivations not under the direct control of the legal process may develop or persist after an official decision of acquittal has been made.

Thus two legal principles conflict in practice. On the one hand, "a man is innocent until proven guilty." On the other, the accused is systematically treated as guilty under the administration of criminal law until a functionary or official body—police, magistrate, prosecuting attorney, or trial judge or jury—decides that he is entitled to be free. Even then, the results of treating him as guilty persist and may lead to serious consequences.

The conflict could be eased by measures aimed at reducing the deprivations imposed on the accused, before and after acquittal. Some legal attention has been focused on pretrial deprivations. The provision of bail and counsel, the availability of habeas corpus, limitations on the admissibility of coerced confessions, and civil actions for false arrest are examples of measures aimed at protecting the rights of the accused before trial. Although these are often limited in effectiveness, especially for individuals of lower socioeconomic status, they at least represent some concern with implementing the presumption of innocence at the pretrial stage.

By contrast, the courts have done little toward alleviating the post-acquittal consequences of legal accusation. One effort along these lines has been employed in the federal courts, however. Where an individual has been accused and exonerated of a crime, he may petition the federal courts for a "Certificate of Innocence" certifying this fact.[8] Possession of a such a document might be expected to alleviate post-acquittal deprivations.

Some indication of the effectiveness of such a measure is found in the responses of the final treatment group. Their folder, it will be recalled, contained information on the accusation and acquittal of the applicant, but also included a letter from a judge addressed "To whom it may concern" certifying the applicant's acquittal and reminding the reader of the presumption of innocence. Such a letter might have had a boomerang effect, by re-emphasizing the legal involvement of the applicant. It was important, therefore, to determine empirically whether such a communication would improve or harm the chances of employment. Our findings indicate that it increased employment opportunities, since the letter folder elicited six positive responses. Even though this fell short of the nine responses to the "no record" folder, it doubled the number for the "accused but acquitted" and created a significantly greater number of job offers than those elicited by the convicted record. This suggests that the procedure merits consideration as a means of offsetting the occupational loss resulting from accusation. It should be noted, however, that repeated use of this device might reduce its effectiveness.

The results of the experiment are summarized in Table 1. The differences in outcome found there indicate that various types of legal records are systematically related to job opportunities. It seems fair to infer also that the trend of job losses corresponds with the apparent punitive intent of the authorities. Where the

Table 1
Effect of Four Types of Legal Folder on Job Opportunities
(in Per Cent)

	No record (N = 25)	Acquitted with letter (N = 25)	Acquitted without letter (N = 25)	Convicted (N = 25)	Total (N = 100)
Positive response	36	24	12	4	19
Negative response	64	76	88	96	81
Total	100	100	100	100	100

man is convicted, that intent is presumably greatest. It is less where he is accused but acquitted and still less where the court makes an effort to emphasize the absence of a finding of guilt. Nevertheless, where the difference in punitive intent is ideally greatest, between conviction and acquittal, the difference in occupational harm is very slight. A similar blurring of this distinction shows up in a different way in the next study.

Study II: The Effects on Defendants of Suits for Medical Malpractice. As indicated earlier, the second study differed from the first in a number of ways: method of research, social class of accused, relationship between the accused and his "employer," social support available to accused, type of offense and its possible relevance to occupational adequacy. Because the two studies differ in so many ways, the reader is again cautioned to avoid thinking of them as providing a rigorous comparative examination. They are presented together only to demonstrate that legal accusation can produce unanticipated deprivations, as in the case of Study I, or unanticipated benefits, as in the research now to be presented. In the discussion to follow, some of the possible reasons for the different outcomes will be suggested.

The extra-legal effects of a malpractice suit were studied by obtaining the records of Connecticut's leading carrier of malpractice insurance. According to these records, a total of 69 doctors in the State had been sued in 64 suits during the post World War II period covered by the study, September, 1945, to September, 1959.[9] Some suits were instituted against more than one doctor, and four physicians had been sued twice. Of the total of 69 physicians, 58 were questioned. Interviews were conducted with the approval of the Connecticut Medical Association by Robert Wyckoff, whose extraordinary qualifications for the work included possession of both the M.D. and LL.B. degrees. Dr. Wyckoff was able to secure detailed response to his inquiries from all doctors contacted.

Twenty of the respondents were questioned by personal interview, twenty-eight by telephone, and the remainder by mail. Forty-three of those reached practiced principally in cities, eleven in suburbs, and four in rural areas. Seventeen were engaged in general practice and forty-one were specialists. The sample proved comparable to the doctors in the State as a whole in age, experience, and professional qualifications.[10] The range was from the lowest professional stratum to chiefs of staff and services in the State's most highly regarded hospitals.

Of the fifty-seven malpractice cases reported, doctors clearly won thirty-eight; nineteen of these were dropped by the plaintiff and an equal number were won in court by the defendant doctor. Of the remaining nineteen suits, eleven were settled out of court for a nominal amount, four for approximately the amount the plaintiff claimed and four resulted in judgment for the plaintiff in court.

The malpractice survey did not reveal widespread occupational harm to the physicians involved. Of the fifty-eight respondents, fifty-two reported no negative effects of the suit on their practice, and five of the remaining six, all specialists, reported that their practice *improved* after the suit. The heaviest loser in court (a radiologist), reported the largest gain. He commented, "I guess all the doctors in town felt sorry for me because new patients started coming in from doctors who had not sent me patients previously." Only one doctor reported adverse consequences to his practice. A winner in court, this man suffered physical and emotional stress symptoms which hampered his later effectiveness in surgical work. The temporary drop in his practice appears to have been produced by neurotic symptoms and is therefore only indirectly traceable to the malpractice suit. Seventeen other doctors reported varying degrees of personal dissatisfaction and anxiety during and after the suit, but none of them reported impairment of practice. No significant relationship was found between outcome of the suit and expressed dissatisfaction.

A protective institutional environment helps to explain these results. No cases were found in which a doctor's hospital privileges were reduced following the suit. Neither was any physician unable later to obtain malpractice insurance, although a handful found it necessary to pay higher rates. The State Licensing Commission, which is headed by a doctor, did not intervene in any instance. Local medical societies generally investigated charges through their ethics and grievance committees, but where they took any action, it was almost always to recommend or assist in legal defense against the suit.

Discussion

Accusation has different outcomes for unskilled workers and doctors in the two studies. How may these be explained? First, they might be nothing more than artifacts of research method. In the field experiment, it was possible to see behavior directly, i.e., to determine how employers act when confronted with what appears to them to be a realistic opportunity to hire. Responses are therefore not distorted by the memory of the respondent. By contrast, the memory of the doctors might have been consciously or unconsciously shaped by the wish to create the impression that the public had not taken seriously the accusation leveled against them. The motive for such a distortion might be either to protect the respondent's self-esteem or to preserve an image of public acceptance in the eyes of the interviewer, the profession, and the public. Efforts of the interviewer to assure his subjects of anonymity—intended to offset these effects—may have succeeded or may, on the contrary, have accentuated an awareness of the danger. A related type of distortion might have stemmed from a desire by doctors to affect public attitudes toward malpractice. Two conflicting motives might have been expected to enter here. The doctor might have tended to exaggerate the harm caused by an accusation, especially if followed by acquittal, in order to turn public opinion toward legal policies which would limit malpractice liability. On the other hand, he might tend to underplay extra-legal harm caused by a legally insufficient accusation in order to discourage potential plaintiffs from instituting suits aimed at securing remunerative settlements and/or revenge for grievances. Whether these diverse motives operated to distort doctors' reports and, if so, which of them produced the greater degree of distortion is a matter for speculation. It is only suggested here that the interview method is more subject to certain types of distortion than the direct behavioral observations of the field experiment.

Even if such distortion did not occur, the results may be attributable to differences in research design. In the field experiment, a direct comparison is made between the occupational position of an accused and an identical individual not accused at a single point in time. In the medical study, effects were inferred through retrospective judgment, although checks on actual income would have no doubt confirmed these judgments. Granted that income had increased, many other explanations are available to account for it. An improvement in practice after a malpractice suit may have resulted from factors extraneous to the suit. The passage of time in the community and increased experience may have led to a larger practice and may even have masked negative effects of the suit. There may have been a general increase in practice for the kinds of doctors involved in these suits, even greater for doctors not sued than for doctors in the sample. Whether interviews with a control sample could have yielded sufficiently precise data to rule out these possibilities is problematic. Unfortunately, the resources available for the study did not enable such data to be obtained.

A third difference in the two designs may affect the results. In the field experiment, full information concerning the legal record is provided to all of the relevant decision makers, i.e., the employers. In the medical study, by contrast, the results depend on decisions of actual patients to consult a given doctor. It may be assumed that such decisions are often based on imperfect information, some patients knowing little or nothing about the malpractice suit. To ascertain how much information employers usually have concerning the legal record of the employee and then supply that amount would have been a desirable refinement, but a difficult one. The alternative approach would involve turning the medical study into an experiment in which full information concerning malpractice (e.g., liable, accused but acquitted, no record of accusation) was supplied to potential patients. This would have permitted a comparison of the effects of legal accusation in two instances where information concerning the accusation is constant. To carry out such an experiment in a field situation would require an unlikely degree of cooperation, for instance by a medical clinic which might ask patients to choose their doctor on the basis of information given them. It is difficult to conceive of an experiment along these lines which would be both realistic enough to be valid and harmless enough to be ethical.

If we assume, however, that these methodological problems do not invalidate the basic finding, how may it be explained? Why would unskilled workers accused but acquitted of assault have great difficulty getting jobs, while doctors accused of malpractice —whether acquitted or not—are left unharmed or more sought after than before?

First, the charge of criminal assault carries with it the legal allegation and the popular connotation of intent to harm. Malpractice, on the other hand, implies negligence or failure to exercise reasonable care. Even though actual physical harm may be greater in malpractice, the element of intent suggests that the man accused of assault would be more likely to repeat his attempt and to find the mark. However, it is dubious that this fine distinction could be drawn by the lay public.

Perhaps more important, all doctors and particularly specialists may be immune from the effects of a malpractice suit because their services are in short supply.[11] By contrast, the unskilled worker is one of many and therefore likely to be passed over in favor of someone with a "cleaner" record.

Moreover, high occupational status, such as is demonstrably enjoyed by doctors,[12] probably tends to insulate the doctor from imputations of incompetence. In general, professionals are assumed to possess uniformly high ability, to be oriented toward community service, and to enforce adequate standards within their own organization.[13] Doctors in particular receive deference, just because they are doctors, not only from the population as a whole but even from fellow professionals.[14]

Finally, individual doctors appear to be protected from the effects of accusation by the sympathetic and powerful support they receive from fellow members of the occupation, a factor absent in the case of unskilled, unorganized laborers.[15] The medical society provides advice on handling malpractice actions, for instance, and referrals by other doctors sometimes increase as a consequence of the sympathy felt for the malpractice suit victim. Such assistance is further evidence that the professional operates as "a community within a community,"[16] shielding its members from controls exercised by formal authorities in the larger society.

In order to isolate these factors, additional studies are needed. It would be interesting to know, for instance, whether high occupational status would protect a doctor acquitted of a charge of assault. Information on this question is sparse. Actual instances of assaults by doctors are probably very rare. When and if they do occur, it seems unlikely that they would lead to publicity and prosecution, since police and prosecutor discretion might usually be employed to quash charges before they are publicized. In the rare instances in which they come to public attention, such accusations appear to produce a marked effect because of the assumption that the pressing of charges, despite the status of the defendant, indicates probable guilt. Nevertheless, instances may be found in which even the accusation of first-degree murder followed by acquittal appears to have left the doctor professionally unscathed.[17] Similarly, as a test of the group protection hypothesis, one might investigate the effect of an acquittal for assault on working men who are union members. The analogy would be particularly instructive where the union plays an important part in employment decisions, for instance in industries which make use of a union hiring hall.

In the absence of studies which isolate the effect of such factors, our findings cannot readily be generalized. It is tempting to suggest after an initial look at the results that social class differences provide the explanation. But subsequent analysis and research might well reveal significant intraclass variations, depending on the distribution of other operative factors. A lower-class person with a scarce specialty and a protective occupational group who is acquitted of a lightly regarded offense might benefit from the accusation. Nevertheless, class in general seems to correlate with the relevant factors to such an extent that in reality the law regularly works to the disadvantage of the already more disadvantaged classes.

Conclusion

Legal accusation imposes a variety of consequences, depending on the nature of the accusation and the characteristics of the accused. Deprivations occur, even though not officially intended, in the case of unskilled workers who have been acquitted of assault charges. On the other hand, malpractice actions—even when resulting in a judgment against the doctor—are not usually followed by negative consequences and sometimes have a favorable effect on the professional position of the defendant. These differences in outcome suggest two conclusions: one, the need for more explicit clarification of legal goals; two, the importance of examining the attitudes and social structure of the community outside the courtroom if the legal process is to hit intended targets, while avoiding innocent bystanders. Greater precision in communicating goals and in appraising consequences of present practices should help to make the legal process an increasingly equitable and effective instrument of social control.

1. Legal sanctions are defined as changes in life conditions imposed through court action.
2. Richard D. Schwartz, "The Effectiveness of Legal Controls: Factors in the Reporting of Minor Items of Income on Federal Income Tax Returns." Paper presented at the annual meeting of the American Sociological Association, Chicago, 1959.
3. The generality of these results remains to be determined. The effects of criminal involvement in the Catskill area are probably diminished, however, by the temporary nature of employment, the generally poor qualifications of the work force, and the excess of demand over supply of unskilled labor there. Accordingly, the employment differences among the four treatment groups found in this study are likely, if anything to be *smaller* than would be expected in industries and areas where workers are more carefully selected.

4. Employers were not approached in preselected random order, due to a misunderstanding of instructions on the part of the law student who carried out the experiment during a three and one-half week period. Because of this flaw in the experimental procedure, the results should be treated with appropriate caution. Thus, chi-squared analysis may not properly be utilized. (For those used to this measure, $P<.05$ for Table 1.)

5. Sol Rubin, *Crime and Juvenile Delinquency*, New York: Oceana, 1958, 151-156.

6. Harold Garfinkel, "Conditions of Successful Degradation Ceremonies," *American Journal of Sociology*, 61 (March, 1956), 420-424.

7. Severe negative effects of conviction on employment opportunities have been noted by Sol Rubin, *Crime and Juvenile Delinquency*, *op. cit.* A further source of employment difficulty is inherent in licensing statutes and security regulations which sometimes preclude convicts from being employed in their preconviction occupation or even in the trades which they may have acquired during imprisonment. These effects may, however, be counteracted by bonding arrangements, prison associations, and publicity programs aimed at increasing confidence in, and sympathy for, exconvicts. See also, B. F. McSally, "Finding Jobs for Released Offenders," *Federal Probation*, 24 (June, 1960), 12-17; Harold D. Lasswell and Richard C. Donnelly, "The Continuing Debate over Responsibility: An Introduction to Isolating the Condemnation Sanction," *Yale Law Journal*, 68 (April, 1959), 869-899; and Johs Andeneas, "General Prevention—Illusion or Reality?" *J. Criminal Law*, 43 (July-August, 1952), 176-198.

8. 28 United States Code, Secs. 1495, 2513.

9. A spot check of one county revealed that the Company's records covered every malpractice suit tried in the courts of that county during this period.

10. No relationship was found between any of these characteristics and the legal or extra-legal consequences of the lawsuit.

11. See Eliot Freidson, "Client Control and Medical Practice," *American Journal of Sociology*, 65 (January, 1960), 374-382. Freidson's point is that general practitioners are more subject to client control than specialists are. Our findings emphasize the importance of professional as compared to client control, and professional protection against a particular form of client control, extending through both branches of the medical profession. However, what holds for malpractice situations may not be true of routine medical practice.

12. National Opinion Research Center, "Jobs and Occupations: A Popular Evaluation," *Opinion News*, 9 (Sept., 1947), 3-13. More recent studies in several countries tend to confirm the high status of the physician. See Alex Inkeles, "Industrial Man: The Relation of Status to Experience, Perception and Value," *American Journal of Sociology*, 66 (July, 1960), 1-31.

13. Talcott Parsons, *The Social System*, New York: The Free Press of Glencoe, 1951, 454-473; and Everett C. Hughes, *Men and their Work*, New York: The Free Press of Glencoe, 1958.

14. Alvin Zander, Arthur R. Cohen, and Ezra Stotland, *Role Relations in the Mental Health Professions*, Ann Arbor: Institute for Social Research, 1957.

15. Unions sometimes act to protect the seniority rights of members who, discharged from their jobs upon arrest, seek re-employment following their acquittal.

16. See William J. Goode, "Community Within a Community: The Professions," *American Sociological Review*, 22 (April, 1957), 194-200.

17. For instance, the acquittal of Dr. John Bodkin Adams after a sensational murder trial, in which he was accused of deliberately killing several elderly women patients to inherit their estates, was followed by his quiet return to medical practice. *New York Times*, Nov. 24, 1961, p. 28, col. 7. Whether the British regard acquittals as more exonerative than Americans is uncertain.

DEVIANCE DISAVOWAL:
THE MANAGEMENT OF
STRAINED INTERACTION
BY THE VISIBLY HANDICAPPED

FRED DAVIS

A recurring issue in social relations is the refusal of those who are viewed as deviant[1] to concur in the verdict. Or, if in some sense it can be said that they do concur, they usually place a very different interpretation on the fact or allegation than do their judges. In our society this is especially true of deviance which partakes to ascription (e.g., the Negro) as against that which partakes to some significant degree of election (e.g., the homosexual). And, while it may be conjectured that ultimately neither the Negro nor the homosexual would be cast in a deviant role were it not for society's devaluation of these attributes in the first place, barring such a hypothetical contingency it remains the more persuasive argument in a democracy to be able to claim that the social injury from which one suffers was in no way self-inflicted.

In these pages I wish to discuss another kind of non self-in-

The study from which this paper derives was supported by a grant from the Association for the Aid of Crippled Children. I am indebted to Stephen A. Richardson and David Klein of the Association for their help and advice. I also wish to thank Frances C. Macgregor, Cornell Medical Center, New York, for having so generously made available to me case materials from her research files on persons with facial disfigurements. See Frances C. Macgregor *et al.*, *Facial Deformities and Plastic Surgery: A Psychosocial Study*, Springfield, Ill.: Charles C. Thomas, 1953.

flicted social injury, the visible physical handicap. My aim though is not to survey and describe the many hardships of the visibly handicapped,[2] but to analyze certain facets of their coping behavior as it relates to the generalized imputations of deviance they elicit from society, imputations which many of them feel it necessary to resist and reject.

There are, of course, many areas in which such imputations bear heavily upon them: employment, friendship, courtship, sex, travel, recreation, residence, education. But the area I treat here is enmeshed to some extent in all of these without being as categorically specific as any. I refer to situations of sociability, and more specifically to that genre of everyday intercourse which has the characteristics of being: (1) face-to-face, (2) prolonged enough to permit more than a fleeting glimpse or exchange, but not so prolonged that close familiarity immediately ensues, (3) intimate to the extent that the parties must pay more than perfunctory attention to one another, but not so intimate that the customary social graces can be dispensed with, and (4) ritualized to the extent that all know in general what to expect, but not so ritualized as to preclude spontaneity and the slightly novel turn of events. A party or other social affair, a business introduction, getting to know a person at work, meeting neighbors, dealing with a salesman, conversing with a fellow passenger, staying at a resort hotel—these are but a few of the everyday social situations which fall within this portion of the spectrum of sociability, a range of involvement which can also be thought of as the zone of first impressions.

In interviews I conducted with a small number of very articulate and socially skilled informants who were visibly handicapped[3] I inquired into their handling of the imputation that they were not "normal, like everyone else." This imputation usually expresses itself in a pronounced stickiness of interactional flow and in the embarrassment of the normal by which he conveys the all too obvious message that he is having difficulty in relating to the handicapped person[4] as he would to "just an ordinary man or woman." Frequently he will make *faux pas,* slips of the tongue, revealing gestures and inadvertent remarks which overtly betray this attitude and place the handicapped person in an even more delicate situation.[5] The triggering of such a chain of interpersonal incidents is more likely with new persons than with those with whom the handicapped have well-established and continuing relations. Hence, the focus here on more or less sociable occasions, it being these in which interactional discomfort is felt most acutely and coping behavior is brought into relief most sharply.

Because the visibly handicapped do not comprise a distinct minority group or subculture, the imputations of generalized deviance that they elicit from many normals are more nearly genuine interactional emergents than conventionalized sequelae to intergroup stereotyping as, for example, might obtain between a Negro and white. A sociable encounter between a visibly handicapped person and a normal is usually more subject to ambiguity and experimentation in role postures than would be the case were the parties perceived by each other primarily in terms of member group characteristics. The visibly handicapped person must with each new acquaintance explore the *possibilities* of a relationship. As a rule there is no ready-made symbolic shorthand (e.g., "a Southerner can't treat a Negro as a social equal," "the Irish are anti-Semitic," "working class people think intellectuals are effeminate") for anticipating the quality and degree of acceptance to be accorded him. The exchange must be struck before its dangers and potentialities can be seen and before appropriate corrective maneuvers can be fed into the interaction.[6]

The Handicap as Threat to Sociable Interaction

Before discussing how the visibly handicapped cope with difficult interaction, it is appropriate to first consider the general nature of the threat posed to the interactional situation *per se* as a result of their being perceived routinely (if not necessarily according to some prevalent stereotype) as "different," "odd," "estranged from the common run of humanity," etc.; in short, other than normal. (Achieving ease and naturalness of interaction with normals serves naturally as an important index to the handicapped person of the extent to which his preferred definition of self—i.e., that of someone who is merely different physically but not socially deviant—has been accepted. Symbolically, as long as the interaction remains stiff, strained or otherwise mired in inhibition, he has good reason to believe that he is in effect being denied the status of social normalcy he aspires to or regards as his due.) The threat posed by the handicap to sociability is, at minimum, fourfold: its tendency to become an exclusive focal point of the interaction, its potential for inundating expressive boundaries, its discordance with other attributes of the person and, finally, it ambiguity as a predicator of joint activity. These are not discrete entities in themselves as much as varying contextual emergents which, depending on the particular situation, serve singly or in combination to strain the framework of normative rules and assumptions in which sociability develops. Let us briefly consider each in turn.

A Focal Point of Interaction. The rules of sociable interaction stipulate a certain generality and diffuseness in the attentions that parties are expected to direct to each other. Even if only superficially, one is expected to remain oriented to the whole person and to avoid the expression of a precipitous or fixed concern with any single attribute of his, however noteworthy or laudable it may be.[7] When meeting someone with a visible handicap, a number of perceptual and interpretative responses occur which make adherence to this rules tenuous for many. First, there is the matter of visibility as such. By definition, the visibly handicapped person cannot control his appearance sufficiently so that its striking particularity will not call a certain amount of concentrated attention to itself.[8] Second, the normal, while having his attention so narrowly channeled, is immediately constrained by the requirements of sociability to act as if he were oriented to the totality of the other rather than to that which is uppermost in his awareness, i.e., the handicap. Although the art of sociability may be said to thrive on a certain playful discrepancy between felt and expressed interests, it is perhaps equally true that when these are too discrepant strain and tension begin to undermine the interaction. (Conversely, when not discrepant enough, flatness and boredom frequently ensue.)[9] Whether the handicap is overtly and tactlessly responded to as such or, as is more commonly the case, no explicit reference is made to it, the underlying condition of heightened, narrowed, awareness causes the interaction to be articulated too exclusively in terms of it. This, as my informants described it, is usually accompanied by one or more of the familiar signs of discomfort and stickiness: the guarded references, the common everyday words suddenly made taboo, the fixed stare elsewhere, the artificial levity, the compulsive loquaciousness, the awkward solemnity.[10]

Second-order interactional elaborations of the underlying impedance are also not uncommon. Thus, for example, the normal may take great pains to disguise his awareness, an exertion that is usually so effortful and transparent that the handicapped person is then enjoined to disguise his awareness of the normal's disguise. In turn, the normal sensing the disguise erected in response to his disguise . . . and so forth. But unlike the infinitely multiplying reflections of an object located between opposing mirrors, this process cannot sustain itself for long without the pretense of unawareness collapsing, as witness the following report by a young woman:

I get suspicious when somebody says, "Let's go for a uh, ah [imitates confused and halting speech] push with me down the hall," or something like that. This to me is suspicious because it means that they're aware, really aware, that there's a wheelchair here, and that this is probably uppermost with them. . . . A lot of people in trying to show you that they don't care that you're in a chair will do crazy things. Oh, there's one person I know who constantly kicks my chair, as if to say, "I don't care that you're in a wheelchair. I don't even know that it's there." But that is just an indication that he *really* knows it's there.

Inundating Potential. The expressive requirements of sociability are such that rather strict limits obtain with respect to the types and amount of emotional display that are deemed appropriate. Even such fitting expressions as gaiety and laughter can, we know, reach excess and lessen satisfaction with the occasion. For many normals, the problem of sustaining sociable relations with someone who is visibly handicapped is not wholly that of the discrepancy of the inner feeling evoked, e.g., pity, fear, repugnance, avoidance. As with much else in sociability, a mere discrepancy of the actor's inner state with the social expectation need not result in a disturbance of interaction. In this instance it is specifically the marked dissonance of such emotions with those outward expressions deemed *most* salient for the occasion (e.g., pleasure, identification, warm interest) that seems to result frequently in an inundation and enfeeblement of the expressive controls of the individual. With some persons, the felt intrusion of this kind of situationally inappropriate emotion is so swift and overwhelming as to approximate a state of shock, leaving them expressively naked, so to speak. A pointed incident is told by a young blind girl:

> One night when I was going to visit a friend two of the people from my office put me into a taxi. I could tell that at first the taxi driver didn't know I was blind because for a while there he was quite a conversationalist. Then he asked me what these sticks were for [a collapsible cane]. I told him it was a cane, and then he got so different. . . . He didn't talk about the same things that he did at first. Before this happened he joked and said, "Oh, you're a very quiet person. I don't like quiet people, they think too much." And he probably wouldn't have said that to me had he known I was blind because he'd be afraid of hurting my feelings. He didn't say anything like that afterwards.

The visibly handicapped are of course aware of this potential for inundating the expressive boundaries of situations and many take precautions to minimize such occurrences as much as possible. Thus, an interior decorator with a facial deformity would when admitted to a client's house by the maid station himself whenever he could so that the client's entrance would find him in a distantly direct line of vision from her. This, he stated, gave the client an opportunity to compose herself, as she might not be able to were she to come upon him at short range.

Contradiction of Attributes. Even when the inundating potential is well contained by the parties and the normal proves fully capable of responding in a more differentiated fashion to the variety of attributes presented by the handicapped person (e.g., his occupational identity, clothes, speech, intelligence, interests, etc.), there is frequently felt to be an unsettling discordance between these and the handicap. Sociable interaction is made more difficult as a result because many normals can only resolve the seeming incongruence by assimilating or subsuming (often in a patronizing or condescending way) the other attributes to that of the handicap, a phenomenon which in analogous connections has been well described by Hughes.[11] Thus, one informant, a strikingly attractive girl, reports that she frequently elicits from new acquaintances the comment, "How strange that someone so pretty should be in a wheelchair." Another informant, a professional worker for a government agency, tells of the fashionable female client who after having inquired on how long the informant had been in her job remarked, "How nice that you have something to do." Because the art of sociability deigns this kind of reductionism of the person, expressions of this type, even when much less blatant, almost invariably cast a pall on the interaction and embarrass the recovery of smooth social posture. The general threat inherent in the perceived discordance of personal attributes is given pointed expression by still another informant, a paraplegic of upper middle class background who comments on the attitude of many persons in his class:

> Now, where this affects them, where this brace and a crutch would affect them, is if they are going someplace or if they are doing something, they feel that, first, you would call attention and, second —you wouldn't believe this but it's true; I'll use the cruelest words I can—no cripple could possibly be in their social stratum.

Ambiguous Predicator. Finally, to the extent to which sociability is furthered by the free and spontaneous initiation of joint activity (e.g., dancing, games, going out to eat; in short, "doing things") there is frequently considerable ambiguity as regards the ability of the handicapped person to so participate and as regards the propriety of efforts which seek to ascertain whether he wants to. For the normal who has had limited experience with the handicapped it is by no means always clear whether, for example, a blind person can be included in a theater party or a crippled person in a bowling game. Even if not able to engage in the projected activity as such, will he want to come along mainly for the sake of company? How many his preferences be gauged without, on the one hand, appearing to "make a thing" out of the proposal or, on the other, conveying the impression that his needs and limitations are not being sufficiently considered? Should he refuse, is it genuine or is he merely offering his hosts a polite, though half-hearted, out? And, for each enigma thus posed for the normal, a counter-enigma is posed for the handicapped person. Do they really want him? Are they merely being polite? In spite of the open invitation, will his acceptance and presence lessen somehow their enjoyment of the activity? It is easy to see how a profusion of anticipatory ambiguities of this kind can strain the operative assumptions underlying sociable relations.

Process of Deviance Disavowal and Normalization

The above features, then, may be said to comprise the threat that a visible handicap poses to the framework of rules and assumptions that guide sociability. We may now ask how socially adept handicapped persons cope with it so as to either keep it at bay, dissipate it, or lessen its impact upon the interaction. In answering this question we will not consider those broad personality adjustments of the person (e.g., aggression, denial, compensation, dissociation, etc.) which at a level once removed, so to speak, can be thought of as adaptive or maladaptive for, among other things, sociability. Nor, at the other extreme, is it possible in the allotted space to review the tremendous variety of specific approaches, ploys and stratagems that the visibly handicapped employ in social situations. Instead, the analysis will attempt to delineate in transactional terms the stages through which a sociable relationship with a normal typically passes, assuming, of course, that the confrontation takes place and that both parties possess sufficient social skill to sustain a more than momentary engagement.

For present purposes we shall designate these stages as: (1) fictional acceptance, (2) the facilitation of reciprocal role-taking around a normalized projection of self and (3) the institutionalization in the relationship of a definition of self that is normal in its moral dimension, however qualified it may be with respect to its situational contexts. As we shall indicate, the unfolding of these stages comprises what may be thought of as a process of deviance disavowal or normalization,[12] depending on whether one views the process from the vantage point of the "deviant" actor or his alters.[13]

Fictional Acceptance. In Western society the overture phases of a sociable encounter are to a pronounced degree regulated by highly elastic fictions of equality and normalcy. In meeting those with whom we are neither close nor familiar, manners dictate that we refrain from remarking on or otherwise reacting too obviously to those aspects of their persons which in the privacy of our thoughts betoken important differences between ourselves. In America at least, these fictions tend to encompass sometimes marked divergencies in social status as well as a great variety of expressive styles; and, it is perhaps the extreme flexibility of such fictions in our culture rather than, as is mistakenly assumed by many foreign observers, their absence that accounts for the seeming lack of punctiliousness in American manners. The point is nicely illustrated in the following news item:

NUDE TAKES A STROLL IN MIAMI

MIAMI, Fla., Nov. 13 (UPI)—A shapely brunette slowed traffic to a snail's pace here yesterday with a 20-minute nude stroll through downtown Miami. . . .

"The first thing I knew something was wrong," said Biscayne Bay bridge-tender E. E. Currey, who was working at his post about one block away, "was when I saw traffic was going unusually slow."

Currey said he looked out and called police. They told him to stop the woman, he said.

Currey said he walked out of his little bridge house, approached the woman nervously, and asked, "Say, girl, are you lost?"

"Yes," she replied. "I'm looking for my hotel."

Currey offered help and asked, "Say, did you lose your clothes?"

"No," he said the woman replied, "Why?"

Currey said that he had to step away for a moment to raise the bridge for a ship and the woman walked away. . . .[14]

Unlike earlier societies and some present-day ones in which a visible handicap automatically relegates the person to a castelike, inferior, status like that of mendicant, clown or thief—or more rarely to an elevated one like that of oracle or healer—in our society the visibly handicapped are customarily accorded, save by children,[15] the surface acceptance that democratic manners guarantee to nearly all. But, as regards sociability, this proves a mixed blessing for many. Although the polite fictions do afford certain entrée rights, as fictions they can too easily come to serve as substitutes for "the real thing" in the minds of their perpetrators. The interaction is kept starved at a bare subsistence level of sociability. As with the poor relation at the wedding party, so the reception given the handicapped person in many social situations: sufficient that he is here, he should not expect to dance with the bride.

At this stage of the encounter, the interactional problem confronting the visibly handicapped person is the delicate one of not permitting his identity to be circumscribed by the fiction while at the same time playing along with it and showing appropriate regard for its social legitimacy. For, as transparent and confining as the fiction is, it frequently is the only basis upon which the contact can develop into something more genuinely sociable. In those instances in which the normal fails or refuses to render even so small a gesture toward normalizing the situation, there exists almost no basis for the handicapped person to successfully disavow his deviance.[16] The following occurrence related by a young female informant is an apt, if somewhat extreme, illustration:

> I was visiting my girl friend's house and I was sitting in the lobby waiting for her when this woman comes out of her apartment and starts asking me questions. She just walked right up. I didn't know her from Adam, I never saw her before in my life. "Gee, what do you have? How long have you been that way? Oh gee, that's terrible." And so I answered her questions, but I got very annoyed and wanted to say, "Lady, mind your own business."

"Breaking Through"—Facilitating Normalized Role-Taking. In moving beyond fictional acceptance what takes place essentially is a redefinitional process in which the handicapped person projects images, attitudes and concepts of self which encourage the normal to identify with him (i.e., "take his role") in terms other than those associated with imputations of deviance.[17] Coincidentally, in broadening the area of minor verbal involvements, this also functions to drain away some of the stifling burden of unspoken awareness that, as we have seen, so taxes ease of interaction. The normal is cued into a larger repertoire of appropriate responses, and even when making what he, perhaps mistakenly, regards as an inappropriate response (for example, catching him-

self in the use of such a word as cripple or blind) the handicapped person can by his response relieve him of his embarrassment. One young informant insightfully termed the process "breaking through":

> The first reaction a normal individual or good-legger has is, "Oh gee, there's a fellow in a wheelchair," or "there's a fellow with a brace." And they don't say, "Oh gee, there is so-and-so, he's handsome" or "he's intelligent," or "he's a boor," or what have you. And then as the relationship develops they don't see the handicap. It doesn't exist any more. And that's the point that you as a handicapped individual become sensitive to. You know after talking with someone for awhile when they don't see the handicap any more. That's when you've broken through.

What this process signifies from a social psychological standpoint is that as the handicapped person expands the interactional nexus he simultaneously disavows the deviancy latent in his status; concurrently, to the degree to which the normal is led to reciprocally assume the redefining (and perhaps unanticipated) self-attitudes proffered by the handicapped person, he comes to normalize (i.e., view as more like himself) those aspects of the other which at first connoted deviance for him. (Sometimes, as we shall see, the normal's normalizing is so complete that it is unwittingly applied to situations in which the handicapped person cannot possibly function "normally" due to sheer physical limitations.) These dynamics might also be termed a process of identification. The term is immaterial, except that in "identifying" or "taking the role of the other" much more is implicated sociologically than a mere subjective congruence of responses. The fashioning of shared perspectives also implies a progressively more binding legitimation of the altered self-representations enacted in the encounter; that is, having once normalized his perception of the handicapped person, it becomes increasingly more compromising —self-discrediting, as it were—for the normal to revert to treating him as a deviant again.

The ways in which the visibly handicapped person can go about disavowing deviance are, as we have stated, many and varied. These range from relatively straightforward conversational offerings in which he alludes in passing to his involvement in a normal round of activities, to such forms of indirection as interjecting taboo or privatized references by way of letting the normal know that he does not take offense at the latter's uneasiness or regard it as a fixed obstacle toward achieving rapport. In the above quote, for example, the informant speaks of "good-leggers," an in-group term from his rehabilitation hospital days, which along with "dirty normals" he sometimes uses with new acquaintances "because it has a humorous connotation . . . and lots of times it puts people at their ease."[18]

Still other approaches to disavowing deviance and bridging fictional acceptance include: an especially attentive and sympathetic stance with respect to topics introduced by the normal, showing oneself to be a comic, wit or other kind of gifted participant, and, for some, utilizing the normalization potential inherent in being seen in the company of a highly presentable normal companion.[19] These, and others too numerous to mention, are not of course invariably or equally successful in all cases; neither are such resources equally available to all handicapped persons, nor are the handicapped equally adept at exploiting them. As a class of corrective strategies however, they have the common aim of overcoming the interactional barrier that lies between narrow fictional acceptance and more spontaneous forms of relatedness.

Inextricably tied in with the matter of approach are considerations of setting, activity and social category of participants, certain constellations of which are generally regarded as favorable for successful deviance disavowal and normalization while others are thought unfavorable. Again, the ruling contingencies appear to be the extent to which the situation is seen as containing elements in it which: (1) contextually reduce the threat posed by the visible handicap to the rules and assumptions of the particular sociable occasion, and (2) afford the handicapped person opportunities for "breaking through" beyond fictional acceptance.

The relevance of one or both of these is apparent in the following social situations and settings about which my informants expressed considerable agreement as regards their preferences, aversions and inner reactions. To begin with, mention might again be made of the interactional rule violations frequently experienced at the hands of small children. Many of the informants were quite open in stating that a small child at a social occasion caused them much uneasiness and cramped their style because they were concerned with how, with other adults present, they would handle some barefaced question from the child. Another category of persons with whom many claimed to have difficulty is the elderly. Here the problem was felt to be the tendency of old people to indulge in patronizing sympathy, an attitude which peculiarly resists re-definition because of the fulsome virtue it attributes to itself. In another context several of the informants laid great stress on the importance of maintaining a calm exterior whenever the physical setting unavoidably exposed them to considerable bodily awkwardness. (At the same time, of course, they spoke of the wisdom of avoiding, whenever possible, such occasions altogether.) Their attitude was that to expressively reflect gracelessness and a loss of control would result in further interactional obstacles toward assimilating the handicapped person to a normal status.

It makes me uncomfortable to watch anyone struggling, so I try to do what I must as inconspicuously as possible. In new situations or in strange places, even though I may be very anxious, I will maintain a deadly calm. For example, if people have to lift the chair and I'm scared that they are going to do it wrong, I remain perfectly calm and am very direct in the instructions I give.

As a final example, there is the unanimity with which the informants expressed a strong preference for the small, as against the large or semipublic social gathering. Not only do they believe that, as one handicapped person among the non-handicapped, they stand out more at large social gatherings, but also that in the anonymity which numbers further there resides a heightened structural tendency for normals to practice avoidance relations with them. The easy assumption on such occasions is that "some other good soul" will take responsibility for socializing with the handicapped person. Even in the case of the handicapped person who is forward and quite prepared to take the initiative in talking to others, the organization and ecology of the large social gathering is usually such as to frustrate his attempts to achieve a natural, non-deviant, place for himself in the group. As one young man, a paraplegic, explained:

The large social gathering presents a special problem. It's a matter of repetition. When you're in a very large group of people whom you don't know, you don't have an opportunity of talking to to three, four or five at a time. Maybe you'll talk to one or two usually. After you've gone through a whole basic breakdown in making a relationship with one—after all, it's only a cocktail party— to do it again, and again, and again, it's wearing and it's no good. You don't get the opportunity to really develop something.

Institutionalization of the Normalized Relationship. In "break- ing through" many of the handicapped are confronted by a delicate paradox, particularly in those of their relationships which continue beyond the immediate occasion. Having disavowed de- viance and induced the other to respond to him as he would to a normal, the problem then becomes one of sustaining the normal- ized definition in the face of many small amendments and quali- fications that must frequently be made to it. The person confined to a wheelchair, for example, must brief a new acquaintance on what to do and how to help when they come to stairs, doorways, vehicle entrances, etc. Further briefings and rehearsals may be required for social obstructions as well: for example, how to act in an encounter with—to cite some typical situations at random— an overly helpful person, a waitress who communicates to the handicapped person only through his companion, a person who stares in morbid fascination.[20]

Generally, such amendments and special considerations are as much as possible underplayed in the early stages of the relation- ship because, as in the case of much minority group protest, the fundamental demand of the handicapped is that they first be granted an irreducibly equal and normal status, it being only then regarded as fitting and safe to admit to certain incidental incapaci- ties, limitations and needs. At some point however, the latter must be broached if the relationship to the normal is to endure in viable form. But to integrate effectively a major claim to "nor- malcy" with numerous minor waivers of the same claim is a tricky feat and one which exposes the relationship to the many situational and psychic hazards of apparent duplicity: the tension of transferring the special arrangements and understandings worked out between the two to situations and settings in which everyone else is "behaving normally"; the sometimes lurking suspicion of the one that it is only guilt or pity that cements the relationship, of the other that the infirmity is being used exploitatively, and of onlookers that there is something "neurotic" and "unhealthy" about it all.[21]

From my informants' descriptions it appears that this third, "normal, but . . ." stage of the relationship, if it endures, is institutionalized mainly in either one of two ways. In the first, the normal normalizes his perceptions to such an extent as to suppress his effective awareness of many of the areas in which the handicapped person's behavior unavoidably deviates from the normal standard. In this connection several of the informants complained that a recurring problem they have with close friends is that the latter frequently overlook the fact of the handicap and the restrictions it imposes on them. The friends thoughtlessly make arrangements and involve them in activities in which they, the handicapped, cannot participate conveniently or comfortably.

The other major direction in which the relationship is sometimes institutionalized is for the normal to surrender some of his normalcy by joining the handicapped person in a marginal, half-alienated, half-tolerant, outsider's orientation to "the Philistine world of normals."[22] Gowman[23] nicely describes the tenor and style of this relationship and its possibilities for sharply disabusing normals of their stereotyped approaches to the handicapped. *Epater le bourgeois* behavior is often prominently associated with it, as is a certain strictly in-group license to lampoon and mock the handicap in a way which would be regarded as highly offensive were it to come from an uninitiated normal. Thus, a blind girl relates how a sighted friend sometimes chides her by calling her "a silly blink." A paraplegic tells of the old friend who tries to revive his flagging spirits by telling him not to act "like a helpless cripple." Unlike that based on overnormalization, the peculiar strength of this relationship is perhaps its very capacity to give expressive scope to the negative reality of the larger world of which it is inescapably a part while simultaneously removing itself from a primary identification with it.

Implications

Two, more general, implications seem worth drawing from this analysis.[24]

First, in studies which trace the process wherein an actor who deviates comes to be increasingly defined as a deviant (e.g., the pre-mental patient, the pre-alcoholic, the pre-juvenile delinquent), unusual prominence is given to the normalizing behavior of those close to him (spouse, parents, friends, etc.). The picture that emerges is one of these persons assuming nearly the whole burden—by rationalizing, denying and overlooking his offensive acts—of attempting to re-establish a socially acceptable relationship with him. He is depicted typically as compulsively wedded to his deviance and incapable or uninterested in making restitutive efforts of his own. Finally, following some critical act of his, normalization fails *in toto* and community agencies are called in to relieve the primary group of its unmanageable burden.

There is much about this picture that is doubtlessly true and consonant with the ascertainable facts as we later come to learn of them from family, friends, police, courts and social agencies. We may question, however, whether it is a wholly balanced picture and whether, given the situational biases of these informational sources, all of the relevant facts have had an equal chance to surface. The perspective developed here suggests that it may be useful to consider whether, and to what extent, the deviator himself is not also engaged, albeit ineffectively, in somehow trying to sustain a normal definition of his person. Were research to indicate that such is the case, we might then ask what it is about his reparative efforts and the situations in which they occur that, as contrasted with the subjects of this study, so often lead to failure and an exacerbation of the troublesome behavior. (We probably will never know, except inferentially by gross extrapolation, of the possibly many cases in which some such interactive process succeeds in favorably resolving the deviating behavior.) In other words, as against the simplistic model of a compulsive deviant and a futile normalizer we would propose one in which it is postulated that both are likely to become engaged in making corrective interactional efforts toward healing the breach. And, when such efforts fail, as they frequently do, it is as important in accounting for the failure to weigh the interactional dynamics and situational contexts of these efforts as it is the nature of the deviant acts and the actor.

Second, we would note that the interactional problems of the visibly handicapped are not so dissimilar from those which all of us confront, if only now and then and to a lesser degree. We too on occasion find ourselves in situations in which some un-camouflageable attribute of our jars the activity and the expectations of our company. We too, if we wish to sustain—and, as is typically the case, our company wishes us to sustain—a fitting and valued representation of ourselves, will tacitly begin to explore with them ways of redressing, insulating and separating the discrepant attribute from ourselves.[25] Our predicament though is much less charged with awareness, more easily set to rights, than that of the visibly handicapped person and his company. But it is precisely this exaggeration of a common interactional predicament that affords us an added insight into the prerequisites and unwitting assumptions of sociable behavior in general. Put differently, it can be said that our understanding of a mechanism is often crude and incomplete until it breaks down and we try to repair it. Breakdown and repair of interaction is what many of the visibly handicapped experience constantly in their lives. In studying this with them we are also studying much about ourselves of which we were heretofore unaware.

1. Following Lemert, as used here the term deviant (or deviance) refers (1) to a person's deviation from prevalent or valued norms, (2) to which the community-at-large reacts negatively or punitively, (3) so as to then lead the person to define his situation largely in terms of this reaction. All three conditions must be fulfilled for it to be said that deviance exists (secondary deviation, in Lemert's definition). In this sense the Negro, the career woman, the criminal, the Communist, the physically handicapped, the mentally ill, the homosexual, to mention but a few, are all deviants, albeit in different ways and with markedly different consequences for their life careers. Edwin M. Lemert, *Social Pathology*, New York: McGraw-Hill, 1951, 75-77.

2. Comprehensive and excellent reviews are to be found in R. G. Barker *et al.*, *Adjustment to Physical Handicap and Illness: A Survey of the Social Psychology of Physique and Disability*, New York: Soc. Sci. Res. Council, 1953, Bulletin 55, 2nd ed., and Beatrice A. Wright, *Physical Disability, A Psychological Approach*, New York: Harper, 1960.

3. Six were orthopedically handicapped, three blind and two facially disfigured. Additional detailed biographical and clinical materials were secured on

one blind and four facially disfigured persons, making for a total of sixteen records.

4. Throughout this paper, whether or not the term "handicap" or "handicapped" is joined by the qualifier "visible," it should be read in this way. Unfortunately, it will not be possible to discuss here that which sociologically distinguishes the situation of the visibly handicapped from that of persons whose physical handicaps are not visible or readily apparent, and how both differ from what is termed the "sick role." These are, though, important distinctions whose analysis might illuminate key questions in the study of deviance.

5. In the sections that follow, the discussion draws heavily on the framework of dramaturgic analysis developed by Erving Goffman. See especially his "Alienation from Interaction," *Human Relations*, 10 (1957), 47-60; "Embarrassment and Social Organization," *American Journal of Sociology*, 62 (November, 1956), 264-271; *Presentation of Self in Everyday Life*, New York: Doubleday and Co., Inc., 1959.

6. Cf. Anselm Strauss, *Mirrors and Masks*, New York: The Free Press of Glencoe, 1959, 31-43.

7. Kurt H. Wolff, ed., *The Sociology of Georg Simmel*, New York: The Free Press of Glencoe, 1950, 45-46.

8. Cf. R. K. White, B. A. Wright and T. Dembo, "Studies in Adjustment to Visible Injuries," *Journal of Abnormal and Social Psychology*, 43 (1948), 13-28.

9. In a forthcoming paper, "Fun in Games: An Analysis of the Dynamics of Social Interaction," Goffman discusses the relationship between spontaneous involvement in interaction and the manner in which "external attributes"—those which in a formal sense are not situationally relevant—are permitted to penetrate the situation's boundaries.

10. Cf. Goffman on "other-consciousness" as a type of faulty interaction. "Alienation from Interaction," *op. cit.*

11. Everett C. Hughes, *Men and Their Work*, New York: The Free Press of Glencoe, 1958, 102-106.

12. As used here the term "normalization" denotes a process whereby alter for whatever reason comes to view as normal and morally acceptable that which initially strikes him as odd, unnatural, "crazy," deviant, etc., irrespective of whether his perception was in the first instance reasonable, accurate or justifiable. Cf. Charlotte G. Schwartz, "Perspectives on Deviance—Wives' Definitions of their Husbands' Mental Illness," *Psychiatry*, 20 (August, 1957), 275-291.

13. Because of the paper's focus on the visibly handicapped person, in what follows his interactional work is highlighted to the relative glossing over of that of the normal. Actually, the work of normalization calls for perhaps as much empathic expenditure as that of deviance disavowal and is, obviously, fully as essential for repairing the interactional breach occasioned by the encounter.

14. *San Francisco Chronicle*, November 14, 1960.

15. The blunt questions and stares of small children are typically of the "Emperor's Clothes" variety. "Mister, why is your face like that?" "Lady, what are you riding around in that for? Can't you walk?" Nearly all of my informants spoke of how unnerving such incidents were for them, particularly when other adults were present. None the less, some claimed to value the child's forthrightness a good deal more than they did the genteel hypocrisy of many adults.

16. On the other side of the coin there are of course some handicapped persons who are equally given to undermining sociable relations by intentionally flaunting the handicap so that the fiction becomes extremely difficult to sustain. An equivalent of the "bad nigger" type described by Strong, such persons were (as in Strong's study) regarded with a mixture of admiration and censure by a number of my informants. Admiration, because the cruel stripping away of pretenses and forcing of issues was thought morally refreshing, especially since,

as the informants themselves recognized, many normals refuse to grant anything more than fictional acceptance while at the same time imagining themselves ennobled for having made the small sacrifice. Censure, because of the conviction that such behavior could hardly improve matters in the long run and would make acceptance even more difficult for other handicapped persons who later came into contact with a normal who had received such treatment. Cf. Samuel M. Strong, "Negro-White Relations as Reflected in Social Types," *American Journal of Sociology*, 52 (July, 1946), p. 24.

17. George H. Mead, *Mind, Self and Society*, Chicago: University of Chicago Press, 1934. See also the discussion on interaction in Strauss, *op. cit.*, 44-88.

18. Parallel instances can easily be cited from minority group relations as, for example, when a Jew in conversation with a non-Jew might introduce a Yiddish phrase by way of suggesting that the other's covert identification of him as a Jew need not inhibit the interaction unduly. In some situations this serves as a subtle means of declaring, "O.K., I know what's bothering you. Now that I've said it, let's forget about it and move on to something else."

19. Alan G. Gowman, "Blindness and the Role of the Companion," *Social Problems*, 4 (July, 1956).

20. *Ibid.*

21. The rhetoric of race relations reflects almost identical rationalizations and "insights" which are meant among other things to serve as cautions for would-be transgressors. "Personally I have nothing against Negroes [the handicapped], but it would be bad for my reputation if I were seen socializing with them." "She acts nice now, but with the first argument she'll call you a dirty Jew [good-for-nothing cripple]." "Regardless of how sympathetic you are toward Negroes [the disabled], the way society feels about them you'd have to be a masochist to marry one."

22. Students of race relations will recognize in this a phenomenon closely akin to "inverse passing" as when a white becomes closely identified with Negroes and passes into a Negro subculture.

23. Gowman, *op. cit.*

24. I am indebted to Sheldon Messinger for his valuable comments in these connections.

25. Goffman, "Embarrassment and Social Organization," *op. cit.*

THE MENTAL HOSPITAL
AND MARITAL FAMILY TIES

HAROLD SAMPSON, SHELDON L. MESSINGER,
ROBERT D. TOWNE and DAVID ROSS, FLORINE LIVSON,
MARY-DEE BOWERS, LESTER COHEN, KATE S. DORST

The devices for controlling major forms of deviance continue to entail removal of the deviant from his natural community setting. Whatever the rationale for removal—humane, protective, punitive, therapeutic—it is seldom envisioned as permanent. Instead, it is represented and understood as temporary if possible, and in the interest of eventually returning the deviant to his community as a functioning member. Thus, a strategic problem is engendered for those who man remedial institutions: to help preserve and reinforce those ties which link the deviant to the world beyond the walls. If these ties are severed, the task of returning him to a viable community context becomes a formidable piece of social engineering.[1]

One type of deviance which frequently involves removal and return is mental illness. The mental patient's ties to intimates and to significant social roles have become attenuated or gravely threatened by events preceding hospitalization. The prolonged

This report is based on a study carried out by the California Department of Mental Hygiene and partially supported by a grant (#3M-9124) from the National Institute of Mental Health. The general perspective adopted owes much to conversations with and published and unpublished writings by Harold Garfinkel. See, for example, his "Conditions of Successful Degradation Ceremonies," *American Journal of Sociology*, 61 (1956), 420-424, and "Some Sociological Concepts and Methods for Psychiatrists," *Psychiatric Research Reports*, 6 (1956), 181-195. The report has benefited from suggestions made by Erving Goffman.

separation of the patient from his family and other relationships, a traditional concomitant of mental hospitalization, intensifies the risk that the patient may adapt permanently to an intramural identity and a new life within the institution,[2] and that others may adapt to his absence, close ranks behind him, and resist his eventual return.[3]

In the situations we have observed, hospitalization has initiated processes which achieved a measure of success in restoring conditions which made it possible for intimate relationships to be resumed. These social processes, which block further attenuation of intimate relationships and facilitate their repair, have received little systematic attention in the literature. This omission may be due, in the first instance, to medical-psychiatric focus on the patient's illness and its therapies.[4] The more recent social psychiatric and sociological literature has tended to emphasize the way hospitalization may undermine relationships and impede recovery.[5] The present report attempts to supplement these perspectives with an analysis of some of those processes which operate against the permanent withdrawal or expulsion of the patient from his personal community.

The network of intimate relationships which will directly concern us is the marital family. Our data are drawn from a study of seventeen marital families in which a wife with young children at home was hospitalized in a California state mental institution, diagnosed as schizophrenic.

We attempted to select only first admissions for mental illness, but our study group includes three deviations from this criterion. In two cases, a brief psychiatric hospitalization in a county hospital had occurred earlier. In the third case, the woman had been hospitalized in a private sanitarium for one month earlier in the same year she entered the state institution.

All family members were white. The wives ranged in age from twenty-six to forty years; their mean age was about thirty-two years. The husbands' ages ranged from twenty-four to forty-five years, averaging about thirty-five years. Nine of the wives had been married to their current husbands from two to ten years; eight, from eleven to sixteen years. Five wives had been previously married; this was true of two husbands. The wives had from one to five children at home, and the children's ages ranged from six months to sixteen years. Most of the families had incomes of less than $7000 a year, but the annual income of one family was close to $10,000 and of another about $16,000.

Twelve wives were admitted to the hospital by the courts; five were self-admitted. Their mean stay in the state hospital from first admission to first release was about nineteen weeks. One stayed only six weeks, another stayed sixty-four weeks. None of the women received individual psychotherapy at the hospital; all received relatively small and intermittent dosages of tranquilizing drugs. Ten of the seventeen received electroshock therapy at some time during their hospital stay.

Our contacts with most adult family members were frequent and prolonged. All informants knew our purpose to be research, whatever other roles they attempted to assign to us in fantasy or in practice. Each wife was interviewed from the point of her admission to the hospital for a period ranging from one to over two years. Husbands were also routinely interviewed during the same period, although in some few instances with less success. We averaged over fifty interviews with each marital pair.

In addition, we interviewed hospital personnel, other relatives such as patients' mothers, and a variety of community professionals including internists, psychiatrists, and social workers who had had contact with the patient or her family over the years. A further supplement was provided by such private and agency records as we could locate and had permission to obtain. In these various ways, we were able to construct a history of these marital families and to gain some grasp of the impact of hospitalization upon their members. We obtained the least information, and thus shall have the least to say, about the impact of hospitalization upon the children.

Our observations suggest that the wife's schizophrenic episode occurred as part of a process of marital disintegration. Her manifest illness did not ordinarily precede and produce marital disintegration, rather it arose in the context of chronically conflicting or recently decayed marital family relations. Hospitalization routinely took place at a relatively late stage of both family and personal disorganization.

The period of hospitalization thus stood in a sequence of events leading toward some modification of already deteriorated relationships. The direction of modification was influenced by certain social processes, initiated through hospitalization, which *tended* to halt marital disintegration and to sustain the marital family. Our selection procedures produced cases in which one or both partners had resisted disassembly of the family as a possible solution to marital difficulties. The processes we shall discuss, thus, ordinarily operated in a context in which natural forces were already present which worked toward marital reintegration. The conservative or restitutional effects of these processes were sometimes obscured, however, by the bitter dramas of marital alienation which often accompanied commitment.[6] Further, doubts about the maintenance of the marital family were commonly experienced by one or both partners during hospitalization and were accompanied by the actual dismemberment of some marriages during hospitalization or shortly after the patient's return to the community. In short, the processes which countered the wife's withdrawal or expulsion from the family were sometimes blurred or even nullified by the magnitude of disruptive forces.

Two other points should be noted before we turn to a description of these social processes. First, we do not propose that the preservation of the marital family was necessarily beneficial to the patient or other family members. It is true that in most cases the wife conceived of only threatening alternatives to conflictful participation in her marital family roles. But our data suggest that the "conservative" solution was frequently a very limited, tenuous, and unsatisfactory one for the wife or husband.

Second, the processes we shall describe were *initiated* by hospitalization, but they were not *guided* in any explicit, cogent, or case-specific way by hospital personnel. Hospital personnel had very limited communication with either patients or relatives, obtained little information on which specific planning could have been based, and tended to operate with limited interest in and insight about the social network of the patients.

We shall consider the processes which tended to counter marital disintegration under three headings. First, hospitalization tended to *interrupt* the divisive processes at work in the marital family, narrowing opportunities for conflict and delaying permanent withdrawal by or exclusion of an errant member. Next, other processes served to *neutralize* the divisive forces, creating conditions under which relationships could be resumed in the face of severely disruptive events. Last, some features of hospitalization tended to *motivate* marital family members to reintegrate their relationships.

I

The separation of the wife from other family members directly blocked action, impulses to action, and defaults of inaction which threatened irremediable disruption of family life. The wife may have feared or wished to kill herself, her children, or her husband. She may have berated herself and others with violent reproaches or withdrawn from interaction and role performance into inaccessible preoccupations. In every case, she had come to find it impossible to fulfill daily responsibilities, and, whether she viewed the source of her difficulty as within or without, she had attempted to communicate the feeling that she could not go on.

Mrs. Arlen said, "I got into a panic, had no place to turn. I can't handle anything. My husband keeps forcing things on me and I panic. Can't take care of my babies. I just want to die, that's all. I was afraid I might kill myself or my babies."

The husband, for his part, may have felt angry, perplexed, or frightened by pre-hospital events, but he too in time had come to feel unable to cope with the situation, to alleviate it, or to endure it.

The removal of the wife from the family, thus, interrupted a threatening or "impossible" situation. The separation which was accomplished was moreover *legitimated* through the act of hospitalization, which ratified the wife as ill and in need of special isolation and treatment.[7] This fact was decisive in blocking self and other reproaches for the withdrawal or exclusion entailed in hospitalization. The negative moral implications of interruption, especially its interpersonal implications, were blunted and redefined. The wife's withdrawal or the husband's action to hospitalize her were validated not as alienative actions, but as actions of an involuntary nature required by and serving the present and future interests of the patient and her family.

Some husbands faced a *fait accompli* through action on the part of their wives and cooperating authorities.

In the context of repeated arguments over his treatment of her and several discontinued attempts to leave him, Mrs. Sand went to the hospital voluntarily without notifying her husband in advance. She telephoned him from the hospital grounds, telling him that she had been admitted and adding that he would have to come out to pick up the car, which she had taken to drive to the institution. Mr. Sand was furious. He told the research interviewer as well as Mrs. Sand that his wife was not mentally ill but only spiteful, and that she had gone to the hospital in another attempt to hurt, embarrass, and inconvenience him.

Mr. Sand remained bitter and unconvinced for several weeks. Indeed, it was only when his wife went off one week-end with a male patient that he came to feel she was mentally ill and that her hospitalization was justified. In these circumstances, he could find no other "explanation" for his wife's conduct, and he came to find his own moral indignation inappropriate.

The tenacity with which Mr. Sand held his initial view of his wife's withdrawal was atypical. For most husbands, the hospital's acceptance of their wives as patients was enough to confirm the legitimacy of separation and to suppress overt reproaches of abandonment.

In the more common situation, the husband actively participated in his wife's admission. Such participation frequently represented a counter-force to the widely observed phenomenon of ignoring, denying, or otherwise minimizing the "mental illness" of an intimate.[8] But having actively participated in his wife's admission to the mental hospital, the husband sometimes had to face *her* accusations of betrayal and abandonment. In this event, the socially validated reality that she "belonged" in the hospital helped to mute and deflect reproaches.

Mrs. Karr's mother and husband were quite concerned during the early hospital period that Mrs. Karr would feel they had "betrayed" her by having approved commitment. Their feelings were closely related to the fact that they had taken her to a psychiatrist on the pretext of taking her for "a ride" and in the face of her insistence that they were taking her to a "bug doctor." On the other hand, once at the psychiatrist's office, Mrs. Karr refused to leave even though the psychiatrist at first suggested out-patient treatment. The police were called to take Mrs. Karr to the mental hospital, and her husband signed commitment papers when Mrs. Karr's mother seemed reluctant to do so.

When electroshock therapy had dimmed Mrs. Karr's memory of these events, her mother and husband entered a pact not to reveal the facts to her. The pact was broken by Mr. Karr at his wife's urging during a joint research interview. As Mr. Karr took responsibility for the commitment, Mrs. Karr offered phrasing which relieved his guilt. She told him it was "the best thing" he could have done, and the "only thing." She added, "Who knows what might have happened. I might have tried to kill the babies or set fire to the house."

It should be added that during the course of hospitalization, as well as upon admission and after release, reproaches were short-circuited, including those by the wife that the husband was not making sufficient effort to have her released, and those by the husband that the wife was defecting from her duties. In the face of both sorts of reproaches there was an appeal to the impersonal authority of the hospital personnel. The argument ran, in both cases, that she was presumably not "well enough" yet, and that only professionals could decide when she was "well enough."

Finally, self-reproaches were blocked, as well as those from and to the patient. Self-reproaches by the husband were often expressed as fear of reproaches from the wife. Likewise, the wife-patient was afforded an opportunity to rationalize her withdrawal from domestic roles, particularly the mother role. The wives we observed were uniformly concerned with their abilities as mothers and with the possible effects of separation upon their children. This was handled by emphasis on the necessity of hospitalization and its function in preparing them to be "better" mothers (and wives). This context of guilt is one factor which helps account for patient insistence on the constraints of patienthood.

Hospitalization thus interrupted a situation which was experienced by one or both partners as "impossible," cutting down the chance of irremediable action, and did so in a way which blocked reproaches for withdrawal or exclusion. Hospitalization also placed constraints upon any actions that would formally confirm a breach of marital relationships. The husband was pressed to defer definitive action. The wife was not permitted to define her activity as having abrogated the marital or parental relationships. In brief, the separation effected by hospitalization was defined as a suspension rather than an abrogation of family commitments. This impeded dissolution of the marriage at a time when disjunctive forces were likely to be maximal.

Husbands who had been planning to separate from or divorce their wives met legal obstacles. Besides these, they experienced moral constraints, from within and without, which often moved them to reconsider their decision. Usually, these constraints operated "automatically": husbands shared definitions of their situations with others which precluded formal breaching action so long as their wives were incapacitated. When the husband did not respond "automatically," social pressures were brought to bear upon him to make him "wait and see how things worked out."

Mrs. Quinn's mother and sisters attempted to persuade Mr. Quinn to postpone his divorce plans until his wife recovered. He refused to do so. Subsequently, they wrote to the ward physician, informing him that the husband was planning a divorce, and that they had unsuccessfully tried to convince him to wait a while. The physician responded that he agreed it would be better for the husband to wait. "In general," the physician said, "it is bad for people to start divorces during the acute illness, since at that time judgment is often bad on the part of both parties."

During the early period of hospitalization, Mr. Quinn concealed from his wife the definiteness of his intention to proceed with divorce. He said in rationalizing this concealment, "she's in no condition to understand." He also initially obscured his intentions in conversations with hospital personnel, but sought in such contacts confirmation for his view that his wife was hopelessly ill, or would recover so partially that she could never be expected to resume the responsibilities of marriage. When hospital personnel suggested a more hopeful prognosis, Mr. Quinn lost faith in their competence and attempted to minimize further contact with them. Following his wife's release from the mental hospital and during preparations for a divorce, Mr. Quinn came to appreciate the radical recovery his wife had made, despite her claims otherwise.

Not just Mr. Quinn, but the several husbands who planned to disengage themselves from sick wives, generally tended to avoid contact with persons whom they regarded as remedial agents.

This was true of the pre-hospital, as well as the hospital and post-hospital periods. We found it particularly difficult to arrange interviews with such husbands, and we found it even more difficult to sustain any long-term contact with them. They also encouraged their wives to break contact with hospital personnel, with private helpers, and with us. We infer that they experienced all such contacts as occasions when they might be induced to confront uneasy feelings about leaving a sick wife or encouraged to continue their involvement with her.

When the wife was considering separation or divorce, the immediate effect of hospitalization was not only to defer definitive action, but also to cast doubt upon the validity of her motivation. If she had sought psychiatric assistance prior to hospitalization, she was likely to have been advised, implicitly or explicitly, to wait until she was less upset before making any final decision. Following admission to the mental hospital, she found it difficult to make gestures of marital renunciation which were taken literally by others. Such gestures were for the most part understood as expressions of her illness, thus depriving them of much of their social validity and social consequence.

Mrs. White was hospitalized following an inverse marital ceremony. Late one night she went to church and placed her wedding ring on the altar. Although this performance was in itself socially invalid, its alienative import was comprehensively negated by the hospitalization which followed it.

In the hospital, Mrs. White avoided home visits and, at one point, forbade her husband to come to see her. He complied with this edict for a while, but then sought out the ward physician to discuss the advisability of further compliance. The ward physician suggested that he visit her notwithstanding her expressed objections. In this and other maneuvers around visiting and not visiting, Mrs. White's actions were not defined as serious, literal abrogations of marital involvement.

The constraints placed upon marital interaction by mental hospitalization, then, had three major effects. They separated the disputants, thereby cutting down the opportunities for a definitive breach to develop. They blocked reproaches for withdrawal or exclusion. They deferred formalization of a marital breach, allowing time for other solutions to be considered and attempted.

An inevitable counterpart of these constraints, however, was the potentiality for undesirable equivocation and postponement of necessary decisions, or for a pathological reconciliation instead of an ultimately beneficial breach. They also encouraged the coercive exploitation of illness by the wife, and hence an investment in remaining ill.

Mr. Baker would accuse his wife of being an "unfit wife and mother" and of being "crazy." She would admit this, saying, "I know I'm crazy. Why don't you help me?"

Following a violent and extended quarrel over Mr. Baker's "taking up" with another woman, he told his wife that he had "had enough" and was determined to leave her. Mrs. Baker didn't exactly blame him for this attitude, feeling that she had brought it on through her own imperfections. She also believed that once her husband came to appreciate her mental condition, which accounted for her imperfections, he might not leave her.

She went to a physician, but was concerned that he wouldn't take her "seriously." Her opening remark, remembered by both her and the physician, was, "If you smile, I'll hit you right in the mouth." The physician, presumably unsmiling, suggested that Mrs. Baker might want to see a psychiatrist. She replied, "To hell with a psychiatrist. If I have to go home, I'll end it all." She also rejected an offer of "nerve pills," later recalling that the offer made her feel she wanted "to smack" the physician. Through insisting that if she went home she might "do something" to her children or herself, Mrs. Baker convinced the physician he should take immediate action in hospitalizing her. On the day of her admission, she told the interviewer, "my husband has to know about this or it isn't going to help me much."

After several months, Mrs. Baker came to feel that her husband was determined to leave her no matter what she did, and she changed her stance. Having discovered that release comes more quickly to married patients who have intact marriages, she conspired with her husband to pretend that their marriage had been repaired, even though they had agreed to separate. Mr. Baker cooperated fully in this deception, including visiting his wife on the ward and engaging in pleasant-appearing chit-chat.

Finally, as we have noted above, these constraints may have contributed to the husband's resistance to recognizing the gravity of his wife's disturbance and, concomitantly, to his failure to support her involvement with remedial agents.

II

Alienative acts already realized during the pre-hospital period may jeopardize future resumption of marital roles. There is a work of "undoing" which must be accomplished if reciprocal role expectations consistent with the reintegration of the marital family are to be restored.

We may conceive of a continuum of increasingly serious situations arising in the pre-hospital period which stand in the way of eventual reintegration of the family unit. In the least difficult situation, the wife quietly withdrew from role performances, experienced severe but largely uncommunicated distress, and was tormented by fears that unless she was removed from the situation something catastrophic would happen. Her fears were usually relatively specific: she would harm herself, her children, her husband. If the wife entered the hospital at this time, uneasiness was likely to focus about her motivation and capacity to return to the family. This uneasiness on the part of the patient and others —that she would *continue* to be the "defective person" hospitalization ratified her as being—had to be undone.

In a more common and difficult situation, the wife's withdrawal from role performances provoked resentment in the husband and marked guilt in the wife; she communicated distress to her husband in the form of bizarre, hostile, and frightening ideas; and she experienced her fantasies of catastrophe as realized rather than impending. In these circumstances, the resumption of marital roles was complicated by devastating memories of rejection, anger, terror, and sin.

Finally, in the most difficult situation, the wife was not hospitalized until she had committed an action which so violated her self-regard as a wife and mother that her resumption of family roles at first seemed irreparably blocked. The situation was exemplified by the wives in the group who were hospitalized following attempts to kill their daughters, and the wife who set her house on fire because she "couldn't stand" the place any more.

In these circumstances, patients and their spouses often assigned remarkable diagnostic acumen and therapeutic efficacy to the hospital, and they strained to view eventual release as a carefully determined medical judgment of recovery. In addition, two other readily identifiable processes facilitated undoing. The first was the isolation of deviant behavior and ideation from the "real" self of the wife and from her "real" relations to intimates. Deviant behavior and ideation was assimilated to a conception of "mental illness," or a functional substitute was found, such as the notion of a "nervous breakdown" or even a physiological imbalance. Hospital usage favored the first conception, but there was little explicit opposition to the second. Even the notion of a physiological imbalance got by, provided there was no insistence on it by the patient or others. All the categories employed suggested or specified non-responsibility in a moral sense, and inauthenticity and non-literalness in an interpersonal sense. The conception of a distinctive "episode," common in psychiatric thought, also facilitated the process of isolation.

Mr. Mark had experienced his wife's withdrawal from sexual relations as a personal criticism and attack upon himself. After her hospitalization, he reinterpreted this and other rejections as manifestations of her illness. He felt that "rejection" did not express her "real" feelings toward him.

The other undoing process may be described as the construction, by the patient and her intimates, of currently acceptable selves for each other. This may be seen as a part of the construction of a new "working consensus."[9] It was often described by the parties to the task as "becoming my (her) 'old self' again," but it involved leaving incongruent attributes of persons and events outside of the day-to-day reality honored by the spouses and others.

We refer here not only to suppression or repression at the individual level, but to a shared process. Memories which were incongruent with the role expectations family members were attempting to reconstruct were left unspoken, and more or less implicit agreements were reached to ignore a threatening past. Some patients and spouses spoke of "sweeping those things under the rug," some of trying to avoid "rehashing the past," and others of "letting sleeping dogs lie."

This process became most visible when it partially failed. Then, action became necessary to restore the suppressive agreement.

Late in the hospitalization, Mr. Yale reminded his wife of earlier delusions. Mrs. Yale laughed nervously, expressed surprise, and then told her husband that it would be better if she were allowed to recapture memories, lost since a course of electroshock therapy, on her own. Mr. Yale desisted from further reminders.

Although guilt and embarrassment doubtless helped motivate forgetting and not-mentioning, this example also calls attention to the specific effects of electroshock therapy in blurring memories incongruent with the selves the patient and her intimates are reconstituting. Patients were seldom if ever told that the purpose of electroshock therapy was to make them forget—indeed, they were seldom if ever told anything about it—but they uniformly came to interpret the hospital's purpose in this way. Our data suggest that they learned this interpretation from other patients, to the extent that it was learned. An interpersonal consequence was the support of shared forgetting.

Mrs. Karr received several electroshock "treatments" before she realized that she was receiving them. At first she believed they "strengthened" her memory. Later, she discovered that her memory was impaired; for example, she learned that she had forgotten the existence of her youngest child. During the post-hospital period, on the occasion of her mother "bringing up" embarrassing incidents connected with her psychotic episode, Mrs. Karr told her: "Mama, stop telling me those things! I went to the hospital and they made me forget them. Now don't keep bringing them up! You're not doing me any good!" When asked if her mother had stopped, Mrs. Karr said, "Well, in her way."

Mr. Karr, for his part, expressed pleasure to the research interviewer that electroshock therapy had made his wife forget her hostile outburst against him in the pre-hospital period.

In addition to the specific assist received from electroshock therapy and its interpretation, relatives received much advice not to "upset" patients. Indeed, such a conception is implicit in the notion of "illness." This often led to delicate handling of patients by relatives and, in the absence of specific advice as to what to avoid, to some tendency to follow the patient's lead in the skirting of touchy subjects.

These processes contributed to the reconstruction of threatened or shattered role expectations. But, as with other reparative processes initiated by hospitalization, they were typically unguided. They sometimes miscarried in two important ways. Persistent family tensions were sometimes obscured without being alleviated, thus restoring an untenable situation. In this instance, that which was ignored or forgotten today only reappeared in new guise tomorrow. The other danger inherent in these processes was the fostering of a kind of covert identity as mental patient for the wife, an identity which was only precariously isolated from her "real" self. Thus, while the processes may be observed to be a part of the work of repair, they involved burdens and costs which in the long run sometimes undermined constructive adaptations.

Hospitalization also tended to neutralize marital disruption by permitting only a graduated resumption of relatedness. This was fostered by the personnel's notion that recovery, above all, takes time.[10]

At first, husband and wife were permitted to see each other only briefly on the hospital ward, a setting which drastically limited the possibilities—and demands—of marital interaction. The children were not allowed to visit the hospital ward.

After the patient had been transferred to the acute treatment ward, she could apply for a pass home and was likely to receive one within a few weeks. The first pass frequently did not permit her to remain away from the hospital overnight. On these short passes, the husband sometimes did not take his wife home, but rather to a nearby town to eat and wander about until it was time to return. The pass was sometimes spent on the hospital grounds. The wife might or might not see her children. In any event, she was unlikely to be expected to do anything by way of cooking or child care, though she may have chosen to do so. The opportunity —which often meant the threat—of having sexual relations often did not arise.

If the first pass did not disturb the patient or spouse too severely, subsequent visits were likely to be longer, and the wife tended to assume some of her domestic duties. On a three-day week-end pass, the husband typically went to work on Monday, and the wife cared for the children during the day, prepared her husband's dinner that evening, and then returned to the hospital.

The limitation of interaction possibilities and demands

sheltered the patient and other family members from repeated failures of role integration and from repeated confrontation of disruptive and frightening affects. The hospital enforced and legitimated this partial moratorium on interaction. The hospital was thus likely to be viewed ambivalently as an undependable protection against dangerous possibilities and as an unreasonable obstacle to marital and maternal intimacies. On learning of an impending pass, husbands frequently wondered if their wives were "ready," expressing this concern by a preoccupation about medication during the visit and by careful planning to avoid potentially disturbing situations. One wife, still reluctant to have sexual relations, told her husband that the hospital did not consider her ready yet for this form of activity.

This partial protection against premature resumption of marital and parental duties was enhanced by the trial nature of visits. We refer to the cautious, tentative rebuilding of role expectations through "voluntary" experiments in the resumption of domestic responsibilities, maternal duties, and intimacy.

Mrs. Arlen told the interviewer that she asked the ward physician for "a ten-day leave. I told him that I wanted it because I wanted to see if I could live with my mother-in-law without getting too nervous and upset, and he said that was a little unusual, that request, and he would have to discuss it with the nurse and everything."

This interchange suggests again the unguided way reparative processes work in the mental hospital. Although visits are widely rationalized as a means of providing graduated trials, a specific request couched in these terms may not be appreciated.

The graduated, trial framework within which the rebuilding of role expectations proceeded was conducive to the discounting of failures. Failures might be seen as a product of a well-intentioned trying too much too soon. Thus, a relative said, "She'll be better next week"; and a patient said, "I guess I wasn't strong enough yet." This process sometimes received a specific assist from personnel. The most frequent responses of hospital physicians to the worried inquiries of relatives as to the patient's progress— or regress—were that "it's about as expected," part of the "ups and downs" of "such" patients. The physicians tended to interpret changes in a patient's state, if they were noticed, either as part

of the expectable course of the illness or as due to specific reme-
dies applied in the hospital. Most of the time, there were so many
potential factors affecting a patient's state that, in the absence
of a controlled experiment, one explanation seemed at least as
good as any other. And, if failures might be discounted within
the trial framework, "success" might be extended to matters that
otherwise seemed trivial or were taken for granted. This is perhaps to be seen as one of the latent consequences of emphasis
on the seriousness of the patient's disability.

Finally, in this framework the "negotiation" of marital disputes
often proceeded under the cover of concern for the wife's "health."
This worked to protect everyone's conception of himself as a
responsible person. Thus, such potentially explosive issues as
whether the husband needed to work such long hours, whether
they should move away from his or her mother, or how they might
share more interests and activities were discussed in terms of the
supposed effects of rearrangements on the wife's well-being. Although such negotiation often represented a step forward in the
confrontation of marital difficulties, their outcome was ordinarily
a limited and transient reorganization of the surface of marital life.

These processes, too, were potentially double-edged in their
consequences. The enforced limitation of role performances was
experienced by most wives as a grave threat to defensive and
adaptive efforts to preserve a valued identity as wife and mother,
and their protest that it was only the hospital which prevented
them from full participation reflected their desperate struggle to
preserve crucial object relations. Further, the trial nature of role
resumptions, with circumspection on the part of both partners,
was occasionally prolonged well into the post-hospital period, so
that what began as a moratorium ended as social invalidism.

III

Hospitalization thus initiated processes which tended to interrupt and neutralize the forces of marital disintegration. It also
tripped off processes serving in a more positive way to move family
members to reintegrate their strained relationships.

Various effects of absence sometimes served to make the heart grow fonder. Thus, removal from the conflict situation often weakened the intensity of the wife's fears, decreased her need and wish to withdraw, and thereby revived positive ties and feelings. Analogous effects could also be observed in some husbands. In two of our families, an informal and almost unacknowledged ceremony commemorated the sense of a fresh start and a recommitment to the marriage. Mr. Yale, who had never given his wife a wedding ring, did so shortly before her release. The Ureys had both lost their wedding rings in the year preceding hospitalization, and he purchased a new pair of rings during the hospital period.

Absence also made the heart grow fonder because of a push from behind rather than the pull of positive attractions. The wife's motivation to resume her marital family roles achieved a fierce and desperate intensity from the defensive and adaptive struggle to preserve the remnants of a valued identity and valued object relations. The urgent wish to be reunited with husband and children often occurred in the context of fears stimulated by hospitalization: fears of "going berserk" intensified by observation of other patients; fears of loss of residual ties to reality, expressed as concern about abandonment or permanent hospitalization; and fears of passivity, helplessness, and infantilism, countered by images of being needed, valued, and useful. The patient thus clung to her outside identity, and condensed diverse conflicts into a single battle: to go home to her family where she could be a good wife and mother.

For the husband, the dislocations of family life caused by the wife's hospitalization sometimes seemed at first negligible after the turbulence and commotion preceding admission. The husband might frankly acknowledge a sense of relief:

Mr. Yale said, "Actually it doesn't bother me too much to do the housework, laundry, cooking, and taking care of the child. I was a bachelor for a long time. And I'm really getting more rest than when she was here. She used to keep me up talking. And I'm not as worried now."

Thus, at first, the wife's absence initially meant one *less* person to take care of. But most husbands in time complained of the additional burdens they were carrying. If a housekeeper or relative was brought in to assist, this introduced new financial or relational problems. At the first signs of improvement, the husband often began to pleasurably anticipate his wife's return and resumption of responsibilities. In some cases, the husband brought pressure on the hospital for his wife's release at just that point when there was a breakdown of substitute household arrangements; for example, when the patient's mother was ill and unable to continue to take care of the children. Then expressed wishes of the children for their mother's return were often intensified by home visits, and this constituted a powerful emotional pressure on both wife and husband for early family reintegration. The separation of the wife from her family thus set in motion various counterforces to marital disintegration, motivating family members to seek reunion.

A second factor tending to facilitate reintegration was the establishment of a reciprocal role in which the husband became the responsible relative and the wife's objective dependency upon him was increased. Hospital personnel treated the husband as *the* person who *should be* responsible for his wife, and as someone concerned about her and eager for her recovery and early return to the family. The staff often privately appreciated the ambivalence that was involved, but officially this ambivalence was not honored. The working definition of the situation was such as to emphasize the continued responsibility and involvement of the husband with his wife.

This induction process often began in the pre-hospital period, as pressures were brought to bear on the husband by the wife or by remedial agents. Many husbands resisted involvement in their wives' complaints, or were reluctant to press for medical or psychiatric treatment, until the very prelude of hospitalization. But in the emergency situations which developed, it was the husbands who were called upon by remedial agents to assume responsibility for their wives and to arrange for admission. Often this was done not only in the name of helping a distressed wife, but in order to protect defenseless children, a particularly powerful rationale. Even when the wife was self-admitted, she often viewed hospitalization as a response to the wishes or actions of her husband. This may have reflected actual pressure by the husband; it also emphasized her continuing commitment to the marital family and the husband's assumed continued involvement with her.

The effect of induction of the husband into the role of responsible relative was most dramatic in those families in which the husband and wife had constructed over the years almost separate lives. The husband may have been working long hours for six or seven days a week, or he may in some other way have become detached from his family. The wife may have become absorbed in an intense and conflicted relationship to her own mother and to her children. The marital partners, in such instances, seemed to have achieved a precarious kind of equilibrium based on emotional distance and lack of explicit demands upon each other.

From the time of her first pregnancy, a few months after marriage, Mrs. Thorne withdrew from sexual relations, became intolerant of affectionate displays, and was reluctant to go out with her husband. Mr. Thorne was at first disturbed by these changes in his wife's conduct, later accepted them, and finally even subtly encouraged them.

The Thornes lived in increasingly separate worlds. Mr. Thorne found occasion to go to work seven days a week, and he often sought companionship and recreation with work colleagues. Mrs. Thorne became preoccupied with her children in a worried, overprotective, and irritable way, and she retained a very close relationship to her mother.

Mrs. Thorne visited her mother or asked her mother to stay with her whenever her husband worked evenings. When he was home, she would spend hours conversing with her mother on the telephone. Mr. Thorne purchased an extension telephone for the bedroom so that his wife could spend the evenings talking to her mother while he watched television. As he said, he didn't want to be disturbed by "all that yak-yak." Mr. Thorne's eventual involvement with another woman, beginning a few months before his wife's psychotic episode, only further symbolized the emotional alienation of the marital partners.

When the manifest illness of the wife in such cases began to obtrude itself into family life, it was initially experienced by the husband as a demand for his interest, concern, involvement, and love. This experienced demand was not ordinarily acceded to until hospitalization signaled the seriousness of the situation and emphasized the concern expected from the responsible relative. In such sequences, hospitalization served—if often only transiently—to dramatize the collapse of a marital equilibrium based upon emotional distance, and to reinstitute a relationship of concern and involvement expressed in the idiom of illness and recovery.

Mrs. Rand suffered from a variety of somatic complaints and a sense of impending personal disorganization for about two years prior to hospitalization. When she attempted to communicate her distress to her husband, he minimized her concerns, emphasized the demands placed upon him by his work, and urged her not to bother him.

One afternoon, after an argument about a new work responsibility her husband had just assumed, Mrs. Rand spent a frantic two hours searching for an ironing board she had just set up. She became panic stricken. She telephoned her minister, who rushed over and found her frightened and somewhat incoherent. The minister wanted to call her husband, but she insisted that he must not be disturbed. When Mr. Rand came home that evening, and his wife told him of the incident, he laughed it off as something that sometimes happens to everyone.

A few weeks later, Mrs. Rand could not sleep. She woke her husband, who told her that he was tired and urged her to try and sleep. At dawn she arose, wrote her husband a brief note, and drove to church. She entered the minister's office, said, "God help me!" and dissolved into tears. Once again, when the minister wanted to call her husband, she urged not disturbing him. This time the minister disregarded her. Within an hour a worried and concerned husband was at her side and arrangements were under way to hospitalize her.

During and after hospitalization, Mrs. Rand commented that her husband no longer ignored her and seemed concerned with her feelings.

Thus, a frequent effect of induction of the husband into the role of responsible relative was to increase marital communication, while focusing it on illness and recovery. We have discussed in an earlier section the process of "negotiation" which may be facilitated by this focus.

The reciprocal of inducting the husband into the role of responsible relative was an increase in the wife's social dependence on him. While the wife was in the hospital, the husband ordinarily served as her primary source of information about the children and other outside interests. As the responsible relative in the eyes of the hospital, the husband's power to limit his wife's contacts with others was usually recognized, if he cared to exert it.

The wives, sensing their own social weightlessness, routinely encouraged their husbands to intervene between them and hospital personnel. This was sometimes indirect, as when Mrs. Yale urged her husband to show more manifest pleasure when coming to pick her up, so that hospital personnel would know he wanted her home. In an extreme case, in which the wife correctly appreciated her husband's reluctance to cooperate in her return, she forged a letter over his signature to the ward physician indicating that she was missed and needed at home. Typically, it was the husband who had to come to get the wife if she was to go on pass; he signed her out and vouchsafed her return. The hospital ordinarily anticipated discharging her "to" him, that is, to his care. The wife was expected—by hospital personnel and by fellow patients—to want to visit home, to want to go home permanently, and to avail herself of every opportunity to proceed along that graduated series of visits which led toward release. The patient culture insistently pointed out that those patients were released first who had a home to go to; in the case of married patients, the home was assumed to be the marital one. Hospital personnel tended to worry about that patient who didn't take advantage of visit opportunities and encouraged her to show more interest in her family.

The process of inducting the husband into the role of responsible relative, with its reciprocal of increasing the wife's objective dependence on him, thus served to channel the wife's pathway to the community through him, intensifying her motivation toward marital integration. Every case gave evidence of pressure to cover over and play down marital dispute, emphasizing the extent to which the wife's experienced social dependence on her husband pressed her toward some semblance of marital reintegration. More generally, the establishment of the reciprocal roles tended to emphasize family values and to foster efforts at collaboration between the marital partners.

The reorganization of the family with the husband in the responsible caretaker role and the wife in the dependent patient role posed various dangers. The husband sometimes used his position to block his wife's return. The couple might be driven toward a façade of reintegration, sometimes deceiving themselves as well as the hospital. But the most characteristic danger was that the role allocations might become stable, so that in the post-hospital period the family was reorganized around an ex-patient who was cared for as a dependent, scrutinized for symptoms, and perhaps by mutual consent excluded from normal participation in family life.

IV

Our observations suggest that an important if implicit function of mental hospitalization is to preserve and reinforce the patient's ties to a personal community. These ties have become attenuated or threatened prior to hospitalization. The admission process may further weaken them. Prolonged hospitalization may sever them completely. We have described social processes, initiated by hospitalization, which tend to counter the permanent withdrawal or expulsion of the patient from his social nexus. The patients we have described were wives and mothers, and the social nexus which has immediately concerned us is the marital family.

We have noted that the immediate effect of hospitalization, prior to specific therapies, is to define the wife as mentally ill and to remove her from the family. These radical procedures initiate a personal and social moratorium. During the moratorium, the wife's role obligations are suspended without being abrogated; past and present expressions of alienation may be reinterpreted, isolated, and forgotten by the patient and her intimates; and critical relationships may be negotiated, modified, and resumed under conditions of limited contact and experimental tentativeness.

We have stressed the typically conservative consequences of the moratorium imposed by this first state hospitalization, for this is what the trend of our observations disclosed. In no case did the wife become permanently detached from the community through this admission. Four women were rehospitalized within a year of release. In fifteen of seventeen cases, the wife returned to the marital family and resumed for at least a time her roles as wife and mother. In most cases, it should be added, this represented a tenuous return to a stressful *status quo ante*.

We have suggested, but not developed in detail, potentially dysfunctional consequences of the type of moratorium imposed by state mental hospitalization. Here we come to the border of our own observations. We must wait on comparable analysis of such alternatives as brief treatment within a community hospital and treatments which attempt to sustain the patient within the home to learn more about these less radical and potentially less dangerous means of accomplishing the work of social reparation.

We must also raise the question of the place of *more* radical procedures, such as family oriented psychotherapies, which do not rely so heavily on suppression, repression, and isolation, but rather attempt to alter the balance of forces which have sustained and shaped individual and family pathology. Here, too, our data, derived from a state hospital, cannot carry us, except insofar as they suggest the therapeutic limitations of more usual procedures.

Finally, we believe that our findings suggest a more general point, one that extends beyond a concern with mental illness to all of the "deviances." It has usually been stressed that deviant conduct provides an occasion and rationale for the casting of persons out of their communities. It has also been frequently suggested that, whatever their intentions, those concerned with the control and reduction of deviant conduct contribute to this effect. It has less frequently been observed that the processes which define persons as deviants and which attempt to redirect their conduct sometimes—and perhaps frequently—have just the opposite effect, namely, halting processes of alienation and stimulating reintegrative processes. We believe that this aspect of the processes of social definition and control deserves explicit attention.

1. See the discussion by Charlotte Green Schwartz in "Rehabilitation of Mental Hospital Patients," *Public Health Monograph No. 17*, Washington, D.C.: U.S. Government Printing Office, 1953, especially 45-48, and the bibliography there cited.

2. Erving Goffman discusses the various forms of adaptation of inmates of "total institutions" in "Some Characteristics of Total Institutions," *Asylums*, Garden City, New York: Doubleday and Co., Inc., 1961.

3. See the thorough discussion of this problem in Elaine Cumming and John Cumming, *Closed Ranks*, Cambridge, Mass.: Harvard University Press, 1957. Schwartz, *op. cit.*, also considers the problem.

4. Thus, even when the relation between the hospital and the family is the topic, it is usual for the effects of this relation on the personal balance of individuals to be emphasized. See, *e.g.*, Theodore Lidz, Georgina Hotchkiss, and Milton Greenblatt, "Patient-Family-Hospital Interrelationships: Some General Conclusions," in *The Patient and the Mental Hospital*, edited by Milton Greenblatt, Daniel J. Levinson, and Richard H. Williams, New York: The Free Press

of Glencoe, 1957, 535-543. Thomas S. Szasz provides a clear exception to this tendency. See, especially, his "Civil Liberties and the Mentally Ill," *Cleveland-Marshall Law Review*, 9 (1960), 399-416. Szasz suggests that hospitalization for mental illness poses "a question of *which value should have preference: the integrity of the family or the autonomy of the individual?* Commitment (and commitment laws) tacitly favor the former." (414-415, italics in the original.) There is, of course, a very large and growing literature on the relations between the family and mental illness. See *e.g.*, the articles by Theodore Lidz and Stephen Fleck, Murray Bowen, John H. Weakland, and Maleta J. Boatman and S. A. Szurek, and the literature cited by them, in *The Etiology of Schizophrenia*, edited by Don D. Jackson, New York: Basic Books, Inc., 1960.

5. *E.g.*, see Erving Goffman's "The Moral Career of the Mental Patient," *Asylums, op. cit.*, in which the role of admission procedures in alienating intimates is emphasized. A notable exception to this emphasis may be found in Talcott Parsons and Renee C. Fox, "Illness, Therapy, and the Modern Urban American Family," *Journal of Social Issues*, 13 (1952), 31-44.

6. Goffman, "The Moral Career of the Mental Patient," *op. cit.*

7. Talcott Parsons has pointed out that, in general, the "sick role" serves to exempt persons from normal responsibilities, and that the physician acts as a legitimatizing agent. See his *The Social System*, New York: The Free Press of Glencoe, 1947, Chapter X. *Effective* legitimation seems more difficult to bring about in the case of mental illness; hospitalization, a radical procedure, partially serves to compensate this difficulty.

8. See Marian Radke Yarrow, Charlotte Green Schwartz, Harriet S. Murphy, and Leila Calhoun Deasy, "The Psychological Meaning of Mental Illness in the Family," *The Journal of Social Issues*, 11 (1955), 12-24; Charlotte Green Schwartz, "Perspectives on Deviance—Wives' Definitions of Their Husbands' Mental Illness," *Psychiatry*, 20 (1957), 275-291; August B. Hollingshead and Frederick C. Redlich, *Social Class and Mental Illness*, New York: John Wiley and Sons, Inc., 1958), especially 172-179; and Cumming and Cumming, *op. cit.*, especially 81-108.

9. Erving Goffman has developed this conception in *The Presentation of Self in Everyday Life*, Garden City, N.Y.: Doubleday and Co., Inc. 1959.

10. See Vilhelm Aubert and Sheldon L. Messinger, "The Criminal and the Sick," *Inquiry*, 1 (1958), 137-160, for a brief discussion of time perspectives on deviance as illness.

THE CYCLE OF ABSTINENCE
AND RELAPSE
AMONG HEROIN ADDICTS

MARSH B. RAY

Those who study persons addicted to opium and its derivatives are confronted by the following paradox: A cure from physiological dependence on opiates may be secured within a relatively short period, and carefully controlled studies indicate that use of these drugs does not cause psychosis, organic intellectual deterioration, or any permanent impairment of intellectual function.[1] But, despite these facts, addicts display a high rate of recidivism. On the other hand, while the rate of recidivism is high, addicts continually and repeatedly seek cure. It is difficult to obtain definitive data concerning the number of cures the addict takes, but various studies of institutional admissions indicate that it is relatively high,[2] and there are many attempts at home cure that go unrecorded.

This paper reports on a study[3] of abstinence and relapse in which attention is focused on the way the addict or abstainer orders and makes meaningful the objects of his experience, including himself as an object,[4] during the critical periods of cure and of relapse and the related sense of identity or of social isola-

I wish to thank Howard S. Becker for his interest, encouragement, and valuable suggestions as I worked out the ideas for this paper. In addition, thanks are also due G. Lewis Penner, Executive Director of the Juvenile Protective Association of Chicago, who made office space available for some of the interviews.

tion the addict feels as he interacts with significant others. It is especially concerned with describing and analyzing the characteristic ways the addict or abstainer defines the social situations he encounters during these periods and responds to the status dilemmas he experiences in them.

Secondary Status Characteristics of Addicts

The social world of addiction contains a loose system of organizational and cultural elements, including a special language or argot, certain artifacts, a commodity market and pricing system, a system of stratification, and ethical codes. The addict's commitment to these values gives him a status and an identity.[5] In addition to these direct links to the world of addiction, becoming an addict means that one assumes a number of secondary status characteristics in accordance with the definitions the society has of this activity.[6] Some of these are set forth in federal and local laws and statutes, others are defined by the stereotypic thinking of members of the larger society about the causes and consequences of drug use.

The addict's incarceration in correctional institutions has specific meanings which he finds reflected in the attitudes adopted toward him by members of non-addict society and by his fellow addicts. Additionally, as his habit grows and the demands for drugs get beyond any legitimate means of supply, his own activities in satisfying his increased craving give him direct experiential evidence of the criminal aspects of self. These meanings of self as a criminal become internalized as he begins to apply criminal argot to his activities and institutional experiences. Thus shoplifting becomes "boosting," the correctional settings become "joints," and the guards in such institutions become "screws."

The popular notion that the addict is somehow psychologically inadequate is supported by many authorities in the field. In addition, support and definition is supplied by the very nature of the institution in which drug addicts are usually treated and have a large part of their experience since even the names of these institutions fix this definition of addiction. For example, one of the out-patient clinics for the treatment of addicts in Chicago was located at Illinois Neuropsychiatric Institute, and the connotations of Bellevue Hospital in New York City, another treatment center for addicts, are socially well established. Then, too, the composition of the staff in treatment centers contributes substantially to the image of the addict as mentally ill, for the personnel are primarily psychiatrists, psychologists, and psychiatric social workers. How such a definition of self was brought forcefully home to one addict is illustrated in the following quotation:

> When I got down to the hospital, I was interviewed by different doctors and one of them told me, "You now have one mark against you as crazy for having been down here." I hadn't known it was a crazy house. You know regular people [non-addicts] think this too.

Finally, as the addict's habit grows and almost all of his thoughts and efforts are directed toward supplying himself with drugs, he becomes careless about his personal appearance and cleanliness. Consequently non-addicts think of him as a "bum" and, because he persists in his use of drugs, conclude that he lacks "will power," is perhaps "degenerate," and is likely to contaminate others.

The addict is aware that he is judged in terms of these various secondary social definitions, and while he may attempt to reject them, it is difficult if not impossible to do so when much of his interpersonal and institutional experience serves to ratify these definitions. They assume importance because they are the medium of exchange in social transactions with the addict and non-addict world in which the addict identifies himself as an object and judges himself in relation to addict and non-addict values. Such experiences are socially disjunctive and become the basis for motivated acts.

The Inception of Cure

An episode of cure begins in the private thoughts of the addict rather than in his overt behavior. These deliberations develop as a result of experience in specific situations of interaction with important others that cause the addict to experience social stress, to develop some feeling of alienation from or dissatisfaction with his present identity, and to call it into question and examine it in all of its implications and ramifications. In these situations the addict engages in private self-debate in which he juxtaposes the values and social relationships which have become immediate and concrete through his addiction with those that are sometimes only half remembered or only imperfectly perceived.

I think that my mother knew that I was addicted because she had heard rumors around the neighborhood. Around that time [when he first began to think about cure] she had been telling me that I looked like a "bum," and that my hair was down the back of my neck and that I was dirty. I had known this too but had shoved it down in the back of my mind somewhere. She used to tell me that to look like this wasn't at all like me. I always wanted to look presentable and her saying this really hurt. At that time I was going to [college] and I wanted to look my best. I always looked at myself as the clever one—the "mystery man"—outwitting the "dolts." I always thought that no one knew, that when I was in my room they thought I was studying my books when actually I wasn't studying at all.

After mother said those things I did a lot of thinking. I often used to sit around my room and think about it and even look at myself in the mirror and I could see that it was true. What is it called . . . ? When you take yourself out of a situation and look at yourself . . . ? "Self-appraisal" . . . I guess that's it. Well I did this about my appearance and about the deterioration of my character. I didn't like it because I didn't want anything to be master over me because this was contrary to my character. I used to sit and look at that infinitesimal bit of powder. I felt it changed my personality somehow.

I used to try staying in but I would get sick. But because I had money I couldn't maintain it [withstand the demands of the withdrawal sickness] and when the pain got unbearable, at least to me it was unbearable, I would go out again. I wanted to be independent of it. I knew then that if I continued I would have to resort to stealing to maintain my habit and this I couldn't tolerate because it was contrary to my character. The others were robbing and stealing but I couldn't be a part of that. I first talked with my uncle about it because my mother was alive then and I thought she would crack up and maybe not understand the problem. I didn't want to be reprimanded, I knew I'd done wrong. I had been through a lot and felt I wanted to be rid of the thing. He was very understanding about it and didn't criticize me. He just talked with me about going to the hospital and said he thought this would be the best way to do it.

But the social psychological prerequisites to the inception of an episode of abstinence need not precede physical withdrawal of the drug. It is frequently the case that following the enforced withdrawal that begins a period of confinement in a correctional institution or hospital, the addict engages in self-debate in which the self in all of its ramifications emerges as an object and is brought under scrutiny. Such institutional situations constrain the addict's perspectives about himself and have a dual character. On the one hand, they serve to ratify a secondary status characteristic, while on the other, as addicts interact with older inmates of jails and hospitals, they provide daily concrete models of what life may be like in later years as a consequence of continued use of drugs.

On occasion, however, the addict group itself, rather than non-addict society, provides the socially disjunctive experience that motivates the addict to abstain, although the non-addict world and its values are still the reference point. An addict who had been addicted for several years and had had several involuntary cures in correctional institutions describes such an experience as follows:

When I first started using we were all buddies, but later we started "burning" each other. One guy would say, "Well, I'll go "cop'" [buy drugs]. Then he'd take the "bread" [money] and he'd never come back. I kicked one time because of that. I didn't have no more money and I got disgusted. First I started to swear him up and down but then my inner conscience got started and I said maybe he got "busted" [arrested]. Then I said, "Aw, to hell with him and to hell with all junkies—they're all the same." So I went home and I tried to read a couple of comic books to keep my mind off it. I was very sick but after a couple of days I kicked.

While the above situation may not be typical, it illustrates the same process to be observed in the other examples—a disruption of the social ordering of experience that has become familiar, a calling into question of the addict identity, and the rejection of this identity and the values associated with it. The more typical situations that evoke such conduct would appear to involve a non-addict or some concrete aspect of the non-addict world as the catalytic agent.

The Addict Self in Transition

The addict who has successfully completed withdrawal is no longer faced with the need to take drugs in order to avert the disaster of withdrawal sickness, and now enters a period which might best be characterized as a "running struggle" with his problems of social identity. He could not have taken such a drastic step had he not developed some series of expectations concerning the nature of his future relationships with social others. His anticipations concerning these situations may or may not be realistic; what matters is that he has them and that the imagery he holds regarding himself and his potentialities is a strong motivating force in his continued abstinence. Above all, he appears to desire ratification by significant others of his newly developing identity, and in his interactions during an episode of abstinence he expects to secure it.

In the early phases of an episode of cure, the abstainer manifests considerable ambivalence about where he stands in addict and non-addict groups, and in discussions of addiction and addicts, he may indicate his ambivalence through his alternate use of the pronouns "we" and "they" and thus his alternate membership in addict and non-addict society. He may also indicate his ambivalence through other nuances of language and choice of words. Later, during a successful episode of abstinence, the ex-addict indicates his non-membership in the addict group through categorizations that place addicts clearly in the third person, and he places his own addiction and matters pertaining to it in the past tense. For example, he is likely to preface a remark with the phrase "When I was an addict. . . ." But of equal or greater importance is the fact that the ex-addict who is successful in remaining abstinent relates to new groups of people, participates in their experience, and to some extent begins to evaluate the conduct of his former associates (and perhaps his own when he was an addict) in terms of the values of the new group.

I see the guys around now quite often and sometimes we talk for a while but I don't feel that I am anything like them any more and I always leave before they "make up" [take drugs]. I tell them, "You know what you are doing but if you keep on you'll just go to jail like I did." I don't feel that they are wrong to be using but just that I'm luckier than they are because I have goals. It's funny, I used to call them "squares" for not using and now they call me "square" for not using. They think that they are "hip" and they are always talking about the old days. That makes me realize how far I've come. But it makes me want to keep away from them, too, because they always use the same old vocabulary—talking about "squares" and being "hip."

Thus, while some abstainers do not deny the right of others to use drugs if they choose, they clearly indicate that addiction is no longer a personally meaningful area of social experience for them. In the above illustration the abstainer is using this experience as something of a "sounding board" for his newly developed identity. Of particular note is the considerable loss of meaning in the old symbols through which he previously ordered his experience and his concern with one of the inevitable consequences of drug use. This is a common experience for those who have maintained abstinence for any length of time.

During the later stages of the formation of an abstainer identity, the ex-addict begins to perceive a difference in his relations with significant others, particularly with members of his family. Undoubtedly their attitudes, in turn, undergo modification and change as a result of his apparent continued abstinence, and they arrive at this judgment by observing his cleanliness and attention to personal neatness, his steady employment, and his re-subscription to other values of non-addict society. The ex-addict is very much aware of these attitudinal differences and uses them further to bolster his conception of himself as an abstainer.

Lots of times I don't even feel like I ever took dope. I feel released not to be dependent on it. I think how nice it is to be natural without having to rely on dope to make me feel good. See, when I was a "junkie" I lost a lot of respect. My father wouldn't talk to me and I was filthy. I have to build up that respect again. I do a lot of things with my family now and my father talks to me again. It's like at parties that my relatives give, now they are always running up to me and giving me a drink and showing me a lot of attention. Before they wouldn't even talk to me. See, I used to feel lonely because my life was dependent on stuff and I felt different from regular people. See, "junkies" and regular people are two different things. I used to feel that I was out of place with my relatives when I was on junk. I didn't want to walk with them on the street and do things with them. Now I do things with them all the time like go to the show and joke with them and I go to church with my uncle. I just kept saying to myself that "junkies" are not my people. My relatives don't say things behind my back now and I am gaining their respect slow but sure.

In this illustration there may be observed a budding sense of social insight characteristic of abstainers in this period of their development. Another characteristic feature is the recognition that subscription to non-addict values must be grounded in action— in playing the role of non-addict in participation with non-addicts and thus sharing in their values and perspectives.

The Process of Relapse

The tendency toward relapse develops out of the meanings of the abstainer's experience in social situations when he develops an image of himself as socially different from non-addicts, and relapse occurs when he redefines himself as an addict. When his social expectations and the expectations of others with whom he interacts are not met, social stress develops and he is required to re-examine the meaningfulness of his experience in non-addict society and in so doing question his identity as an abstainer. This type of experience promotes a mental realignment with addict values and standards and may be observed in the abstainer's thoughts about himself in covert social situations, in his direct interpersonal relations with active addicts, and in his experience with representatives of non-addict society. It is in these various settings that his developing sense of self as an abstainer is put to the test.

Experiences with other addicts that promote relapse. Re-addiction most frequently occurs during the period immediately following the physical withdrawal of the drug—the period described earlier as a time of "running struggle" with identity problems for the ex-addict. It is at this point, when the old values and old meanings he experienced as an addict are still immediate and the new ordering of his experience without narcotics is not well established, that the ex-addict seems most vulnerable to relapse.

Sometimes the experiences that provoke the questioning of identity that precedes relapse occur within the confines of the very institution where the addict has gone to seek cure. The social expectations of other addicts in the hospital are of vital importance in creating an atmosphere in which identification with the values of non-addict society is difficult to maintain.

[The last time we talked you said that you would like to tell me about your experiences in the hospital. What were they like?]
Well, during the first time I was at the hospital most of the fellows seemed to hate [to give] the "square" impression, not hate it exactly but refuse to admit [to] it. My own feelings were that everyone should have been a little different in expressing themselves that I would like to accept the extreme opposite. But I felt that I would have disagreements about this with the fellow inmates. They thought I was a very queer or peculiar person that constantly showed disagreement about the problem as they saw it. I never did reach an understanding with them about the problem.

But addicts do not always relapse on first contact with members of the old group. In fact, there is nothing to indicate that addicts relapse only as a result of association. Instead, contacts may go on for some time during which the ex-addict carries on much private self-debate, feeling at one point that he is socially closer to addicts and at another that his real interest lies in future new identities on which he has decided. Typically he may also call to mind the reason he undertook cure in the first place and question the rationality of relapsing. An interesting example of the dilemma and ambivalence experienced under these circumstances and the partial acceding to social pressures from the addict group by applying the definitions of that group to one's own conduct are the experiences of another addict.

[He had entered the hospital "with the key" and after completing withdrawal he stayed at the hospital for three weeks before voluntarily signing out, although the required period of treatment for a medical discharge at the time was four and one-half months.]
This one kid who was a friend of mine came to me one night and said, "Let's get out of here." So I went and checked out too. Then I got to thinking, "I don't want to go home yet—I'm still sick—and what did I come down here for anyway." So I went up and got my papers back from the officer and tore them up. Then I found this

kid and told him that I was staying and he said, "Oh we knew you weren't going to do it—we knew you'd chicken out." Then I went back and put my papers through again. I felt they were trying to "put me down."

When we got out I could have had a shot right away because one of these guys when we got to town said he knew a croaker who would fix us up, but I didn't go with them. I didn't care what they thought because I got to figuring that I had went this far and I might as well stay off.

When I got home I stayed off for two months but my mother was hollering at me all the time and there was this one family in the neighborhood that was always "chopping me up." I wanted to tell this woman off because she talked all right to my face but behind my back she said things like she was afraid I would turn her son on because I was hanging around with him. She would tell these things to my mother. I never turned anybody on! She didn't know that but I wanted to tell her. Finally I just got disgusted because nobody wanted to believe me and I went back on.

The experiences of this addict provide an interesting denial of the notion that addicts relapse because of association *per se* and support the thesis that relapse is a function of the kind of object ex-addicts make of themselves in the situations they face.

Relations with non-addicts as a prelude to relapse. While the ex-addict's interaction with addict groups is often a source of experiences which cause him to question the value to him of an abstainer identity, experiences with non-addict groups also play a vital role. In most instances the addict has established a status for himself in the eyes of non-addicts who may be acquainted with his case—members of his family, social workers, law enforcement officers, physicians, and so forth. Through gestures, vocal and otherwise, these non-addicts make indications to the ex-addict concerning his membership and right to participation in their group, for example, the right to be believed when he attempts to indicate to the non-addict world that he believes in and subscribes to its values. In his contacts with non-addicts, the former addict is particularly sensitive to their cues.

During the early phases of an episode of abstinence the abstainer enters various situations with quite definite expectations concerning how he should be defined and treated. He indicates his desire for ratification of his new status in many ways, and finds it socially difficult when he sees in the conduct of others toward him a reference to his old identity as an addict. He is not unaware of these doubts about his identity.

My relatives were always saying things to me like "Have you really quit using that drug now?" and things like that. And I knew that they were doing a lot of talking behind my back because when I came around they would stop talking but I overheard them. It used to burn my ass.

On the other hand, the non-addicts with whom he has experience during this period have their own expectations concerning the abstainer's probable conduct. Based in part on the stereotypic thinking of non-addict society concerning additction, in part on unfortunate previous experiences, they may exhibit some skepticism concerning the "cure" and express doubt about the abstainer's prognosis.[7]

The Social Psychological Meaning of Relapse

On an immediate concrete level, relapse requires that the individual reorient himself to the market conditions surrounding the sale of illicit drugs. He must re-establish his sources of supply and, if he has been abstinent for very long, he may have to learn about new fads and fashions in drug use. He may learn, for example, that dolophin is more readily available than heroin at the moment of his return to drug use, that it requires less in the way of preparation, that it calls for such and such amount to safely secure a certain effect, what the effects will be, and so on.

But the ex-addict's re-entrance into the social world of addiction has much deeper meanings. It places demands and restraints upon his interactions and the meaningfulness of his experience. It requires a recommitment to the norms of addiction and limits the degree to which he may relate to non-addict groups in terms of the latter's values and standards. It demands participation in the old ways of organizing conduct and experience and, as a consequence, the readoption of the secondary status characteristics of addiction. He again shows a lack of concern about his personal appearance and grooming. Illicit activities are again engaged in to get money for drugs, and as a result the possibility of more firmly establishing the criminal aspect of his identity becomes a reality.

The social consequence of these experiences and activities is the re-establishment of the sense of social isolation from the non-addict group and a recaptured sense of the meaningfulness of experience in the social world of addiction. It is through these familiar meanings and the reapplication of the symbolic meanings of the addict world to his own conduct that identity and status as an addict are reaffirmed. The ex-addict who relapses is thus likely to comment, "I feel like one of the guys again," or as Street has put it, "It was like coming home."[8]

While repeated relapse on the addict's part may more firmly convince him that "once a junkie, always a junkie" is no myth but instead a valid comment on his way of life, every relapse has has within it the genesis of another attempt at cure. From his however brief or lengthy excursions into the world of non-addiction, the relapsed addict carries back with him an image of himself as one who has done the impossible—one who has actually experienced a period when it was unnecessary to take drugs to avoid the dreaded withdrawal sickness. But these are not his only recollections. He recalls, too, his identification of himself as an abstainer, no matter how tentatively or imperfectly this may have been accomplished. He thinks over his experiences in situations while he occupied the status of abstainer and speculates about the possible other outcomes of these situations had he acted differently.

[Originally from Chicago, he experienced the only voluntary period of abstinence in a long career of addiction while living with his wife in Kansas City, Missouri. After an argument with his wife, during which she reminded him of his previous addiction and its consequences for her, he left her and returned to Chicago, where he immediately relapsed. After three weeks he was using about $12 worth of morphine daily.] He reports on his thoughts at the time as follows:

Now and then I'm given to rational thinking or reasoning and somehow I had a premonition that should I remain in Chicago much longer, shoplifting and doing the various criminal acts I did to get money for drugs, plus the criminal act of just using the drug, I would soon be in jail or perhaps something worse, for in truth one's life is at stake each day when he uses drugs. I reflected on the life I had known in Kansas City with Rose in contrast to the one I had returned to. I didn't know what Rose thought had become of me. I thought that more than likely she was angry and thoroughly disgusted and glad that I was gone. However, I wanted to return but first thought it best to call and see what her feelings were.

[At his wife's urging he returned to Kansas City and undertook a "cold turkey" cure in their home. He remained abstinent for a considerable period but subsequently relapsed again when he returned to Chicago.]

Reflections of the above kind provide the relapsed addict with a rich body of material for self-recrimination and he again evaluates his own conduct in terms of what he believes are the larger society's attitudes toward addicts and addiction. It is then that he may again speculate about his own potential for meaningful experiences and relationships in a non-addict world and thus set into motion a new attempt at cure.

Summary

Addiction to narcotic drugs in our society commits the participant in this activity to a status and identity that has complex secondary characteristics. These develop through shared roles and common interpersonal and institutional experience, and as a consequence addicts develop perspectives about themselves and about non-addict values. They evaluate social situations, and in turn are evaluated by the other participants in these situations, in these terms, often with the result that the value of the addict's identity relative to the social world of addiction is brought into question. When this happens the identification of oneself as an addict, committed to the values and statuses of the addict group, is contrasted with new or remembered identities and relationships, resulting in a commitment to cure with its implications of intense physical suffering. In the period following physical withdrawal from heroin, the addict attempts to enact a new social reality which coincides with his desired self-image as an abstainer, and he seeks ratification of his new identity from others in the situations he faces.

But the abstainer's social expectations during a period when he is off drugs are frequently not gratified. Here again, socially disjunctive experiences bring about a questioning of the value of an abstainer identity and promote reflections in which addict and non-addict identities and relationships are compared. The abstainer's realignment of his values with those of the world of addiction results in the redefinition of self as an addict and has as a consequence the actions necessary to relapse. But it should be noted that the seed of a new attempt at abstinence are sown, once addiction has been re-established, in the self-recriminations engaged in upon remembrance of a successful period of abstinence.

1. See as examples: C. Knight Aldrich, "The Relationship of the Concept Formation Test to Drug Addiction and Intelligence," *Journal of Nervous and Mental Diseases,* 100 (July, 1944), 30-34; Margaret E. Hall, "Mental and Physical Efficiency of Women Drug Addicts," *Journal of Abnormal and Social Psychology,* 33 (July, 1938), 332-345; A. Z. Pfeffer and Dorothy Cleck, "Chronic Psychoses and Addiction to Morphine," *Archives of Neurology and Psychiatry,* 56 (December, 1946), 665-672.

2. Michael J. Pescor, *A Statistical Analysis of the Clinical Records of Hospitalized Drug Addicts,* Supplement No. 143 to the Public Health Reports, United States Public Health Service, Washington: Government Printing Office, 1943, p. 24; Victor H. Vogel, "Treatment of the Narcotic Addict by the U.S. Public Health Service," *Federal Probation,* 12 (June, 1948), 45-50.

3. The basic data consisted of case histories collected in repeated depth interviews with 17 addicts and abstainers over a two-year period. During this time several of the active addicts became abstainers and vice versa. Additional material was gathered while the author worked for a year as a social worker in a rehabilitation program for addicts.

4. "Object" is employed here in the sense intended by George Herbert Mead in his development of the concept in *Mind, Self and Society,* Chicago: University of Chicago Press, 1934, Part III, 135-226. Two earlier studies have applied this kind of thinking in studying the behavior of addicts, see: L. Guy Brown, "The Sociological Implications of Drug Addiction," *Journal of Educational Sociology,* 4 (February, 1931), 358-369, and Alfred R. Lindesmith, *Opiate Addiction,* Bloomington, Indiana: Principia Press, 1947.

5. Marsh B. Ray, "Cure and Relapse Among Heroin Addicts," Unpublished M.A. thesis, Department of Sociology, University of Chicago, 1958.

6. For a general discussion of the important role that auxiliary status characteristics play in social situations, see Everett C. Hughes, "Dilemmas and Contradictions in Status," *American Journal of Sociology,* 50 (March, 1945), 253-259.

7. Family members may have been subjected to thefts by the addict, or other kinds of trickery, and they tend to be on their guard lest the experience be repeated. Interestingly, the matter of thefts of either money or small household objects (a radio or a clock) is often used by family members as an index as to whether "he's back on that stuff again" or not. His physical appearance is another gauge.

8. Leroy Street (pseudonym) and D. Loth, *I Was A Drug Addict*, Pyramid Books, New York: Random House, 1953, p. 71.

PART THREE

ORGANIZED DEVIANCE AND DEVIANT ROLES

THE SOCIAL INTEGRATION
OF QUEERS AND PEERS

ALBERT J. REISS, JR.

Sex delinquency is a major form of behavior deviating from the normative prescriptions of American society. A large number of behaviors are classified as sex delinquency—premarital heterosexual intercourse, pederasty, and fellation, for example.

Investigation of sex behavior among males largely focuses on the psychological structure and dynamic qualities of adult persons who are described as "sexual types" or on estimating the incidence, prevalence, or experience rates of sex acts for various social groups in a population. There is little systematic research on the social organization of sexual activity in a complex social system unless one includes descriptive studies of the social organization of female prostitution.

An attempt is made in this paper to describe the sexual relation between "delinquent peers" and "adult queers" and to account for its social organization. This transaction is one form of homosexual prostitution between a young male and an adult male fellator. The adult male clients pays a delinquent boy prostitute a sum of money in order to be allowed to act as a fellator. The transaction is limited to fellation and is one in which the boy

---

The word "queer" is of the "straight" and not the "gay" world. In the "gay" world it has all the qualities of a negative sterotype but these are not intended in this paper. The paper arose out of the perspective of boys in the "straight" world.

I am particularly indebted to Howard S. Becker, Evelyn Hooker, Everett Hughes, John Kitsuse, Ned Polsky, H. Laurence Ross, and Clark Vincent for their helpful suggestions and encouragement in publishing this article.

develops no self-conception as a homosexual person or sexual deviator, although he perceives adult male clients as sexual deviators, "queers" or "gay boys."

There has been little research on social aspects of male homosexual prostitution; hence the exploratory nature of the investigation reported here and the tentative character of the findings. Although there are descriptions of "marriage" and of the "rigid caste system of prison homosexuality"[1] which contribute to our understanding of its social organization in the single sex society of deviators, little is known about how homosexual activity is organized in the nuclear communities of America.

A few recent studies discuss some organizational features of male prostitution.[2] Ross distinguishes three types of male homosexual prostitutes on the basis of the locus of their hustling activity.[3] (1) the *bar-hustler* who usually visits bars on a steady basis in search of queer clients; (2) the *street-hustler,* usually a teen-aged boy who turns "tricks" with older men; and (3) the *call-boy* who does not solicit in public. The street-hustler has the lowest prestige among hustlers, partly because his is the more hazardous and less profitable form of activity. One might expect their prestige status in the organized "gay world" to be low since they apparently are marginal to its organization. Street-hustlers, therefore, often become bar-hustlers when they are able to pass in bars as of legal age.

The boys interviewed for this study could usually be classified as street-hustlers, given the principal locus of their activity. Yet, the street-hustlers Ross describes are oriented toward careers as bar-hustlers, whereas none of the boys I studied entered hustling as a career. For the latter, hustling is a transitory activity, both in time and space.

There apparently are crucial differences among hustlers, however, in respect to the definition of the hustler role and the self-concept common to occupants in the role. The hustlers Ross studied are distinguished by the fact that they define themselves as both prostitute and homosexual. The boys I studied *do not define themselves either as hustlers or as homosexual.* Most of these boys see themselves as "getting a queer" only as a substitute activity or as part of a versatile pattern of delinquent activity.[4]

The absence of a shared definition of one another as hustlers to-gether with shared definitions of when one "gets a queer" serve to insulate these boys from self-definitions either as street-hustlers or as homosexual.

The boys interviewed in this study regard hustling as an accept-able substitute for other delinquent earnings or activity. Although the sexual transaction itself may occur in a two-person *or* a larger group setting, the prescribed norms governing this transaction are usually learned from peers in the delinquent gang. Furthermore, in many cases, induction into the queer-peer transaction occurs through participation in the delinquent group. They learn the prescribed form of behavior with adult fellators and are inducted into it as a business transaction by means of membership in a group which carries this knowledge in a common tradition and controls its practices. In particular, it will be shown that the peer group controls the amount of activity and the conditions under which it is permitted. Finally, it is postulated that this is a shared organizational system between peer hustlers and adult fellators.

There apparently exist the other possible types of males who engage in homosexual sex acts based on the elements of self-definition as homosexual and hustler. John Rechy in several vignettes describes a third type who conceive of themselves as hustlers but do not define themselves as homosexual.[5]

> . . . the world of queens and male-hustlers and what they thrive on, the queens being technically men but no one thinks of them that way—always "she"—their "husbands" being the masculine vagrants—"fruithustlers"—fleetingly sharing the queens' pads—never considering they're involved with another man (the queen), and as long as the hustler goes only with queens—and with fruits only for scoring (which is making or taking sexmoney, getting a meal, making a pad) *he is himself not considered queer*. (Italics mine.)[6]

The importance of being defined as nonhomosexual while acknowledging one's role as a hustler is brought forth in this passage:

> Like the rest of us on that street—who played the male role with other men—Pete was touchy about one subject—his masculinity. In Bickford's one afternoon, a good looking masculine young man walked in, looking at us, walks out again hurriedly. "That cat's queer,"

Pete says, glaring at him. "I used to see him and I thought he was hustling, and one day he tried to put the make on me in the flix. It bugged me, him thinking I'd make it with him for free. I told him to f . . . off, go find another queer like him." He was moodily silent for a long while and then he said almost belligerently: "No matter how many queers a guy goes with, if he goes for money, that don't make him queer. You're still straight. It's when you start going for free, with other young guys, that you start growing wings.[7]

The literature on male homosexuality, particularly that written by clinicians, is abundant with reference to the fourth possible type—those who define themselves as homosexual but not as hustlers.

The Data

Information on the sexual transaction and its social organization was gathered mostly by interviews, partly by social observation of their meeting places. Though there are limitations to inferring social organization from interview data (particularly when the organization arises through behavior that is negatively sanctioned in the larger society), they provide a convenient basis for exploration.

Sex histories were gathered from 18.6 per cent of the 1008 boys between the ages of twelve and seventeen who were interviewed in the Nashville, Tennessee, SMA for an investigation of adolescent conforming and deviating behavior. These represent all of the interviews of one of the interviewers during a two-month period, together with interviews with all Nashville boys incarcerated at the Tennessee State Training School for Boys.

As Table 1 discloses, the largest number of interviews was taken with lower-class delinquent boys. There is a reason for this: when it was apparent that delinquents from the lowest social class generally had some contact with adult male fellators, an attempt was made to learn more about how this contact was structured and controlled. Sex histories, therefore, were obtained from all of the white Nashville boys who were resident in the Tennessee State Training School for Boys during the month of June, 1958.

The way sex history information was obtained precludes mak-

Table 1

Type of Sex Experience by Conforming-Deviating Type of Boy

Per Cent by Conforming-Deviating Type

Type of Sex Experience	LOWER CLASS				MIDDLE CLASS				ALL CLASSES		
	Org. career delinquent	Peer oriented delinquent	Conforming non-achiever	Conforming achiever	Peer oriented delinquent	Conforming non-achiever	Conforming achiever	Hyper-conformer	Non-conforming isolate	Conforming isolate	Total
Total	73	166	250	81	38	86	193	56	24	41	1008
Queers, masturbation, and heterosexual	32.5	27.3	5.1	20.0	–	10.0	–	–	37.5	–	17.6
Queers, masturbation, hetero and animal	30.2	4.5	–	–	5.0	–	–	–	–	–	8.5
Heterosexual only	4.7	11.4	–	–	70.0	30.0	–	–	12.5	–	13.4
Heterosexual and masturbation*	25.6	34.1	33.3	40.0	15.0	10.0	40.0	–	25.0	–	27.3
Masturbation only	2.3	15.9	48.7	40.0	–	10.0	40.0	57.1	25.0	100.0	21.9
Denies sex experience	4.7	6.8	12.8	–	10.0	40.0	20.0	42.9	0.0	–	11.2
Subtotal	43	44	39	5	20	10	10	7	8	1	187
No sex history	41.1	73.5	84.4	93.8	47.4	88.4	94.8	87.5	66.7	97.6	81.4

*Includes 3 cases of heterosexual, masturbation, and animal (2 lower-class organized career delinquent and 1 peer oriented delinquent).

ing reliable estimates about the incidence or prevalence of hustling within the Nashville adolescent boy population. Yet the comparisons among types of conformers and deviators in Table 1 provide an informed guess about their life chances for participation in such an activity.[8]

Only two middle-class boys report experience in the peer-queer transaction. In one case, the boy acquiesced once to solicitation; in the other, the boy had acquired experience and associations in the State Training School for Boys which led to continued participation following his release. Within the lower-class group, it seems clear that the career-oriented delinquent is most likely to report sex experiences with fellators. Roughly three of every five boys report such experiences as contrasted with the peer-oriented delinquent, the type with the next highest relative frequency, where only about one in three report such experiences.

Taking into account the proportional distribution of types of conformers and deviators in a school population of adolescent boys and applying in a very rough way the proportional distribution for type of sex deviation set forth in Table 1, the experience rate with fellators is quite low in a population of all adolescent boys. The peer-queer relationship seems almost exclusively limited to lower-class delinquent boys—particularly career-oriented delinquent boys, where the experience rate is probably very high.

While not of direct concern here, it is of interest that the conformers in Table 1 seem to consist about equally of boys who either report a history of heterosexual and masturbation experience, or masturbation only experience, while hyperconformers either report no sex experience or that they masturbate only.

It might also be inferred from Table 1 that the adolescent conforming boy of lower-class origins in our society is very unlikely to report he never masturbates, though a substantial proportion of middle-class conforming boys maintain they never masturbate and never have masturbated. Although there may be age differences among the class levels in age of onset of masturbation, the class difference may yet be genuine. It is possible, of course, that this difference in masturbation experience reflects only a difference in willingness to report masturbation to a middle-class investigator, i.e., middle-class boys are more likely to hide their sexual experience, even that of masturbation, from others. Nevertheless, there may be class differences in the social organization of sexual experiences, since lower-class boys reported masturbating in groups when they first began to masturbate, while this experience was reported much less frequently by middle-class boys, for whom it is more likely a private matter. The same thing is true for heterosexual experience: lower-class boys, particularly delinquent ones, frequently report they participate in group heterosexual activity in "gang-bangs," while heterosexual experience appears to be a more private experience for the middle-class boy, who does not share his sexual partner with peers. All of this may reflect not only greater versatility in the sex experience of the lower-class male but perhaps a greater willingness to use sex as a means to gratification.

How Peers and Queers Meet

Meetings between adult male fellators and delinquent boys are easily made, because both know how and where to meet within the community space. Those within the common culture know that contact can be established within a relatively short period of time, if it is wished. The fact that meetings between peers and queers can be made easily is mute evidence of the organized understandings which prevail between the two populations.

There are a large number of places where the boys meet their clients, the fellators. Many of these points are known to all boys regardless of where they reside in the metropolitan area. This is particularly true of the central city locations where the largest number of contact points is found within a small territorial area. Each community area of the city, and certain fringe areas, inhabited by substantial numbers of lower-class persons, also have their meeting places, generally known only to the boys residing in the area.

Queers and peers typically establish contact in public or quasi-public places. Major points of contact include street corners, public parks, men's toilets in public or quasi-public places such as those in transportation depots, parks or hotels, and "second" and "third-run" movie houses (open around the clock and permitting sitting through shows). Bars are seldom points of contact, perhaps largely because they are plied by older male hustlers who lie outside the peer culture and groups, and because bar proprietors will not risk the presence of under-age boys.

There are a number of prescribed modes for establishing contact in these situations. They permit the boys and fellators to communicate intent to one another privately despite the public character of the situation. The major form of establishing contact is the "cruise," with the fellator passing "queer-corners" or locations until his effort is recognized by one of the boys. A boy can then signal—usually by nodding his head, a hand gesticulation signifying OK, following, or responding to commonly understood introductions such as "You got the time?"—that he is prepared to undertake the transaction. Entrepreneur and client then move to a place where the sexual activity is consummated, usually a place affording privacy, protection, and hasty exit. "Dolly," a three-time loser at the State Training School, describes one of these prescribed forms for making contact:

> Well, like at the bus station, you go to the bathroom and stand there pretendin' like . . . and they're standin' there pretendin' like . . . and then they motions their head and walks out and you follow them, and you go some place. Either they's got a car, or you go to one of them hotels near the depot or some place like that . . . most any place.

Frequently contact between boys and fellators is established when the boy is hitchhiking. This is particularly true for boys' first contacts of this nature. Since lower-class boys are more likely than middle-class ones to hitch rides within a city, particularly at night when such contacts are most frequently made, they perhaps are most often solicited in this manner.

The experienced boy who knows a "lot of queers," may phone known fellators directly from a public phone, and some fellators try to establish continued contact with boys by giving them their phone numbers. However, the boys seldom use this means of contact for reasons inherent in their orientation toward the transaction, as we shall see below.

We shall now examine how the transaction is facilitated by these types of situations and the prescribed modes of contact and communication. One of the characteristics of all these contact situations is that they provide a *rationale* for the presence of *both* peers and queers in the *same* situation or place. This rationale is necessary for both parties, for were there high visibility to the presence of either and no ready explanation for it, contact and communication would be far more difficult. Public and quasi-public facilities provide situations which account for the presence of most persons since there is relatively little social control over the establishment of contacts. There is, of course, some risk to the boys and the fellators in making contact in these situations since they are generally known to the police. The Morals Squad may have "stake-outs," but this is one of the calculated risks and the communication network carries information about their tactics.

A most important element in furnishing a rationale is that these meeting places must account for the presence of delinquent boys of essentially lower-class dress and appearance who make contact with fellators of almost any class level. This is true despite the fact that the social settings which fellators ordinarily choose to establish contact generally vary according to the class level of the fellators. Fellators of high social class generally make contact by "cruising" past street-corners, in parks, or the men's rooms in "better" hotels, while those from the lower class are likely to select the public bath or transportation depot. There apparently is some general equation of the class position of boys and fellators in the peer-queer transaction. The large majority of fellators in the delinquent peer-queer transaction probably are from the lower class ("apes"). But it is difficult to be certain about the class position of the fellator clients since no study was made of this population.

The absence of data from the fellator population poses difficulties in interpreting the contact relationship. Many fellators involved with delinquent boys do not appear to participate in any overt or covert homosexual groups, such as the organized homosexual community of the "gay world."[9]

The "gay world" is the most visible form of organized homosexuality since it is an organized community, but it probably encompasses only a small proportion of all homosexual contact. Even among those in the organized homosexual community, evi-

dence suggests that the homosexual members seek sexual gratification outside their group with persons who are essentially
anonymous to them. Excluding homosexual married couples,
Leznoff and Westley maintain that there is ". . . a prohibition
against sexual relationships within the group. . . ."[10] Ross indicates
that young male prostitutes are chosen, among other reasons, for
the fact that they protect the identity of the client.[11] Both of
these factors tend to coerce many male fellators to choose an
anonymous contact situation.

It is clear that these contact situations provide not only a
rationale for the presence of the parties to the transaction but
also a guarantee of anonymity. The guarantee does not necessarily
restrict social visibility as both the boys and the fellators may
recognize cues (including, but not necessarily, those of gesture
and dress) which lead to mutual role identification.[12] But anonymity is guaranteed in at least two senses: anonymity of presence
is assured in the situation and their personal identity in the
community is protected unless disclosed by choice.

There presumably are a variety of reasons for the requirement
of anonymity. For many, a homosexual relationship must remain
a secret since their other relationships in the community—families,
business relationships, etc.—must be protected. Leznoff and Westley refer to these men as the "secret" as contrasted with the
"overt" homosexuals,[13] and in the organized "gay world" they
are known as "closet fags." For some, there is also a necessity for
protecting identity to avoid blackmail.[14] Although none of the
peer hustlers reported resorting to blackmail, the adult male fellator may nonetheless hold such an expectation, particularly if
he is older or of high social class. Lower-class ones, by contrast,
are more likely to face the threat of violence from adolescent boys
since they more often frequent situations where they are likely
to contact "rough trade."[15] The kind of situation in which the
delinquent peer-queer contact is made and the sexual relationship
consummated tends to minimize the possibility of violence.

Not all male fellators protect their anonymity; some will let
a boy have their phone number and a few "keep a boy." Still,
most fellators want to meet boys where they are least likely to
be victimized, although boys sometimes roll queers by selecting

a meeting place where by prearrangement, their friends can meet them and help roll the queer, steal his car, or commit other acts of violence. Boys generally know that fellators are vulnerable in that they "can't" report their victimization. Parenthetically, it might be mentioned that these boys are not usually aware of their own institutional invulnerability to arrest. An adolescent boy is peculiarly invulnerable to arrest even when found with a fellator since the mores define the boys as exploited.[16]

Situations of personal contact between adolescent boys and adult male fellators also provide important ways to *communicate intent* or to carry out the transaction *without* making the contact particularly visible to others. The wall writings in many of these places are not without their primitive communication value, e.g., "show it hard," and places such as a public restroom provide a modus operandi. The entrepreneur and his customer in fact can meet with little more than an exchange of non-verbal gestures, transact their business with a minimum of verbal communication and part without a knowledge of one another's identity. In most cases, boys report "almost nothing" was said. The sexual transaction may occur with the only formal transaction being payment to the boy.

Induction into the Peer-Queer Transaction

The peer-queer culture operates through a delinquent peer society. Every boy interviewed in this study who voluntarily established contacts with fellators was also delinquent in many other respects. The evidence shows that contact with fellators is an institutionalized aspect of the organization of lower-class delinquency oriented groups. This is not to say that boys outside these groups never experience relationships with adult male fellators: some do, but they are not participants in groups which sanction the activity according to the prescribed group standards described below. Nor is it to say that all delinquent groups positively sanction the peer-queer transaction, since its distribution is unknown.

How, then, do lower-class delinquent boys get to meet fellators? Most boys from the lowest socioeconomic level in large cities are prepared for this through membership in a delinquent group which has a knowledge of how to make contact with fellators and relate to them. This is part of their common culture. Often, too, the peer group socializes the boy in his first experiences or continuing ones with fellators. The behavior is apparently learned within the framework of differential association.

The peer group actually serves as a school of induction for some of its members. The uninitiated boy goes with one or more members of his peer group for indoctrination and his first experience. Doy L., a lower-class boy at a lower-class school and a two-time loser at the State Training School, explains how he got started:

> I went along with these older boys down to the bus station, and and they took me along and showed me how it was done . . . they'd go in, get a queer, get blowed and get paid . . . if it didn't work right, they'd knock him in the head and get their money . . . they showed me how to do it, so I went in too.

In any case, boys are socialized in the subcultural definitions of peer-queer relations by members of their group and many apply this knowledge when an opportunity arises. Within the group, boys hear reports of experiences which supply the cultural definitions: how contacts are made, how you get money if the queer resists, how much one should expect to get, what kind of behavior is acceptable from the queer, which is to be rejected and how. Boys know all this *before* they have any contact with a fellator. In the case of street gangs, the fellators often pass the neighborhood corner; hence, even the preadolescent boy learns about the activity as the older boys get picked up. As the boy enters adolescence and a gang of his own which takes over the corner, he is psychologically and socially prepared for his first experience, which generally occurs when the first opportunity presents itself. Lester H. illustrates this; his first experience came when he went to one of the common points of convergence of boys and fellators—The Empress Theatre—to see a movie. Lester relates:

> I was down in the Empress Theatre and this gay came over and felt me up and asked me if I'd go out . . . I said I would if he'd give me the the money as I'd heard they did, and I was gettin' low on it . . . so he took me down by the river and blowed me.

In a substantial number of cases, a brother introduces the boy to his first experience, much as he introduces him to other first experiences. Jimmie M. illustrates this pattern. Jimmie describes how he was led into his first heterosexual experience:

When I was almost 14, my younger brother said he'd screwed this woman and he told me about it, so I went down there and she let me screw her too.

His induction into the peer-queer transaction also occurred through his younger brother:

Well, my younger brother came home and told me this gay'd blowed him and he told me where he lived . . . And, I was scared to do it, but I figured I'd want to see what it was like since the other guys talked about it and my brother'd done it. So I went down there and he blowed me.

Not all boys belonging to groups which sanction peer hustling accept the practice. Some boys reject the peer-queer transaction while retaining membership in the group. It is not too surprising that such exceptions occur. Although in most delinquent groups some forms of sex activity confer status, it is rarely an absolute requisite for participation in such groups. Some boys in gangs which frequently gang shag, for example, refuse to participate in these activities. "I don't like my meat that raw" appears to be an acceptable "out." Exemption appears possible so long as the boy is acceptable in most, if not all, other respects. A lower-class delinquent boy apparently doesn't "chicken-out" or lose his "rep" if he doesn't want to engage in sex behaviors which most of his peers practice. (The same condition may hold for other practices, such as the use of narcotics.) Jerry P. from a lower-class school is in a group where all the other boys go with fellators; but he refuses to become involved, though he goes so far as to ride in the car with one of the gang's "regular queers." Jerry is in a gang which often gets picked up by a well-known "local gay," a David B. Jerry admits: "I ride with B. a lot, but he's never done anything to me; I just can't go for that." When asked how he knew B. was a queer, he replied, "Oh, all the guys say so and talk about doin' it with him. . . . I could, but I just don't want to." Joe C., at a school which crosscuts the class structure, was asked if he had any other kind of sex experiences. His reply shows his rejection of his peer group's pattern of behavior with fellators. "You mean with queers?" "Un huh." "I don't go with any. Most of my friends queer-bait, but I don't." A friend of his, Roy P., also rejects the activity: "Ain't no sense in queer-baitin'; I don't need the money that bad."

The impression should not be gained that most lower-class boys who are solicited by fellators accept the solicitation. A majority of all solicitations are probably refused when the initial contact is made unless several other conditions prevail. The first is that the boy must be a member of a group which permits this form of transaction, indoctrinates the boy with its codes and sanctions his participation in it. Almost all lower-class boys reported they were solicited by a queer at least once. A majority refused the solicitation. Refusal is apparently easy since boys report that queers are seldom insistent. There apparently is a mutual willingness to forego the transaction in such cases, perhaps because the queer cannot afford the risk of exposure, but perhaps also because the probability of his establishing contact on his next try is sufficiently high so that he can "afford" to accept the refusal. Looked at another way, there must be a set of mutual gains and expectations for the solicitation to be accepted and the transaction to proceed. Boys who refuse to be solicited are not vulnerable for another reason: they usually are members of groups which negatively sanction the activity. Such groups generally "bug" boys who go out with fellators and use other techniques of isolation to discourage the transaction. There also are gangs which look upon queers as "fair game" for their aggressive activity. They beat them, roll, and otherwise put upon them. A third condition that must prevail is that the boy who accepts or seeks solicitation from fellators must view the offer as instrumental gain, particularly monetary gain (discussed below).

There are boys, however, particularly those who are quite young, who report a solicitation from a man which they were unable to refuse but which they subsequently rejected as neither gratifying nor instrumentally acceptable. It is these boys who can be said to be "exploited" by adult fellators in the sense that they are either forced into the act against their will, or are at least without any awareness of how to cope with the situation. One such instance is found in the following report:

> This guy picked me up down at Fourth and Union and said he was going over to East Nashville, so I got in . . . but he drove me out on Dickerson Pike. (What'd he do?) . . . Well, he blowed me and it made me feel real bad inside . . . but I know how to deal with queers now . . . ain't one of 'em gonna do that to me again . . . I hate queers. . . . They're crazy.

There is an important admission in the statement, "But I know how to deal with 'em now." The lower-class boy as he grows older learns how to deal with sexual advances from fellators. Boys exchange experiences on how they deal with them and it becomes quite difficult to "exploit" a lower-class boy who is socialized in a peer group. It is perhaps largely the very young boy, such as the one in the case above, or those isolated from peer groups, who are most vulnerable to solicitation without previous preparation for it.

Lower-class boys, as we have seen, have the highest probability of being in situations where they will be solicited by fellators. But, *the lower-class boy who is a member of a career-oriented gang which positively sanctions instrumental relationships with adult male fellators and which initiates members into these practices, and a boy who at the same time perceives himself as "needing" the income which the transaction provides, is most likely to establish personal contact with adult male fellators on a continuing basis.*

It is suggested that the peer-queer transaction is behavior learned through differential association in delinquent gangs. This cannot be demonstrated without resort to a more specific test of the hypothesis. But, as Sutherland has pointed out, "Criminal behavior is partially a function of opportunities to commit special classes of crimes. . . . It is axiomatic that persons who commit a specific crime have the opportunity to commit that crime. . . . While opportunity may be partially a function of association with criminal patterns and of the specialized techniques thus acquired, it is not entirely determined in this manner, and consequently differential association is not a sufficient cause of criminal behavior."[17] Middle-class boys are perhaps excluded from the peer-queer transaction as much through lack of opportunity to commit this special class of crime in their community of exposure as through any criterion of differential association. The structure of the middle-class area is incompatible with the situational requirements for the peer-queer transaction.

Norms Governing the Transaction

Does the peer society have any norms about personal relations with fellators? Or, does it simply induct a boy into a relationship by teaching him how to effect the transaction? The answer is that there appear to be several clear-cut norms about the relations between peers and queers, even though there is some deviation from them.

The first major norm is that *a boy must undertake the relationship with a queer solely as a way of making money; sexual gratification cannot be actively sought as a goal in the relationship.* This norm does not preclude a boy from sexual gratification by the act; he simply must not seek this as a goal. Put another way, a boy cannot admit that he failed to get money from the transaction unless he used violence toward the fellator and he cannot admit that he sought it as a means of sexual gratification.

The importance of making money in motivating a boy to the peer-queer transaction is succinctly stated by Dewey H:

This guy in the Rex Theatre came over and sat down next to me when I was 11 or 12, and he started to fool with me. I got over and sat down another place and he came over and asked me, didn't I want to and he'd pay me five bucks. I figured it was *easy money* so I went with him . . . I didn't do it before that. That wasn't too long after I'd moved to South Nashville. I was a pretty good boy before that . . . not real good, but I never ran with a crowd that got into trouble before that. But, I met a lot of 'em there. (Why do you run with queers?) It's *easy money* . . . like I could go out and break into a place when I'm broke and get money that way . . . but that's harder and *you take a bigger risk* . . . with a queer it's *easy money.*

Dewey's comments reveal two important motivating factors in getting money from queers, both suggested by the expression, "easy money." First, the money is easy in that it can be made quickly. Some boys reported that when they needed money for a date or a night out, they obtained it within an hour through the sexual transaction with a queer. All a boy has to do is go to a place where he will be contacted, wait around, get picked up, carried to a place where the sexual transaction occurs, and in a relatively short period of time he obtains the money for his service.

It is easy money in another and more important sense for many of these boys. Boys who undertake the peer-queer transaction are generally members of career-oriented delinquent groups. Rejecting the limited opportunities for making money by legitimate means or finding them inaccessible, their opportunities to make money by illegitimate means may also be limited or the risk may be great. Theft is an available means, but it is more difficult and involves greater risk than the peer-queer transaction. Delinquent boys are not unaware of the risks they take. Under most circumstances, delinquents may calculate an act of stealing as "worth the risk." There are occasions, however, when the risk is calculated as too great. These occasions occur when the "heat" is on the boy or when he can least afford to run the risk of being picked up by the police, as is the case following a pickup by the police, being put on probation or parole, or being warned that incarceration will follow the next violation. At such times, boys particularly calculate whether they can afford to take the risk. Gerald L., describing a continuing relationship with a fellator who gave him his phone number, reflects Dewey's attitude toward minimizing risk in the peer-queer transaction: "So twic'd after that when I was gettin' real low and couldn't risk stealin' and gettin' caught, I called him and he took me out and blowed me." Here is profit with no investment of capital and a minimum of risk in social, if not in psychological, terms.

The element of risk coupled with the wish for "easy money" enters into our understanding of the peer-queer relationship in another way. From a sociological point of view, the peer-queer sexual transaction occurs between two major types of deviators— "delinquents" and "queers." Both types of deviators risk negative sanctions for their deviant acts. The more often one has been arrested or incarcerated, the more punitive the sanctions from the larger social system for both types of deviators. At some point, therefore, both calculate risks and seek to minimize them, at least in the very short run. Each then becomes a means for the other to minimize risk.

When the delinquent boy is confronted with a situation in which he wants money and risks little in getting it, how is he to get it without working? Illegitimate activities frequently provide the "best" opportunity for easy money. These activities often are restricted in kind and number for adolescents and the risk of negative sanctions is high. Under such circumstances, the service offered a queer is a chance to make easy money with a minimum of risk.

Opportunities for sexual gratification are limited for the adult male fellator, particularly if he wishes to minimize the risk of detection in locating patrons, to avoid personal involvement and to get his gratification when he wishes it. The choice of a lower-class male, precisely because of his class position, somewhat reduces the risk. If the lower-class male also is a delinquent, the risk is minimized to an even greater degree.

This is not to say that the parties take equal risks in the situation. Of the two, the fellator perhaps is less able to minimize his risk since he still risks violence from his patron, but much less so if a set of expectations arise which control the use of violence as well. The boy is most able to minimize his risk since he is likely to be defined as "exploited" in the situation if caught.

Under special circumstances, boys may substitute other gratifications for the goal of money, provided that these gratifications do not include sexual gratification as a major goal. These special circumstances are the case where an entire gang will "make a night (or time) of it" with one or more adult male fellators. Under these circumstances, everyone is expected from the sub-cultural expectations about making money from the fellator because everyone participates and there is no reason for everyone (or anyone) to make money. For the group to substitute being given a "good time" by a "queer" for the prescribed financial transaction is, of course, the exception which proves the rule.

Several examples of group exemption from the prescribed norm of a financial gain were discovered. Danny S., leader of the Black Aces, tells of his gang's group experiences with queers: "There's this one gay who takes us to the Colonial Motel out on Dickerson Pike . . . usually it's a bunch of us boys and we all get drunk and get blowed by this queer . . . we don't get any money then . . . it's more a drinking party." The Black Aces are a fighting gang and place great stress on physical prowess, particularly boxing. All of its members have done time more than once at the State Training School. During one of these periods, the school employed a boxing instructor whom the boys identified as "a queer," but the boys had great respect for him since he taught them how to box and was a game fighter. Danny refers to him in accepting terms: "He's a real good guy. He's fought with us once or twice and we drink with him when we run into him. . . . He's taken us up to Miter Dam a coupla times; he's got a cabin up there on the creek and he blows us. . . . But mostly we just drink and have a real good time." These examples illustrate the instrumental orientation of the gang members. If the expense of the gang members getting drunk and having a good time are borne by a "queer," each member is released from the obligation to receive cash. The relationship in this case represents an exchange of services rather than that of money for a service.

The second major norm operating in the relationship is that *the sexual transaction must be limited to mouth-genital fellation. No other sexual acts are generally tolerated.*[18] The adult male fellator must deport himself in such a way as to re-enforce the instrumental aspects of the role relationship and to insure affective neutrality.[19] For the adult male fellator to violate the boy's expectation of "getting blowed," as the boys refer to the act, is to risk violence and loss of service. Whether or not the boys actually use violent means as often as they say they do when expectations are violated, there is no way of knowing with precision. Nevertheless, whenever boys reported they used violent means, they always reported some violation of the subcultural expectations. Likewise, they never reported a violation of the subcultural expectations which was not followed by the use of violent means, unless it was clearly held up as an exception. Bobby A. expresses the boys' point of view on the use of violent means in the following exchange: "How much did you usually get?" "Around five dollars; if they didn't give that much, I'd beat their head in." "Did they ever want you to do anything besides blow you?" "Yeh, sometimes . . . like they want me to blow them, but I'd tell them to go to hell and maybe beat them up."

Boys are very averse to being thought of in a queer role or engaging in acts of fellation. The act of fellation is defined as a "queer" act. Most boys were asked whether they would engage in such behavior. All but those who had the status of "punks" denied they had engaged in behavior associated with the queer role. Asking a boy whether he is a fellator meets with strong denial and often with open hostility. This could be interpreted as defensive behavior against latent homosexuality. Whether or not this is the case, strong denial could be expected because the question goes counter to the subcultural definitions of the peer role in the transaction.

A few boys on occasion apparently permit the fellator to perform other sexual acts. These boys, it is guessed, are quite infrequent in a delinquent peer population. Were their acts known to the members of the group, they would soon be defined as outside the delinquent peer society. Despite the limitation of the peer-queer sexual transaction to mouth-genital fellation, there are other sexual transactions which the peer group permits members to perform under special circumstances. They are, for example, permitted to perform the *male* roles in "crimes against nature," such as in pederasty ("cornholing" to the boys), bestiality (sometimes referred to as buggery) and carnal copulation with a man involving no orifice (referred to as "slick-legging" among the boys) provided that the partner is roughly of the same age and not a member of the group and provided also that the boys are confined to the single-sex society of incarcerated delinquent boys. Under no circumstances, however, is the female role in carnal copulation acceptable in any form. It is taboo. Boys who accept the female role in sexual transactions occupy the lowest status position among delinquents. They are "punks."

The third major norm operating on the relationship is that *both peers and queers, as participants, should remain affectively neutral during the transaction.* Boys within the peer society define the ideal form of the role with the fellator as one in which the boy is the entrepreneur and the queer is viewed as purchasing a service. The service is a business deal where a sexual transaction is purchased for an agreed upon amount of money. In the typical case, the boy is neither expected to enjoy or be repulsed by the sexual transaction; mouth-genital fellation is accepted as a service offered in exchange for a fee. It should be kept in mind that self-gratification is permitted in the sexual act. Only the motivation to sexual gratification in the transaction is tabooed. But self-gratification must occur without displaying either positive or negative affect toward the queer. In the prescribed form of the role relationship, the boy sells a service for profit and the queer is to accept it without show of emotion.

The case of Thurman L., one of three brothers who are usually in trouble with the law, illustrates some aspects of the expected pattern of affective neutrality. Thurman has had a continuing relationship with a queer, a type of relationship in which it would be anticipated that affective neutrality would be difficult to maintain. This relationship continued, in fact, with a twenty-one-year-old "gay" until the man was "sent to the pen." When queried about his relationship with this man and why he went with him, Thurman replied:

> Don't know . . . money and stuff like that I guess. (What do you mean? . . . stuff like that?) Oh, clothes. . . . (He ever bought you any clothes?) Sure, by this one gay. . . . (You mind being blowed?) No. (You like it?) Don't care one way or the other. I don't like it, and I don't not like it. (You like this one gay?) Nope, can't say that I liked anythin' about him. (How come you do it then?) Well, the money for one thing. . . . I need that. (You enjoy it some?) Can't say I do or don't.

More typical than Thurman's expression of affective neutrality is the boy who accepts it as "OK" or, "It's all right; I don't mind it." Most frequent of all is some variant of the statement: "It's OK, but I like the money best of all." The definition of affective neutrality fundamentally requires only that there be no positive emotional commitment to the queer *as a person*. The relationship must be essentially an impersonal one, even though the pure form of the business relationship may seldom be attained. Thus, it is possible for a boy to admit self-gratification without admitting any emotional commitment to the homosexual partner.

Although the peer group prescribes affective neutrality toward the queer in the peer-queer transaction, queers must be regarded as low prestige persons, held in low esteem, and the queer role is taboo. The queer is most commonly regarded as "crazy, I guess." Some boys take a more rationalistic view: "They're just like that, I guess" or, "They're just born that way." While there are circumstances under which one is permitted to like a particular fellator, as in the case of all prejudices attached to devalued status, the person who is liked must be the exception which states the rule. Though in many cases both the boy and the fellator are of very low class origins, and in many cases both are altogether repulsive in appearance, cleanliness, and dress by middle-class standards, these are not the standards of comparison used by the boys. The deviation of the queers from the boy's norms of masculine behavior places the fellator in the lowest possible status, even "beneath contempt." If the fellator violates the expected affective relationship in the transaction, he may be treated not only with violence but with contempt as well. The seller of the service ultimately reserves the right to set the conditions for his patrons.

Some boys find it difficult to be emotionally neutral toward the queer role and its occupants; they are either personally offended or affronted by the behavior of queers. JDC is an instance of a boy who is personally offended by their behavior; yet he is unable to use violence even when expectations governing the transaction are violated. He does not rely very much on the peer-queer relationship as a source of income. JDC expresses his view: "I don't really go for that like some guys; I just do it when I go along with the crowd. . . . You know. . . . That, and when I do it for money. . . . And I go along. . . . But . . . I hate queers. They embarrass me." "How?" "Well, like you'll be in the lobby at the theater, and they'll come up and pat your ass or your prick right in front of everybody. I just can't go for that—not me." Most of the boys wouldn't either, but they would have resorted to violent means in this situation.

Two principal types of boys maintain a continuing relationship with a known queer. A few boys develop such relationships to insure a steady income. While this is permitted within peer society for a short period of time, boys who undertake it for extended periods of time do so with some risk, since in the words of the boys, "queers can be got too easy." The boy who is affectively involved with a queer or his role is downgraded in status to a position, "Ain't no better'n a queer." There are also a few boys affectively committed to a continuing relationship with an adult male homosexual. Such boys usually form a strong dependency relationship with him and are kept much as the cabin boys of old. This type of boy is clearly outside the peer society of delinquents and is isolated from participation in gang activity. The sociometric pattern for such boys is one of choice into more than one gang, none of which is reciprocated.

Street-hustlers are also downgraded within the peer society, generally having reputations as "punk kids." The street-hustler pretty much "goes it alone." Only a few street-hustlers were interviewed for this study. None of them was a member of an organized delinquent group. The sociometric pattern for each, together with his history of delinquent activity, placed them in the classification of nonconforming isolates.

A fourth major norm operating on the peer-queer relationship serves as a primary factor in stabilizing the system. This norm holds that *violence must not be used so long as the relationship conforms to the shared set of expectations between queers and peers*. So long as the fellator conforms to the norms governing the transaction in the peer-queer society, he runs little risk of violence from the boys.

The main reason, perhaps, for this norm is that uncontrolled violence is potentially disruptive of any organized system. All organized social systems must control violence. If the fellator clients were repeatedly the objects of violence, the system as it has been described could not exist. Most boys who share the common expectations of the peer-queer relationship do not use violent means unless the expectations are violated. To use violence, of course, is to become affectively involved and therefore another prescription of the relationship is violated.

It is not known whether adult male fellators who are the

clients of delinquent entrepreneurs share the boys' definition of the norm regarding the use of violence. They may, therefore, violate expectations of the peer society through ignorance of the system rather than from any attempt to go beyond the set of shared expectations.

There are several ways the fellator can violate the expectations of boys. The first concerns money: refusal to pay or paying too little may bring violence from most boys. Fellators may also violate peer expectations by attempting to go beyond the mouth-genital sexual act. If such an attempt is made, he is usually made an object of aggression as in the following excerpt from Dolly's sex history:

> (You like it?) It's OK. I don't mind it. It feels OK. (They ever try anything else on you?) They usually just blow and that's all. (Any ever try anything else on you?) Oh sure, but we really fix 'em. I just hit 'em on the head or roll 'em . . . throw 'em out of the car. . . . Once a gay tried that and we rolled him and threw him out of the car. Then we took the car and stripped it (laughs with glee).

Another way the fellator violates a boy's expectations is to introduce considerable affect into the relationship. It appears that affect is least acceptable in two forms, both of which could be seen as "attacks on his masculinity." In one form, the queer violates the affective neutrality requirement by treating the adolescent boy as if he were a girl or in a girl's role during the sexual transaction, as for example, by speaking to him in affectionate terms such as "sweetie." There are many reasons why the feminine sex role is unacceptable to these lower-class boys, including the fact that such boys place considerable emphasis on being "tough" and masculine. Walter Miller, for example, observes that:

> . . . The almost compulsive lower class concern with "masculinity" derives from a type of compulsive reaction-formation. A concern over homosexuality runs like a persistent thread through lower class culture—manifested by the institutionalized practice of "baiting queers," often accompanied by violent physical attacks, an expressed contempt for "softness" or frills, and the use of the local term for "homosexual" as a general pejorative epithet (e.g., higher class individuals or upwardly mobile peers are frequently characterized as "fags" or "queers").[20]

Miller sees violence as part of a reaction-formation against the matriarchal lower-class household where the father often is absent. For this reason, he suggests, many lower-class boys find it difficult to identify with a male role, and the "collective" reaction-formation is a cultural emphasis on masculinity. Violence toward queers is seen as a consequence of this conflict. Data from our interviews suggest that among career-oriented delinquents, violation of the affective-neutrality requirement in the peer-queer relationship is at least as important in precipitating violence toward "queers." There are, of course, gangs which were not studied in this investigation which "queer-bait" for the express purpose of "rolling the queer."

The other form in which the fellator may violate the affective-neutrality requirement is to approach the boy and make suggestive advances to him when he is with his age-mates, either with girls or with his peer group when he is not located for "business." In either case, the sexual advances suggest that the boy is not engaged in a business relationship within the normative expectations of the system, but that he has sexual motivation as well. The delinquent boy is expected to control the relationship with his customers. He is the entrepreneur "looking" for easy money or at the very least he must appear as being merely receptive to business; this means that he is receptive only in certain situations and under certain circumstances. He is not in business when he is with girls and he is not a businessman when he is cast in a female role. To be cast in a female role before peers is highly unacceptable, as the following account suggests:

This gay comes up to me in the lobby of the Empress when we was standin' around and starts feelin' me up and callin' me Sweetie and like that . . . and, I just couldn't take none of that there . . . what was he makin' out like I was a queer or somethin' . . . so I jumps him right then and there and we like to of knocked his teeth out.

The sexual advance is even less acceptable when a girl is involved:

I was walkin' down the street with my steady girl when this gay drives by that I'd been with once before and he whistles at me and calls, "hi Sweetie." . . . And, was I mad . . . so I went down to where the boys was and we laid for him and beat on him 'til he like to a never come to . . . ain't gonna take nothin' like that off'n a queer.

In both of these instances, not only is the boys' masculinity under attack, but the affective-neutrality requirement of the business transaction is violated. The queer's behavior is particularly unacceptable, however, because it occurs in a peer setting where the crucial condition is the maintenance of the boy's status within the group. A lower-class boy cannot afford to be cast in less than a highly masculine role before lower-class girls or risk definition as a queer before peers. His role within his peer group is under threat even if he suffers *no* anxiety about masculinity. Not only the boy himself but his peers perceive such behavior as violating role expectations and join him in violent acts toward the fellator to protect the group's integrity and status.

If violence generally occurs only when one of the major peer norms has been violated, it would also seem to follow that *violence is a means of enforcing the peer entrepreneurial norms of the system*. Violence or the threat of violence is thus used to keep adult male fellators in line with the boys' expectations in his customer role. It represents social control, a punishment meted out to the fellator who violates the cultural expectation. Only so long as the fellator seeks gratification from lower-class boys in a casual pick-up or continuing relationship where he pays money for a "blow-job," is he reasonably free from acts of violence.

There is another, and perhaps more important, reason for the use of violence when the peer defined norms of the peer-queer relationship are violated. The formally prescribed roles for peers and queers are basically the roles involved in all institutionalized forms of prostitution, the prostitute and the client. But in most forms of prostitution, whether male or female, the hustlers perceive of themselves in hustler roles, and furthermore the male hustlers also develop a conception of themselves as homosexual whereas *the peer hustler in the peer-queer relationship develops no conception of himself either as prostitute or as homosexual*.

The fellator risks violence, therefore, if he threatens the boy's self-conception by suggesting that the boy may be homosexual and treats him as if he were.

Violence seems to function, then, in two basic ways for the peers. On the one hand, it integrates their norms and expectations by controlling and combating behavior which violates them. On the other hand, it protects the boy's self-identity as nonhomosexual and reinforces his self-conception as "masculine."

The other norms of the peer society governing the peer-queer transaction also function to prevent boys in the peer-queer society from defining themselves as homosexual. The prescriptions that the goal is money, that sexual gratification is not to be sought as an end in the relationship, that affective neutrality be maintained toward the fellator and that only mouth-genital fellation is permitted, all tend to insulate the boy from a homosexual self-definition. So long as he conforms to these expectations, *his "significant others" will not define him as homosexual;* and this is perhaps the most crucial factor in his own self-definition. The peers define one as homosexual not on the basis of homosexual *behavior* as such, but on the basis of participation in the homosexual *role,* the "queer" role. The reactions of the larger society, in defining the *behavior* as homosexual is unimportant in their own self-definition. What is important to them is the reactions of their peers to violation of peer group norms which define roles in the peer-queer transaction.

Terminating the Role Behavior

Under what circumstances does a boy give up earning money in the peer-queer transaction? Is it altogether an individual matter, or are there group bases for abandoning the practice? We have little information on these questions since interviews were conducted largely with boys who were still participants in the peer-queer culture. But a few interviews, either with boys who had terminated the relationship or spoke of those who had, provide information on how such role behavior is terminated.

Among lower-class adolescent boys, the new roles one assumes with increasing age are important in terminating participation in the peer-queer relationship. Thus older boys are more likely to have given up the transaction as a source of income. Several boys gave as their reason, "I got a job and don't need that kind of money now." An older boy, who recently married, said that he had quit when he was married. Another responded to the question, "When do you think you'll quit?" with, "When I quit school, I reckon. . . . I don't know a better way to make money afore then." A few boys simply said that they didn't care to make money that way any more, or that since they got a steady girl, they had quit.

The reasons older boys have for giving up the peer-queer transaction as a means of making money are perhaps different for the career-oriented than for the peer-oriented delinquent boy. As career-oriented delinquents get older, the more serious crimes direct their activity and the group is more actively involved in activities which confer status. The boy has a "rep" to maintain. The peer hustler role clearly contributes nothing to developing or maintaining a reputation, and the longer one gets money this way, the more one may risk it. The older career-oriented delinquent boy perhaps gives up peer hustling activity, then, just as he often gives up petty theft and malicious destruction of property. These are activities for younger boys.

As peer-oriented delinquents get older, they enter adult groups where a job becomes one of the acceptable ways of behaving. Many of them may also move out of the "tight little island" of the peer group which inducted them into the activity. If one gets enough money from a job, there is no socially acceptable reason for getting money in the peer-queer transaction. One risks loss of status if one solicits at this age, for this is the age to move from one steady girl to another and perhaps even settle on one and get married, as often one "has to."

Regardless of the reasons for moving out, it seems clear that most boys do move out of their roles as peer hustlers and do not go on to other hustling careers. The main reason perhaps that most boys do not move on in hustling careers is that they never conceived of themselves in a hustling role or as participants in a career where there was a status gradation among hustlers. Hustling, to the peer hustler, is simply another one of the activities which characterizes a rather versatile pattern of deviating acts. It is easier, too, to move out when one has never defined oneself as homosexual. It is in this sense, perhaps, that we have reason to conclude that these boys are not involved in the activity primarily for its homosexual basis. Peer hustlers are primarily oriented either toward delinquent, and later criminal, careers, or toward conventional conformity in lower-class society. They become neither hustlers nor queers.

Summary

This paper explores a special form of male prostitution in American society, a homosexual relationship between adult male fellators and delinquents. It is seen as a financial transaction between boys and fellators which is governed by delinquent peer norms. These norms integrate the two types of deviators into an institutionalized form of prostitution and protect the boys from self-definitions either as prostitutes or as homosexuals.

The conclusions offered in this paper must be regarded as tentative, because of limitations inherent in the data. Study of the fellator population might substantially change the conclusions. Cross-cultural studies also are necessary. Discussion of these findings with criminologists in Denmark and Sweden and exploratory investigations in several larger American cities, however, suggest that the description and explanation offered in this paper will hold for other American cities and for some other social systems.

1. Arthur V. Huffman, "Sex Deviation in a Prison Community," *The Journal of Social Therapy,* 6 (Third Quarter, 1960), 170-181; Joseph E. Fishman, *Sex in Prison,* New York: The Commonwealth Fund, 1930; Donald Clemmer, *The Prison Community,* Boston: The Christopher Publishing House, 1940, 260-273.

2. William Marlin Butts, "Boy Prostitutes of the Metropolis," *Journal of Clinical Psychopathology,* 8 (1946-1947), 673-681; H. Laurence Ross, "The 'Hustler' in Chicago," *The Journal of Student Research,* 1 (September, 1959), 13-19; Jens Jersild, *Boy Prostitution,* Copenhagen: C. E. Gad, 1956 (Translation of *Den Mandlige Prostitution* by Oscar Bojesen).

3. H. Laurence Ross, *op. cit.,* p. 15.

4. The distinction made here is not intended to suggest that other types of hustlers do not also define themselves in other deviant roles. Hustlers may occupy a variety of deviant roles which are classified as delinquent or criminal; they may be "hooked," blackmailers, thieves, etc.

5. I am indebted to Ned Polsky for bringing Rechy's stories to my attention.

6. John Rechy, "The Fabulous Wedding of Miss Destiny," *Big Table* 1, Number 3 (1959), p. 15.

7. John Rechy, "A Quarter Ahead," *Evergreen Review,* 5: 19 (July-August, 1961), 18.

8. For a definition of the types of conformers and deviators, see Albert J. Reiss, Jr., "Conforming and Deviating Behavior and the Problem of Guilt," *Psychiatric Research Reports*, 13 (December, 1960), 209-210, and Albert J. Reiss, Jr., and Albert Lewis Rhodes, "The Distribution of Juvenile Delinquency in the Social Class Structure," *American Sociological Review*, 26: 5 (October, 1961), 720-732.

9. See, for example, Maurice Leznoff and William A. Westley, "The Homosexual Community," *Social Problems*, 4 (April 1956), 257-263.

10. *Ibid.*, p. 258.

11. H. Laurence Ross, *op. cit.*, p. 15.

12. The cues which lead to the queer-peer transaction can be subtle ones. The literature on adult male homosexuality makes it clear that adult males who participate in homosexual behavior are not generally socially visible to the public by manner and dress. Cf., Jess Stearn, *The Sixth Man*, Garden City, N.Y.: Doubleday and Co., 1961, Chapters 1 and 3.

13. Leznoff and Westley, *op. cit.*, 260-261.

14. Ross notes that, failing in the con-man role, some hustlers resort to extortion and blackmail since they provide higher income. See Ross, *op. cit.*, p. 16. Sutherland discusses extortion and blackmail of homosexuals as part of the practice of professional thieves. The "muzzle" or "mouse" is part of the role of the professional thief. See Edwin Sutherland, *The Professional Thief*, Chicago: University of Chicago Press, 1937, 78-81. See also the chapter on "Blackmail" in Jess Stearn, *op. cit.*, Chapter 16.

15. Jess Stearn, *op. cit.*, p. 47.

16. Albert J. Reiss, Jr., "Sex Offenses: The Marginal Status of the Adolescent," *Law and Contemporary Problems*, 25 (Spring, 1960), 322-324 and 326-327.

17. Albert Cohen, Alfred Lindesmith, and Karl Schuessler, editors, *The Sutherland Papers*, Bloomington, Indiana: The University of Indiana Press, 1956, p. 31.

18. It is not altogether clear why mouth-genital fellation is the only sexual act which is tolerated in the peer-queer transaction. The act seems to conform to the more "masculine" aspects of the role than do most, but not all, possible alternatives. Ross has suggested to me that it also involves less bodily contact and therefore may be less threatening to the peers' self-definitions. One possible explanation therefore for the exclusiveness of the relationship to this act is that it is the most masculine alternative involving the least threat to peers' self-definition as nonhustler and nonhomosexual.

19. Talcott Parsons in *The Social System*, New York: The Free Press of Glencoe, 1951, Chapter III, discusses this kind of role as ". . . the segregation of specific instrumental performances, both from expressive orientations other than the specifically appropriate rewards and from other components of the instrumental complex." (p. 87.)

20. Walter Miller, "Lower-Class Culture as a Generating Milieu of Gang Delinquency," *The Journal of Social Issues*, 14: 3 (1958), 9.

THE BEHAVIOR OF THE
SYSTEMATIC CHECK FORGER

EDWIN M. LEMERT

The concept of behavior systems in crime was first approximated in this country in Hall's analysis of several types of larceny in terms of their historical, legal, and social contexts.[1] Later the concept was made explicit and formulated into a typology by Sutherland and by Sutherland and Cressey.[2] Although this has hitherto inspired only a few monographic studies, there seems to be a growing consensus that focusing attention on specific orders of crime or making behavior systems the unit of study holds considerable promise for criminological research.[3]

Because this paper proposes to assess the usefulness of Sutherland's formulation of the behavior system in analyzing or understanding the behavior of the systematic check forger, the typology outlined in his study of the professional thief will be employed. The five elements of the behavior system of the thief are as follows: (1) stealing is made a regular business; (2) every act is carefully planned, including the use of the "fix"; (3) technical skills are used, chiefly those of manipulating people; this differentiates the thief from other professional criminals; (4) the thief is migratory but uses a specific city as a headquarters; (5) the thief has criminal associations involving acquaintances, congeniality, sympathy, understandings, rules, codes of behavior, and a special language.[4]

Altogether seventy-two persons currently serving sentences for check forgery and writing checks with insufficient funds were studied. Three additional check offenders were contacted and interviewed outside of prison. The sample included eight women and sixty-seven men, all of whom served time in California correctional institutions.

Thirty of the seventy-five check criminals could be classified as systematic in the sense that they (1) thought of themselves as check men; (2) had worked out or regularly employed a special technique of passing checks; (3) had more or less organized their lives around the exigencies or imperatives of living by means of fraudulent checks. The remaining forty-five cases represented a wide variety of contexts in which bogus check passing was interspersed with periods of stable employment and family life, or was simply an aspect of alcoholism, gambling, or one of a series of criminal offenses having little or no consistency.

Findings

Projected against the typology of professional theft, the behavior of the persons falling into the systematic check forgery category qualified only in a very general way as professional crime. In other words, although it is possible to describe these forgeries as *systematic,* it is questionable whether more than a small portion of them can be subsumed as *professional* under the more general classification of professional theft. A point-by-point comparison will serve to bring out the numerous significant differences between systematic forgery and professional theft.

1. *Forgery as a "regular business."* It is questionable whether check men look upon their crimes as a "regular business" in the same way as do members of "other occupational groups" who "wish to make money in safety."[5] In virtually all cases the motivation proved to be exceedingly complex. This fact was self-consciously recognized and expressed in different ways but all informants revealed an essential perplexity or conflict about their criminal behavior. The following statement may be taken as illustrative:

> Nine out of ten check men are lone wolves. Those men who work in gangs are not real check men. They do it for money; we do it for something else. It gives us something we need. Maybe we're crazy. . . .

The conflicts expressed involved not merely the rightness or wrongness of behavior; they also disclosed a confusion and uncertainty as to the possibility of living successfully or safely by issuing false checks. All of the cases, even the few who had a history of professional thieving, admitted that arrest and imprisonment are inevitable. None knew of exceptions to this, although one case speculated that "It might be done by an otherwise respected businessman who made one big spread and then quit and retired."

The case records of the systematic check forgers gave clear testimony of this. Generally they had but short-lived periods of freedom, ranging from a few months to a year or two at the most, followed by imprisonment. Many of the cases since beginning their forgery careers had spent less total time outside prisons than within, a fact corroborated by the various law-enforcement officers queried on the point.

Many of the check men depicted their periods of check writing as continuous sprees during which they lived "fast" and luxuriously. Many spoke of experiencing considerable tension during these periods, and two cases developed stomach ulcers which caused them to "lay off at resorts." A number gambled and drank heavily, assertedly to escape their internal stress and sense of inevitable arrest. A number spoke of gradual build-up of strain and a critical point just before their arrest at which they became demoralized and after which they "just didn't care any more" or "got tired of running." The arrests of several men having a very long experience with checks resulted from blunders in technique of which they were aware at the time they made them. Some of the men gave themselves up to detectives or F.B.I. agents at this point.

In general the picture of the cool, calculating professional with prosaic, matter-of-fact attitudes toward his crimes as a trade or occupation supported by rationalizations of a subculture was not valid for the cases in question.

2. *Planning as an aspect of forgery.* In regard to the second element of professional theft—planning—the behavior of check forgers is again divergent. Actually the present techniques of check passing either preclude precise planning or make it un-

necessary. Although systematic check passers undeniably pay careful attention to such things as banking hours, the places at which checks are presented, and the kinds of "fronts" they employ, these considerations serve only as generalized guides for their crimes. Most informants held that situations have to be *exploited as they arise,* with variation and flexibility being the key to success. What stands out in the behavior of systematic check forgers is the rapid tempo—almost impulsiveness—with which they work.

The cases seemed to agree that check forgers seldom attempt to use the "fix" in order to escape the consequences of their crimes. The reason for this is that although one or a small number of checks might be made good, the systematic forger has too many bad checks outstanding and too many victims to mollify by offering restitution. Although the forger may be prosecuted on the basis of only one or two checks, ordinarily the prosecuting attorney will have a choice of a large number of complaints upon which to act. About the best the check forger can hope for through fixing activities is a short sentence or a sentence to jail rather than to prison.

3. *Technical skills.* Although the systematic check man relies upon technical skills—those of manipulating others—these are usually not of a high order, nor do they require a long learning period to master. From the standpoint of the appearance of the check or the behavior involved at the time of its passing, there need, of course, be no great difference between passing a bad check and passing a good check. This is particularly true of personal checks, which are at least as favored as payroll checks by check men.

When check men impersonate others or when they assume fictitious roles, acting ability is required. To the extent that elaborate impersonations are relied upon by the forger, his check passing takes on qualities of a confidence game. Most of the check men showed strong preference, however, for simple, fast-moving techniques. A number expressed definite dislike for staged arrangements, such as that of the "out of town real estate buyer" or for setting up a fictitious business in a community, then waiting several weeks or a month before making a "spread" of checks. As they put it, they "dislike the slow build-up involved."

4. *Mobility.* Like the thief, the systematic forger is migratory. Only one check man interviewed spoke of identifying himself with one community, and even he was reluctant to call it a head-quarters. Generally check men are migratory within regions.

5. *Associations.* The sharpest and most categorical difference between professional theft and systematic forgery lies in the realm of associations. In contrast to pickpockets, shoplifters, and con men, whose criminal techniques are implicitly cooperative, most check men with highly developed systems work alone, carefully avoiding contacts and interaction with other criminals. Moreover, their preference for solitude and their secretiveness gives every appearance of a highly generalized reaction; they avoid not only cooperative crime but also any other kinds of association with criminals. They are equally selective and cautious in their contacts and associations with the noncriminal population, preferring not to become involved in any enduring personal relationships.

A descriptive breakdown of the thirty check forgers classified as systematic bears out this point. Only four of the thirty had worked in check passing gangs. Two of these had acted as "fences" who organized the operations. Both were close to seventy years old and had long prison records, one having been a receiver of stolen property, the other having worked as a forger. Both had turned to using gangs of passers because they were too well known to detectives either to pass checks themselves or to permit their handwriting to appear on the checks. The other two forgers who had worked in gangs were female drug addicts who had teamed up with other female addicts.[6]

Three other systematic check forgers did not work directly with other criminals but had criminal associations of a *contractual* nature. One old-time forger familiar with the now little-used methods for forging signatures and raising checks usually sold checks to passers but never had uttered (passed) any of his own forgeries. Two men were passers who purchased either payroll checks from a "hot printer" or stolen checks from burglars. Apart from the minimal contacts necessary to sell or obtain a supply of checks, all three men were lone operators and very seclusive in their behavior.

Six of the thirty systematic forgers worked exclusively with one other person, usually a girl or "broad."[7] The check men seemed to agree that working with a girl was equivalent to working alone. These pairs ordinarily consisted of the check man and some girl not ordinarily of criminal background with whom he had struck up a living arrangement and for whom he felt genuine affection. The girl was used either to make out the checks or to pass them. In some cases she was simply used as a front to distract attention. Some men picked up girls in bars or hotels and employed them as fronts without their knowledge.

The remaining seventeen of the thirty systematic check forgers operated on a solitary basis. The majority of these argued that contact with others is unnecessary to obtain and pass a supply of checks. Most of them uttered personal checks. However, even where they made use of payroll or corporation checks they contrived to manufacture or obtain them without resorting to interaction with criminal associates or intermediaries. For example, one Nisei check man arranged with a printer to make up checks for a fraternal organization of which he represented himself as secretary-treasurer. Another man frequented business offices at noon time, and when the clerk left the office, helped himself to a supply of company checks, in one instance stealing a check-writing machine for his purposes.

It was difficult to find evidence of anything more than rudimentary congeniality, sympathy, understandings, and shared rules of behavior among the check forgers, including those who had worked in gangs. Rather the opposite seemed true, suspicion and distrust marking their relationships with one another. One organizer of a gang, for example, kept careful account of all the checks he issued to his passers and made them return torn off corners of checks in case they were in danger of arrest and had to get rid of them. Only two of the thirty forgers indicated that they had at times engaged in recreational activities with other criminals. Both of these men were lone wolves in their work. One other lone wolf stated that he had on occasion had dinner with another check man he happened to know well and that he had once or twice entered into a rivalry with him to see who could pass a check in the most difficult place.

The two men who had organized gangs of check passers worked with a set of rules, but they were largely improvised and laid down by the fence rather than voluntarily recognized and obeyed by the passers. The other check men with varying degrees of explicitness recognized rules for passing checks—rules learned almost entirely on an individual trial-and-error basis. The informants insisted that "you learn as you go" and that one of the rules was "never use another man's stunt."

Such special morality as was recognized proved to be largely functional in derivation. Thus attitudes toward drinking and toward picking up women for sexual purposes were pretty much the result of individual perceptions of what was likely to facilitate or hamper the passing of checks or lead to arrest. Many of the men stated that since they were dealing primarily with business, professional, and clerical persons, their appearance and behavior had to be acceptable to these people. "Middle class" is probably the best term to describe their morality in most areas.

Careful inquiries were made to discover the extent to which the check men were familiar with and spoke an argot. Findings proved meager. Many of the men had a superficial acquaintance with general prison slang, but only four men could measurably identify and reproduce the argot of check forgery or that of thieves. Three more could be presumed to have some familiarity with it. Only one of these spoke the argot in the prison setting. Another said that he never used the argot either in prison or on the outside, except years previously when once in a great while he had "let down at a thieves' party." There were only two men who spoke of themselves as being "on the scratch."[8]

Interpretation

How can these findings be reconciled with the specific statement of Sutherland's informant that "laying paper" is a form of professional theft most often worked in mobs?[9] The answer to this apparent contradiction requires that a distinction be made between forgery of *the nineteenth and early twentieth centuries and that of the present day.* In the past forgery was a much more complex procedure in which a variety of false instruments such as bank notes, drafts, bills of exchange, letters of credit, registered bonds, and post office money orders as well as checks were manufactured or altered and foisted off. A knowledge of chemicals, papers, inks, engraving, etching, lithography, and penmanship as well as detailed knowledge of bank operations were prime requisites for success. The amounts of money sought were comparatively large, and often they had to be obtained through complex monetary transactions.[10] The technological characteristics of this kind of forgery made planning, timing, specialization, differentiation of roles, morale, and organization imperative. Capital was necessary for living expenses during the period when preparations for the forgeries were being made.[11] Intermediates between the skilled forger and the passers were necessary so that the latter could swear that the handwriting on the false negotiable instruments was not theirs and so that the forger himself was not exposed to arrest. A "shadow" was often used for protection against the passer's temptation to abscond with the money and in order to alert the others of trouble at the bank.[12] "Fall" money was accumulated and supplied to assist the passer when arrested. Inasmuch as forgery gangs worked together for a considerable length of time, understandings, congeniality, and rules of behavior, especially with regard to the division of money, could and did develop. In short, professional forgery was based upon the technology of the period.

Although precise dating is difficult, the heyday of professional forgery in this country probably began after the Civil War and lasted through the 1920's.[13] It seems to have corresponded with the early phases of industrialization and commercial development before business and law-enforcement agencies developed methods and organization for preventing forgery and apprehending the offenders. Gradually technological developments in inks, papers, protectographs, and check-writing machines made the forging of signatures and the manufacture of false negotiable instruments more difficult. According to one source, for example, raised drafts have been virtually nonexistent since 1905.[14] Similarly, at the present time raising of checks is quite rare. The establishment of a protective committee by the American Bankers Association in 1894, related merchants' protective agencies, and improvements in police methods have made the risks of organized professional forgery exceedingly great.[15]

Check gangs have always been vulnerable to arrest but this vulnerability has been multiplied many times by the large amounts of evidence left behind them in the form of countless payroll checks. Vulnerability is also heightened by the swiftness of communication today. If one person of a check-passing gang is arrested and identifies his associates, it becomes a relatively simple matter for police to secure their arrest. A sexually exploited and angered female companion may easily do the same to the check man. This goes far to explain the extreme seclusiveness of systematic check forgers and their almost abnormal fear of stool pigeons or of being "fingered." The type of persons who can be engaged as passers—unattached women, bar waitresses, drug addicts, alcoholics, petty thieves, and transient unemployed persons —also magnifies the probabilities that mistakes will be made and precludes the growth of a morale which might prevent informing to the police. These conditions also explain the fact that when the forger does work with someone it is likely to be one other person upon whom he feels he can rely with implicit confidence. Hence the man-woman teams in which the woman is in love with the man, or the case of the two homosexual girls, or of the two brothers mentioned previously.

Further evidence that organized forgery is a hazardous type of crime, difficult to professionalize under modern conditions, is indicated by the fact that the organizer or fence is apt to be an older criminal with a long record, whose handwriting methods are so well known that he has no choice other than to work through passers. Even then he does it with recognition that arrest is inevitable.

A factor of equal importance in explaining the decline of professional organized forgery has been the increasingly widespread use of business and payroll checks as well as personal checks. Whereas in the past the use of checks was confined to certain kinds of business transactions, mostly involving banks, today it is ubiquitous. Attitudes of business people and their clerical employees have undergone great change, and only the most perfunctory identification is necessary to cash many kinds of checks. Check men recognize this in frequent unsolicited comments that passing checks is "easy." Some argue that the form of the check is now relatively unimportant to passing it, that "you can pass a candy bar wrapper now days with the right front and story."[16] It is for this reason that the systematic check man does not have to resort to criminal associates or employ the more complex professional procedures used in decades past.

These facts may also account for the presence among lone-wolf check forgers of occasional persons with the identification, orientation, skills, codes, and argot of the thief. Case histories as well as the observations of informants show that older professional criminals in recent decades have turned to check passing because they face long sentences for additional crimes or sentencing under habitual criminal legislation. They regard checks as an "easy racket" because in many states conviction makes them subject to jail sentences rather than imprisonment. Check passing may be a last resort for the older criminal.

The presence of the occasional older professional thief in the ranks of check forgers may actually token a general decline and slow disappearance of professional thieving. One professional thief turned check passer had this to say:

I'm a thief—a burglar—but I turned to checks because it's getting to hard to operate. Police are a lot smarter now, and they have better methods. People are different nowadays too; they report things more. It's hard to trust anyone now. Once you could trust cab drivers; now you can't. We live in a different world today.[17]

The Check Forger as an Isolate

The preference of many systematic check forgers for solitary lives and their avoidance of primary-group associations among criminals may also be explicable in terms of their educational characteristics and class origins. The history of forgery reveals that in medieval times it was considered to be the special crime of the clerical class, as indeed it had to be inasmuch as the members of this class monopolized writing skills.[18] It also seems to be true from the later history of the crime that it has held a special attraction for more highly educated persons, for those of higher socioeconomic status and those of "refined" or artistic tastes.[19] The basic method of organized forgery is stated to have been invented and perfected in England, not by criminals but by a practicing barrister of established reputation in 1840.[20] An early gang of forgers organized by a practicing physician is also described by Felstead.[21] A number of studies directed to the differentiating characteristics of check criminals point to an "above average" intelligence and formal education. This refers to the general population as well as to the criminal populations with which they have been compared.[22]

All of this is not to say that less-educated persons do not frequently pass bad checks but rather that the persons who persist in the behavior and develop behavior systems of forgery seem much more likely than other criminals to be drawn from a segment of the population distinguished by a higher socioeconomic status. Generally this was true of the systematic forgers in this study. Eight of the thirty had completed two or more years of college. Fourteen of the thirty had fathers who were or had been in the professions and business, including a juvenile court judge, a minister, a postmaster of a large city, and three very wealthy ranch owners. One woman came from a nationally famous family of farm implement manufacturers. Four others had siblings well established in business and the professions, one of whom was an attorney general in another state. Two of the men had been successful businessmen themselves before becoming check men.

The most important implication of these data is that systematic check forgers do not seem to have had criminal antecedents or early criminal associations.[23] For this reason, as well as for technical reasons, they are not likely to seek out or to be comfortable in informal associations with other criminals who have been products of early and lengthy socialization and learning in a criminal subculture. It also follows that their morality and values remain essentially "middle" or "upper" class and that they seldom integrate these with the morality of the professional criminal. This is reflected in self-attitudes in which many refer to themselves as "black sheep" or as a kind of Dr. Jekyl-Mr. Hyde person. Further support for this interpretation comes from their status in prison where, according to observations of themselves and others, they are marginal so far as participation in the primary groups of the prison is concerned.

Conclusion

The cases and data presented suggest that present-day check forgery exists in systematic form but does not appear to be a professional behavior system acquired or maintained through associations with other criminals. The technical demands of contemporary check forgery preclude efficient operation on an organized, cooperative basis. In addition to these factors the class characteristics and backgrounds of systematic forgers incline them to avoid intimate association with other criminals.

1. Jerome Hall, *Theft, Law and Society*, 2nd Edition, Indianapolis: Bobbs-Merril, 1952.

2. See Edwin H. Sutherland, "The Professional Thief," *Journal of Criminal Law and Criminology*, 28 (July-August, 1937), 161-163; Edwin H. Sutherland and Donald R. Cressey, *Principles of Criminology*, 5th Edition, New York: Lippincott, 1955; Alfred R. Lindesmith and H. Warren Dunham, "Some Principles of Criminal Typology," *Social Forces*, 19 (March, 1941), 307-314; L. Puibaraud, *Les Malfaiteurs de Profession*, Paris: E. Flammarion, 1893; H. W. Gruhle and L. Wetzel, Editors, "Verbrechentype," cited in W. A. Bonger, *Criminality and Economic Conditions*, Boston: Little, Brown, 1916, p. 581; and W. A. Bonger, *ibid.*, 579-589.

3. W. C. Reckless, *The Crime Problem*, 2nd Edition, New York: Appleton-Century, 1955, p. 134.

4. See Edwin H. Sutherland, *The Professional Thief*, Chicago: University of Chicago Press, 1937; Sutherland, "The Professional Thief," *op. cit.*; Marshall B. Clinard, *Sociology of Deviant Behavior*, New York: Rinehart, 1957, 256-262; Reckless, *op. cit., passim*; Ruth Shonle Cavan, *Criminology*, New York: Crowell, 1948, Chapter V; Mabel A. Elliot, *Crime in Modern Society*, New York: Harper & Row, 1942, Chapter IV; D. W. Maurer, *Whiz Mob*, Gainesville, Florida: American Dialect Society, 1955, No. 24; and H. Von Hentig, "The Pickpocket: Psychology, Tactics and Technique," *Journal of Criminal Law and Criminology*, 34 (May-June, 1943), 11-16.

5. Sutherland and Cressey, *op. cit.*, p. 240.

6. One may question whether they were systematic check forgers in a true sense; other informants state that "such people are not real check men; they are just supporting a habit." Their self-definitions and the organization of their lives centers around drug addiction rather than forgery.

7. One of the "pair" workers consisted of two homosexual females. The other non-man-woman pair was made up of two brothers, both of whom had

substantial prison records. They worked up and down the West Coast, alternating in making out checks and playing the part of passer.

8. The attitude of the lone-wolf check man toward the argot is illustrated by the following quotation: "It's just the older men in here [San Quentin] who use argot, or some of the young guys who think they are tough. I know the argot but when I hear it I tell them to talk English. Most people on the outside know it anyway. Why call a gun a heater? What is gained by it. . . .?" These findings coincide with Maurer's. He states that the argot of check forgery is relatively unspecialized and that forgers seldom have an opportunity to use it. D. W. Maurer, "The Argot of Check Forgery," *American Speech*, 16 (December, 1941), 243-250.

9. Sutherland, *The Professional Thief, op. cit.*, p. 77. Maurer, *op. cit.*, refers to check forgery as a branch of the "grift," and also speaks of professional forgers without, however, defining the term. Yet he recognizes that check forgers are usually lone wolves.

10. G. Dilnot, *The Bank of England Forgery*, New York: Scribner's, 1929.

11. See W. A. Pinkerton, "Forgery," paper read before the Annual Convention of the International Association of Chiefs of Police, Washington D.C., 1905; Pinkerton, *Thirty Years a Detective*, New York: G. W. Carleton, 1884, 338-441; and Dilnot, *op. cit.*

12. Pinkerton, in "Forgery," *op. cit.*, enumerates the following roles of the forgery gang: (1) backer, (2) forger, (3) middleman, (4) presenter, (5) shadow. Maurer, in "The Argot of Check Forgery," *op. cit.*, without specifying the historical period to which his description applies, distinguishes the following as check forger roles: (1) connection, (2) fence, (3) passer.

13. J. W. Speare, *Protecting the Nation's Money*, Rochester: Todd Protectograph Co., 1926.

14. *Ibid.*

15. Pinkerton, "Forgery," *op. cit.*, and Maurer, "The Argot of Check Forgery," *op. cit.*

16. Detectives in Santa Monica, California, showed the writer a collection of checks successfully passed with such signatures as: "I. M. A. Fool," "U. R. Stuck," and others not printable. For a discussion of the crudeness of bogus checks accepted by business people, see J. L. Sternitsky, *Forgery and Fictitious Checks*, Springfield, Ill.: Charles C Thomas, 1955.

17. There is evidence that there has been a sharp absolute decline in the number of pickpockets in recent years and that most of the so-called "class cannons" (highly skilled) operating now are fifty years of age or over. See Maurer, *Whiz Mob, op. cit.*

18. T. F. Tout, *Medieval Forgers and Forgeries*, Bulletin of the John Rylands Library, 1919, Nos. 5, 3, 4, 5-31.

19. This is the thesis of Rhodes. Two of the four participants in the famous Bank of England forgery in 1873 were college educated, one being a Harvard graduate. H. T. F. Rhodes, *The Craft of Forgery*, London: J. Murray, 1934. See Dilnot, *The Bank of England Forgery, op. cit.* Forgers coming from "good" families are described by H. L. Adam, in *Oriental Crime*, London: T. Werner Laurie, 1908. Fourteen of the nineteen persons tried for forgery at Newgate Prison in England during the later eighteenth and early nineteenth centuries were what can be termed "middle" and "upper" class, including three army or navy officers (one who commanded the royal yacht of Queen Caroline, consort of George IV), one banker, one physician (Cambridge graduate), one prosecuting attorney, two engravers (one by appointment to George III), three "gentlemen" of good connections, and three bank clerks. Two of the three men who had "poor parents" had married women of "good means." T. Tegg, in *The Chronicles of Crime*, London: Camden Pelham, 1841, Vols. I and II, and Bonger, *op. cit.*, 429, 430, 437, give data from France and Italy which support

this idea. A number of writers have commented on the fact that forgery has been quite common among the educated classes of India, particularly the "wily Brahmins." See, for example, Adam, *op. cit.;* S. M. Edwards, *Crime in India,* London: Oxford University Press, 1924, 3-6; and Hardless and Hardless, *Forgery in India,* Chunar: Sanctuary, 1920.

20. See Rhodes, *op. cit.,* and G. Dilnot, *The Trial of Jim the Penman,* London: Geoffrey Bles, 1930.

21. T. S. Felstead, in *Famous Criminals and Their Trials,* New York: Doran, 1926.

22. See Irwin Berg, "A Comparative Study of Forgery," *Journal of Applied Psychology,* 28 (June, 1944), 232-238; Vernon B. Fox, "Intelligence, Race and Age as Selective Factors in Crime," *Journal of Criminal Law and Criminology,* 37 (July-August, 1946), 141-152; E. A. Hooton, *The American Criminal,* Cambridge: Harvard University Press, 1939, Vol. I, p. 87; and L. Lawes, *Life and Death in Sing Sing,* New York: Sun Dial Press, 1938, p. 40.

23. Edwin Lemert, "An Isolation and Closure Theory of Naive Check Forgery," *Journal of Criminal Law and Criminology,* 44 (September-October, 1953), 296-307; and Lemert, "Generality and Specificity in Criminal Behavior: Check Forgery Considered," paper read before the American Sociological Society, September, 1956.

THIEVES, CONVICTS,
AND THE INMATE CULTURE

JOHN IRWIN and DONALD R. CRESSEY

In the rapidly growing literature on the social organization of correctional institutions, it has become common to discuss "prison culture" and "inmate culture" in terms suggesting that the behavior systems of various types of inmates stem from the conditions of imprisonment themselves. Use of a form of structural-functional analysis in research and observation of institutions has led to emphasis of the notion that internal conditions stimulate inmate behavior of various kinds, and there has been a glossing over of the older notion that inmates may bring a culture with them into the prison. Our aim is to suggest that much of the inmate behavior classified as part of the prison culture is not peculiar to the prison at all. On the contrary, it is the fine distinction between "prison culture" and "criminal subculture" which seems to make understandable the fine distinction between behavior patterns of various categories of inmates.

A number of recent publications have defended the notion that behavior patterns among inmates develop with a minimum of influence from the outside world. For example, in his general discussion of total institutions, Goffman acknowledges that inmates bring a culture with them to the institution, but he argues that upon entrance to the institution they are stripped of this support by processes of mortification and dispossession aimed

We are indebted to the following persons for suggested modifications of the original draft: Donald L. Garrity, Daniel Glaser, Erving Goffman, and Stanton Wheeler.

at managing the daily activities of a large number of persons in
a small space with a small expenditure of resources.[1] Similarly,
Sykes and Messinger note that a central value system seems to
pervade prison populations, and they maintain that "conformity
to, or deviation from, the inmate code is the major basis for clas-
sifying and describing the social relations of prisoners."[2] The
emphasis in this code is on directives such as "don't interfere
with inmate interests," "don't lose your head," "don't exploit inmates," "don't weaken," and "don't be a sucker." The authors'
argument, like the argument in other of Sykes' publications is that
the origin of these values is situational; the value system arises
out of the conditions of imprisonment.[3] Cloward stresses both the
acute sense of status degradation which prisoners experience and
the resulting patterns of prison life, which he calls "structural
accommodation."[4] Like others, he makes the important point that
the principal types of inmates—especially the "politicians" and
the "shots"—help the officials by exerting controls over the general
prison body in return for special privileges. Similarly, he recognizes the "right guy" role as one built around the value system
described by Sykes and Messinger, and points out that it is tolerated by prison officials because it helps maintain the status quo.
Cloward hints at the existence in prison of a *criminal* subculture
when he says that "the upper echelons of the inmate world come
to be occupied by those whose past behavior best symbolizes that
which society rejects and who have most fully repudiated institutional norms." Nevertheless, his principal point is that this superior status, like other patterns of behavior among inmates, arises
from the *internal* character of the prison situation. McCleery also
stresses the unitary character of the culture of prisoners, and he
identifies the internal source of this culture in statements such as:
"The denial of validity to outside contacts protected the inmate
culture from criticism and assured the stability of the social system," "A man's status in the inmate community depended on his
role there and his conformity to its norms," "Inmate culture
stressed the goals of adjustment within the walls and the rejection
of outside contacts," and "Status has been geared to adjustment
in the prison."[5]

The idea that the prison produces its own varieties of behavior represents a break with the more traditional notion that men bring patterns of behavior with them when they enter prison, and use them in prison. Despite their emphasis on "prisonization" of newcomers, even Clemmer and Riemer noted that degree of conformity to prison expectations depends in part on prior, outside conditions.[6] Schrag has for some years been studying the social backgrounds and careers of various types of inmates.[7] Unlike any of the authors cited above, he has collected data on both the pre-prison experiences and the prison experiences of prisoners. He relates the actions of inmates to the broader community as well as to the forces that are more indigenous to prisons themselves.[8] Of most relevance here is his finding that anti-social inmates ("right guys") "are reared in an environment consistently oriented toward illegitimate social norms,"[9] and frequently earn a living via contacts with organized crime but do not often rise to positions of power in the field. In contrast, asocial inmates ("outlaws") are frequently reared in institutions: "The careers of asocial offenders are marked by high egocentrism and inability to profit from past mistakes or to plan for the future."[10]

However, despite these research findings, even Schrag has commented as follows: "Juxtaposed with the official organization of the prison is an unofficial social system originating within the institution and regulating inmate conduct with respect to focal issues, such as length of sentence, relations among prisoners, contacts with staff members and other civilians, food, sex, and health, among others."[11] Garrity interprets Schrag's theory in the following terms, which seem to ignore the findings on the pre-prison careers of the various inmate types:

Schrag has further suggested that all inmates face a number of common problems of adjustment as a consequence of imprisonment and that social organization develops as a consequence. When two or more persons perceive that they share a common motivation or problem of action, a basis for meaningful interaction has been established, and from this interaction can emerge the social positions, roles, and norms which comprise social organization. Schrag suggests that the common problems of adjustment which become the principal axes of prison life are related to time, food, sex, leisure, and health.[12]

Garrity himself uses the "indigenous origin" notion when he says that "the axial values regarding shared problems or deprivations provide the basis for articulation of the broad normative system or 'prison code' which defines positions and roles in a general way but allows enough latitude so that positions and roles take on the character of social worlds themselves."[13] However, he also points out that some prisoners' reference groups are outside the prison, and he characterizes the "right guy" as an "anti-social offender, stable, and oriented to crime, criminals, and inmates."[14] "The 'right guy' is the dominant figure in the prison, and his reference groups are elite prisoners, sophisticated, career-type criminals, and other 'right guys.' "[15] Cressey and Krassowski, similarly, seem confused about any distinction between a criminal subculture and a prison subculture. They mention that many inmates of Soviet labor camps "know prisons and maintain criminalistic values," and that the inmates are bound together by a "criminalistic ideology,"[16] but they fail to deal theoretically with the contradiction between these statements and their observation that the inmate leaders in the labor camps are "toughs" or "gorillas" rather than "right guys" or "politicians." Conceivably, leadership is vested in "toughs" to a greater extent than is the case in American prisons because the orientation is more that of a *prison* subculture than of a criminal subculture in which men are bound together with a "criminalistic ideology."

It is our contention that the "functional" or "indigenous origin" notion has been overemphasized and that observers have overlooked the dramatic effect that external behavior patterns have on the conduct of inmates in any given prison. Moreover, the contradictory statements made in this connection by some authors, including Cressey,[17] seem to stem from acknowledging but then ignoring the deviant subcultures which exist outside any given prison and outside prisons generally. More specifically, it seems rather obvious that the "prison code"—don't inform on or exploit another inmate, don't lose your head, be weak, or be a sucker, etc.—is also part of a *criminal* code, existing outside prisons. Further, many inmates come to any given prison with a record of many terms in correctional institutions. These men, some of whom have institutional records dating back to early childhood, bring with them a ready-made set of patterns which they apply to the new situation, just as is the case with participants in the criminal subculture. In view of these variations, a clear understanding of inmate conduct cannot be obtained simply by viewing "prison culture" or "inmate culture" as an isolated system springing solely from the conditions of imprisonment. Becker and Geer have made our point in more general terms: "The members of a group may derive their understandings from cultures other than that of the group they are at the moment participating in. To the degree that group participants share latent social identities (related to their membership in the same 'outside' social groups) they will share these understandings, so that there will be a culture which can be called *latent,* i.e., the culture has its origin and social support in a group other than the one in which the members are now participating."[18]

We have no doubt that the total set of relationships called "inmate society" is a response to problems of imprisonment. What we question is the emphasis given to the notion that solutions to these problems are found within the prison, and the lack of emphasis on "latent culture"—on external experiences as determinants of the solutions. We have found it both necessary and helpful to divide inmates into three rough categories: those oriented to a criminal subculture, those oriented to a prison subculture, and those oriented to "conventional" or "legitimate" subcultures.

The Two Deviant Subcultures

When we speak of a criminal subculture we do not mean to imply that there is some national or international organization with its own judges, enforcement agencies, etc. Neither do we imply that every person convicted of a crime is a member of the subculture. Nevertheless, descriptions of the values of professional thieves, "career criminals," "sophisticated criminals," and other good crooks indicate that there is a set of values which extends to criminals across the nation with a good deal of consistency.[19] To avoid possible confusion arising from the fact that not all criminals share these values, we have arbitrarily named the system a "thief" subculture. The core values of this subculture correspond closely to the values which prison observers have ascribed to the "right guy" role. These include the important notion that criminals should not betray each other to the police, should be reliable, wily but trustworthy, cool-headed, etc. High status in this subculture is awarded to men who appear to follow these prescriptions without variance. In the thief subculture a man who is known as "right" or "solid" is one who can be trusted and relied upon. High status is also awarded to those who possess skill as thieves, but to be just a successful thief is not enough; there must be solidness as well. A solid guy is respected even if he is unskilled, and no matter how skilled in crime a stool pigeon may be, his status is low.

Despite the fact that adherence to the norms of the thief subculture is an ideal, and the fact that the behavior of the great majority of men arrested or convicted varies sharply from any "criminal code" which might be identified, a proportion of the persons arrested for "real crime" such as burglary, robbery, and larceny have been in close contact with the values of the subculture. Many criminals, while not following the precepts of the subculture religiously, give lip service to its values and evaluate their own behavior and the behavior of their associates in terms relating to adherence to "rightness" and being "solid." It is probable, further, that use of this kind of value is not even peculiarly "criminal," for policemen, prison guards, college professors, students, and almost any other category of persons who evaluate behavior in terms of in-group loyalties. Whyte noted the mutual obligations binding corner boys together and concluded that status depends upon the extent to which a boy lives up to his obligations, a form of "solidness."[20] More recently, Miller identified "toughness," "smartness," and "autonomy" among the "focal concerns" of lower class adolescent delinquent boys; these also characterize prisoners who are oriented to the thief subculture.[21] Wheeler found that half of the custody staff and 60 per cent of the treatment staff in one prison approved the conduct of a hypothetical inmate who refused to name an inmate with whom he had been engaged in a knife fight.[22] A recent book has given the name "moral courage" to the behavior of persons who, like thieves, have shown extreme loyalty to their in-groups in the face of real or threatened adversity, including imprisonment.[23]

Imprisonment is one of the recurring problems with which thieves must cope. It is almost certain that a thief will be arrested from time to time, and the subculture provides members with patterns to be used in order to help solve this problem. Norms which apply to the prison situation, and information on how to undergo the prison experience—how to do time "standing on your head"—with the least suffering and in a minimum amount of time are provided. Of course, the subculture itself is both nurtured and diffused in the different jails and prisons of the country.

There also exists in prisons a subculture which is by definition a set of patterns that flourishes in the environment of incarceration. It can be found wherever men are confined, whether it be in city jails, state and federal prisons, army stockades, prisoner of war camps, concentration camps, or even mental hospitals. Such organizations are characterized by deprivations and limitations on freedom, and in them available wealth must be competed for by men supposedly on an equal footing. It is in connection with the *maintenance* (but not necessarily with the *origin*) of this subculture that it is appropriate to stress the notion that a minimum of outside status criteria are carried into the situation. Ideally, all status is to be achieved by the means made available in the prison, through the displayed ability to manipulate the environment, win special privileges in a certain manner, and assert influence over others. To avoid confusion with writings on "prison culture" and "inmate culture," we have arbitrarily named this system of values and behavior patterns a "convict subculture." The central value of the subculture is utilitarianism, and the most manipulative and most utilitarian individuals win the available wealth and such positions of influence as might exist.

It is not correct to conclude, however, that even these behavior patterns are a consequence of the environment of any particular prison. In the first place, such utilitarian and manipulative behavior probably is characteristic of the "hard core" lower class in the United States, and most prisoners come from this class. After discussing the importance of toughness, smartness, excitement, and fate in this group, Miller makes the following significant observation:

> In lower class culture a close conceptual connection is made between "authority" and "nurturance." To be restrictively or firmly controlled is to be cared for. Thus the overtly negative evaluation of superordinate authority frequently extends as well to nurturance, care, or protection. The desire for personal independence is often expressed in terms such as "I don't need *nobody* to take care of me. I can take care of myself!" Actual patterns of behavior, however, reveal a marked discrepancy between expressed sentiments and what is covertly valued. Many lower class people appear to seek out highly restrictive social environments wherein stringent external controls are maintained over their behavior. Such institutions as the armed forces, the mental hospital, the disciplinary school, the prison or correctional institution, provide environments which incorporate a strict and detailed set of rules defining and limiting behavior, and enforced by an authority system which controls and applies coercive sanctions for deviance from these rules. While under the jurisdiction of such systems, the lower class person generally expresses to his peers continual resentment of the coercive, unjust, and arbitrary exercise of authority. Having been released, or having escaped from these milieux, however, he will often act in such a way as to insure recommitment, or choose recommitment voluntarily after a temporary period of "freedom."[24]

In the second place, the "hard core" members of this subculture as it exists in American prisons for adults are likely to be inmates who have a long record of confinement in institutions for juveniles. McCleery observed that, in a period of transition, reform-school graduates all but took over inmate society in one prison. These boys called themselves a "syndicate" and engaged in a concentrated campaign of argument and intimidation directed toward capturing the inmate council and the inmate craft shop which had been placed under council management. "The move of the syndicate to take over the craft shop involved elements of simple exploitation, the grasp for a status symbol, and an aspect of economic reform."[25] Persons with long histories of institutionalization, it is important to note, might have had little contact with the thief subculture. The thief subculture does not flourish in institutions for juveniles, and graduates of such institutions have not necessarily had extensive criminal experience on the outside. However, some form of the convict subculture *does* exist in institutions for juveniles, though not to the extent characterizing prisons for felons. Some of the newcomers to a prison for adults are, in short, persons who have been oriented to the convict subculture, who have found the utilitarian nature of this subculture acceptable, and who have had little contact with the thief subculture. This makes a difference in their behavior.

The category of inmates we have characterized as oriented to "legitimate" subcultures includes men who are not members of the thief subculture upon entering prison and who reject both the thief subculture and the convict subculture while in prison. These men present few problems to prison administrators. They make up a large percentage of the population of any prison, but they isolate themselves—or are isolated—from the thief and convict subcultures. Clemmer found that 40 per cent of a sample of the men in his prison did not consider themselves a part of any group, and another 40 per cent could be considered a member of a "semi-primary group" only.[26] He referred to these men as "un-grouped," and his statistics have often been interpreted as meaning that the prison contains many men not oriented to "inmate culture" or "prison culture"—in our terms, not oriented to either the thief subculture or the convict subculture. This is not necessarily the case. There may be sociometric isolates among the thief-oriented prisoners, the convict-oriented prisoners, and the legitimately oriented prisoners. Consequently, we have used the "legitimate subcultures" terminology rather than Clemmer's term "ungrouped." Whether or not men in this category participate in cliques, athletic teams, or religious study and hobby groups, they are oriented to the problem of achieving goals through means which are legitimate outside prisons.

Behavior Patterns in Prison

On an ideal-type level, there are great differences in the prison behavior of men oriented to one or the other of the three types of subculture. The hard core member of the convict subculture finds his reference groups inside the institutions and, as indicated, he seeks status through means available in the prison environment.

But it is important for the understanding of inmate conduct to note that the hard core member of the thief subculture seeks status in the broader criminal world of which prison is only a part. His reference groups include people both inside and outside prison, but he is committed to criminal life, not prison life. From his point of view, it is adherence to a widespread criminal code that wins him high status, not adherence to a narrower convict code. Convicts might assign him high status because they admire him as a thief, or because a good thief makes a good convict, but the thief does not play the convicts' game. Similarly, a man oriented to a legitimate subculture is by definition committed to the values of neither thieves nor convicts.

On the other hand, within any given prison, the men oriented to the convict subculture are the inmates that seek positions of power, influence, and sources of information, whether these men are called "shots," "politicians," "merchants," "hoods," "toughs," "gorillas," or something else. A job as secretary to the Captain or Warden, for example, gives an aspiring prisoner information and consequent power, and enables him to influence the assignment or regulation of other inmates. In the same way, a job which allows the incumbent to participate in a racket, such as clerk in the kitchen storeroom where he can steal and sell food, is highly desirable to a man oriented to the convict subculture. With a steady income of cigarettes, ordinarily the prisoners' medium of exchange, he may assert a great deal of influence and purchase those things which are symbols of status among persons oriented to the convict subculture. Even if there is no well-developed medium of exchange, he can barter goods acquired in his position for equally desirable goods possessed by other convicts. These include information and such things as specially starched, pressed, and tailored prison clothing, fancy belts, belt buckles or billfolds, special shoes, or any other type of dress which will set him apart and will indicate that he has both the influence to get the goods and the influence necessary to keeping and displaying them despite prison rules which outlaw doing so. In California, special items of clothing, and clothing that is neatly laundered, are called "bonaroos" (a corruption of *bonnet rouge,* by means of which French prison trusties were once distinguished from the common run of prisoners), and to a lesser degree even the persons who wear such clothing are called "bonaroos."

Two inmates we observed in one prison are somewhat representative of high status members of the convict subculture. One was the prison's top gambler, who bet the fights, baseball games, football games, ran pools, etc. His cell was always full of cigarettes, although he did not smoke. He had a job in the cell block taking care of the laundry room, and this job gave him time to conduct his gambling activities. It also allowed him to get commissions for handling the clothing of inmates who paid to have them "bonarooed," or who had friends in the laundry who did this for them free of charge, in return for some service. The "commissions" the inmate received for doing this service were not always direct; the "favors" he did gave him influence with many of the inmates in key jobs, and he reputedly could easily arrange cell changes and job changes. Shortly after he was paroled he was arrested and returned to prison for robbing a liquor store. The other inmate was the prison's most notorious "fag" or "queen." He was feminine in appearance and gestures, and wax had been injected under the skin on his chest to give the appearance of breasts. At first he was kept in a cell block isolated from the rest of the prisoners, but later he was released out into the main population. He soon went to work in a captain's office, and became a key figure in the convict subculture. He was considered a stool pigeon by the thieves, but he held high status among participants in the convict subculture. In the first place, he was the most desired fag in the prison. In the second place, he was presumed to have considerable influence with the officers who frequented the captain's office. He "married" another prisoner, who also was oriented to the convict subculture.

Since prisoners oriented either to a legitimate subculture or to a thief subculture are not seeking high status within any given prison, they do not look for the kinds of positions considered so desirable by the members of the convict subculture. Those oriented to legitimate subcultures take prison as it comes and seek status through channels provided for that purpose by prison administrators—running for election to the inmate council, to the editorship of the institutional newspaper, etc.—and by, generally, conforming to what they think administrators expect of "good prisoners." Long before the thief has come to prison, his subculture has defined proper prison conduct as behavior rationally calculated to "do time" in the easiest possible way. This means that he wants a prison life containing the best possible combination of a maximum amount of leisure time and a maximum number of privileges. Accordingly, the privileges sought by the thief are different from the privileges sought by the man oriented to prison itself. The thief wants things that will make prison life a little easier—extra food, a maximum amount of recreation time, a good radio, a little peace. One thief serving his third sentence for armed robbery was a dish washer in the officers' dining room. He liked the eating privileges, but he never sold food. Despite his "low status" job, he was highly respected by other thieves, who described him as "right," and "solid." Members of the convict subculture, like the thieves, seek privileges. There is a difference, however, for the convict seeks privileges which he believes will enhance his position in the inmate hierarchy. He also wants to do easy time but, as compared with the thief, desirable privileges are more likely to involve freedom to amplify one's store, such as stealing rights in the kitchen, and freedom of movement around the prison. Obtaining an easy job is managed because it is easy and therefore desirable, but it also is managed for the purpose of displaying the fact that it can be obtained.

In one prison, a man serving his second sentence for selling narcotics (he was not an addict) worked in the bakery during the entire term of his sentence. To him, a thief, this was a "good job," for the hours were short and the bakers ate very well. There were some rackets conducted from the bakery, such as selling cocoa, but the man never participated in these activities. He was concerned a little with learning a trade, but not very seriously. Most of all, he wanted the eating privileges which the bakery offered. A great deal of his time was spent reading psychology, philosophy, and mysticism. Before his arrest he had been a reader of tea leaves and he now was working up some plans for an illegal business involving mysticism. Other than this, his main activity was sitting with other inmates and debating.

Just as both thieves and convicts seek privileges, both seek the many kinds of contraband in a prison. But again the things the thief seeks are those that contribute to an easier life, such as mechanical gadgets for heating water for coffee and cocoa, phonographs and radios if they are contraband or not, contraband books, food, writing materials, socks, etc. He may "score" for food occasionally (unplanned theft in which advantage is taken of a momentary opportunity), but he does not have a "route" (highly organized theft of food). One who "scores" for food eats it, shares it with his friends, sometimes in return for a past or expected favors, but he does not sell it. One who has a "route" is in the illicit food selling business.[27] The inmate oriented to the convict subculture, with its emphasis on displaying ability to manipulate the environment, rather than on pleasure, is the inmate with the "route." The difference is observable in the case of an inmate assigned to the job of clerk in the dental office of one prison. This man was known to both inmates and staff long before he arrived at the institution, for his crime and arrest were highly publicized in the newspapers. It also became known that he had done time in another penitentiary for "real crime," and that his criminal exploits had frequently taken him from one side of the United States to the other. His assignment to the dental office occurred soon after he entered the prison, and some of the inmates believed that such a highly desirable job could not be achieved without "influence" and "rep." It was an ideal spot for conducting a profitable business, and a profitable business was in fact being conducted there. In order to get on the list to see the dentist, an inmate had to pay a price in cigarettes to two members of the convict subculture who were running the dental office. This practice soon changed, at least in reference to inmates who could show some contact with our man's criminal friends, in or out of prison. If a friend vouched for a man by saying he was "right" or "solid," the man would be sitting in the dental chair the next day, free of charge.

Generally speaking, an inmate oriented to the thief subculture simply is not interested in gaining high status in the prison. He wants to get out. Moreover, he is likely to be quietly amused by the concern some prisoners have for symbols of status, but he publicly exhibits neither disdain nor enthusiasm for this concern.

One exception to this occurred in an institution where a thief had become a fairly close friend of an inmate oriented to the prison. One day the latter showed up in a fresh set of bonaroos, and he made some remark that called attention to them. The thief looked at him, laughed, and said, "For Christ's sake, Bill, they're *Levi's* (standard prison blue denims) and they are always going to be Levi's." The thief may be accorded high status in the prison, because "rightness" is revered there as well as on the outside, but to him this is incidental to his being a "man," not to his being a prisoner.

Members of both subcultures are conservative—they want to maintain the status quo. Motivation is quite different, however. The man oriented to the convict subculture is conservative because he has great stock in the existing order of things, while the man who is thief oriented leans toward conservatism because he knows how to do time and likes things to run along smoothly with a minimum of friction. It is because of this conservatism that so many inmates are directly or indirectly in accommodation with prison officials who, generally speaking, also wish to maintain the status quo. A half dozen prison observers have recently pointed out that some prison leaders—those oriented to what we call the convict subculture—assist the officials by applying pressures that keep other inmates from causing trouble, while other prison leaders—those oriented to what we call the thief subculture—indirectly keep order by propagating the *criminal* code, including admonitions to "do your own time," "don't interfere with others' activities," "don't 'rank' another criminal." The issue is not whether the thief subculture and convict subculture are useful to, and used by, administrators; it is whether the observed behavior patterns originate in prison as a response to official administrative practices.

There are other similarities, noted by many observers of "prison culture" or "inmate culture." In the appropriate circumstances, members of both subcultures will participate in fomenting and carrying out riots. The man oriented to the convict subculture does this when a change has closed some of the paths for achieving positions of influence, but the thief does it when privileges of the kind that makes life easier are taken away from him. Thus, when a "prison reform" group takes over an institution, it may inadvertently make changes which lead to alliances between the members of two subcultures who ordinarily are quite indifferent to each other. In more routine circumstances, the thief adheres to a tight system of mutual aid for other thieves—persons who are "right" and "solid"—a direct application in prison of the norms which ask that a thief prove himself reliable and trustworthy to other thieves. If a man is "right," then even if he is a stranger one must help him if there is no risk to himself. If he is a friend, then one must, in addition, be willing to take *some* risk in order to help him. But in the convict subculture, "help" has a price; one helps in order to gain, whether the gain be "pay" in the form of cigarettes, or a guarantee of a return favor which will enlarge one's area of power.

Relationships Between the Two Subcultures

In the routine prison setting, the two deviant subcultures exist in a balanced relationship. It is this total setting which has been observed as "inmate culture." There is some conflict because of the great disparity in some of the values of thieves and convicts, but the two subcultures share other values. The thief is committed to keeping his hands off other people's activities, and the convict, being utilitarian, is likely to know that it is better in the long run to avoid conflict with thieves and confine one's exploitations to the "do rights" and to the members of his own subculture. Of course, the thief must deal with the convict from time to time, and when he does so he adjusts to the reality of the fact that he is imprisoned. Choosing to follow prison definitions usually means paying for some service in cigarettes or in a returned service; this is the cost of doing easy time. Some thieves adapt in a more general way to the ways of convicts and assimilate the prisonized person's concern for making out in the institution. On an ideal-type level, however, thieves do not sanction exploitation of other inmates, and they simply ignore the "do rights," who are oriented to legitimate subcultures. Nevertheless, their subculture as it operates in prison has exploitative effects.[28]

Numerous persons have documented the fact that "right guys," many of whom can be identified as leaders of the thieves, not of the convicts, exercise the greatest influence over the total prison population. The influence is the long-run kind stemming from the ability to influence notions of what is right and proper, what McCleery calls the formulation and communication of definitions.[29] The thief, after all, has the respect of many inmates who are not themselves thieves. The right guy carries a set of attitudes, values, and norms that have a great deal of consistency and clarity. He acts, forms opinions, and evaluates events in the prison according to them, and over a long period of time he in this way determines basic behavior patterns in the institution. In what the thief thinks of as "small matters," however—getting job transfers, enforcing payment of gambling debts, making cell assignments—members of the convict subculture run things.

It is difficult to assess the direct lines of influence the two deviant subcultures have over those inmates who are not members of either subculture when they enter a prison. It is true that if a new inmate does not have definitions to apply to the new prison situation, one or the other of the deviant subcultures is likely to supply them. On the one hand, the convict subculture is much more apparent than the thief subculture; its roles are readily visible to any new arrival, and its definitions are readily available to one who wants to "get along" and "make it" in a prison. Moreover, the inmate leaders oriented to the convict subculture are anxious to get new followers who will recognize the existing status hierarchy in the prison. Thieves, on the other hand, tend to be snobs. Their status in prison is determined in part by outside criteria, as well as by prison conduct, and it is therefore difficult for a prisoner, acting as a prisoner, to achieve these criteria. At a minimum, the newcomer can fall under the influence of the thief subculture only if he has intimate association over a period of time with some of its members who are able and willing to impart some of its subtle behavior patterns to him.

Our classification of some inmates as oriented to legitimate subcultures implies that many inmates entering a prison do not find either set of definitions acceptable to them. Like thieves, these men are not necessarily "stripped" of outside statuses, and they do not play the prison game. They bring a set of values with them when they come to prison, and they do not leave these values at the gate. They are people such as a man who, on a drunken Saturday night, ran over a pedestrian and was sent to the prison for manslaughter, a middle-class clerk who was caught embezzling his firm's money, and a young soldier who stole a car in order to get back from a leave. Unlike thieves, these inmates bring to the prison both anti-criminal and anti-prisoner attitudes. Although it is known that most of them participate at a minimum in primary group relations with either thieves or convicts, their relationships with each other have not been studied. Further, criminologists have ignored the possible effects the "do rights" have on the total system of "inmate culture." It seems a worthy hypothesis that thieves, convicts, and "do rights" all bring certain values and behavior patterns to prison with them, and that total "inmate culture" represents an adjustment or accommodation of these three systems within the official administrative system of deprivation and control.[30] It is significant in this connection that Wheeler has not found in Norwegian prisons the normative order and cohesive bonds among inmates that characterize many American prisons. He observes that his data suggest "that the current functional interpretations of the inmate system in American institutions are not adequate," and that "general features of Norwegian society are imported into the prison and operate largely to offset any tendencies toward the formation of a solidary inmate group. . . ."[31]

Behavior After Release

If our crude typology is valid, it should be of some use for predicting the behavior of prisoners when they are released. However, it is important to note that in any given prison the two deviant subcultures are not necessarily as sharply separated as our previous discussion has implied. Most inmates are under the influence of *both* subcultures. Without realizing it, inmates who have served long prison terms are likely to move toward the middle, toward a compromise or balance between the directives coming from the two sources. A member of the convict subculture may come to see that thieves are the real men with the prestige; a member of the thief subculture or even a "do right" may lose his ability to sustain his status needs by outside criteria. Criminologists seem to have had difficulty in keeping the two kinds of influence separate, and we cannot expect all inmates to be more astute than the criminologists. The fact that time has a blending effect on the participants in the two deviant subcultures suggests that the subcultures themselves tend to blend together in some prisons. We have already noted that the thief subculture scarcely exists in some institutions for juveniles. It is probable also that in army stockades and in concentration camps this subculture is almost nonexistent. In places of short-term confinement, such as city and county jails, the convict subculture is dominant, for the thief subculture involves status distinctions that are not readily observable in a short period of confinement. At the other extreme, in prisons where only prisoners with long sentences are confined, the distinctions between the two subcultures are likely to be blurred. Probably the two subcultures exist in their purest forms in institutions holding inmates in their twenties, with varying sentences for a variety of criminal offenses. Such institutions, of course, are the "typical" prisons of the United States.

Despite these differences, in any prison the men oriented to legitimate subcultures should have a low recidivism rate, while the highest recidivism rate should be found among participants in the convict subculture. The hard core members of this subculture are being trained in manipulation, duplicity and exploitation, they are not sure they can make it on the outside, and even when they are on the outside they continue to use convicts as a reference group. This sometimes means that there will be a wild spree of crime and dissipation which takes the members of the convict subculture directly back to the prison. Members of the thief subculture, to whom prison life represented a pitfall in outside life, also should have a high recidivism rate. However, the thief sometimes "reforms" and tries to succeed in some life within the law. Such behavior, contrary to popular notions, is quite acceptable to other members of the thief subculture, so long as the new job and position are not "anti-criminal" and do not involve regular, routine, "slave labor." Suckers work, but a man who, like a thief, "skims it off the top" is not a sucker. At any rate, the fact that convicts, to a greater extent than thieves, tend to evaluate things from the perspective of the prison and to look upon discharge as a short vacation from prison life suggests that their recidivism rate should be higher than that of thieves.

Although the data collected by Garrity provide only a crude test of these predictions, they do support them. Garrity determined the recidivism rates and the tendencies for these rates to increase or decrease with increasing length of prison terms, for each of Schrag's inmate types. Unfortunately, this typology does not clearly make the distinction between the two subcultures, probably because of the blending process noted above. Schrag's "right guys" or "antisocial offenders," thus, might include both men who perceive role requirements in terms of the norms of the convict subculture, and men who perceive those requirements in terms of the norms of the thief subculture. Similarly, neither his "con politician" ("pseudosocial offender") nor his "outlaw" ("asocial offender") seems to be what we would characterize as the ideal-type member of the convict subculture. For example, it is said that relatively few of the former have juvenile records, that onset of criminality often occurs after a position of respectability has already been attained in the civilian community, and that educational and occupational records are far superior to those of "right guys." Further, outlaws are characterized as men who have been frequently reared in institutions or shifted around in foster homes; but they also are characterized as "undisciplined trouble-makers," and this does not seem to characterize the men who seek high status in prisons by rather peaceful means of manipulation and exploitation. In short, our ideal-type "thief" appears to include only some of Schrag's "right guys"; the ideal-type "convict" seems to include some of his "right guys," some of his "con politicians," and all of his "outlaws." Schrag's "square Johns" correspond to our "legitimate subcultures" category.

Garrity found that a group of "square Johns" had a low parole violation rate and that this rate remained low no matter how much time was served. The "right guys" had a high violation rate that decreased markedly as time in prison increased. In Garrity's words, this was because "continued incarceration [served] to sever his connections with the criminal subculture and thus to increase the probability of successful parole."[32] The rates for the "outlaw" were very high and remained high as time in prison increased. Only the rates of the "con politician" did not meet our expectations—the rates were low if the sentences were rather short but increased systematically with time served.

Noting that the origins of the thief subculture and the convict subculture are both external to a prison should change our expectations regarding the possible reformative effect of that prison. The recidivism rates of neither thieves, convicts, nor "do rights" are likely to be significantly affected by incarceration in any traditional prison. This is not to say that the program of a prison with a "therapeutic milieu" like the one the Wisconsin State Reformatory is seeking, or of a prison like some of those in California, in which group counseling is being used in an atempt to change organizational structure, will not eventually affect the recidivism rates of the members of one or another, or all three, of the categories. However, in reference to the ordinary custodially-oriented prison the thief says he can do his time "standing on his head," and it appears that he *is* able to do the time "standing on his head"—except for long-termers, imprisonment has little effect on the thief one way or the other. Similarly, the routine of any particular custodial prison is not likely to have significant reformative effects on members of the convict subculture—they will return to prison because, in effect, they have found a home there. And the men oriented to legitimate subcultures will maintain low recidivism rates even if they never experience imprisonment. Garrity has shown that it is not correct to conclude, as reformers have so often done, that prisons are the breeding ground of crime. It probably is not true either that any particular prison is the breeding ground of an inmate culture that significantly increases recidivism rates.

1. Erving Goffman, "On the Characteristics of Total Institutions," Chapters 1 and 2 in Donald R. Cressey, Editor, *The Prison: Studies in Institutional Organization and Change,* New York: Holt, Rinehart and Winston, 1961, 22-47.

2. Richard A. Cloward, Donald R. Cressey, George H. Grosser, Richard McCleery, Lloyd E. Ohlin, and Gresham M. Sykes and Sheldon L. Messinger, *Theoretical Studies in Social Organization of the Prison,* New York: Social Science Research Council, 1960, p. 9.

3. *Ibid.,* 15, 19. See also Gresham M. Sykes, "Men, Merchants, and Toughs: A Study of Reactions to Imprisonment," *Social Problems,* 4 (October, 1957),

130-138; and Gresham M. Sykes, *The Society of Captives*, Princeton: Princeton University Press, 1958, 79-82.

4. Cloward, *et al., op. cit.*, 21, 35-41.

5. *Ibid.*, 58, 60, 73.

6. Donald Clemmer, *The Prison Community*, Re-issued Edition, New York: Rinehart, 1958, 229-302; Hans Riemer, "Socialization in the Prison Community," *Proceedings of the American Prison Association*, 1937, 151-155.

7. See Clarence Schrag, *Social Types in a Prison Community*, Unpublished M.S. Thesis, University of Washington, 1944.

8. Clarence Schrag, "Some Foundations for a Theory of Correction," Chapter 8 in Cressey, *op. cit.*, p. 329.

9. *Ibid.*, p. 350.

10. *Ibid.*, p. 349.

11. *Ibid.*, p. 342.

12. Donald R. Garrity, "The Prison as a Rehabilitation Agency," Chapter 9 in Cressey, *op. cit.*, 372-373.

13. *Ibid.*, p. 373.

14. *Ibid.*, p. 376.

15. *Ibid.*, p. 377.

16. Donald R. Cressey and Witold Krassowski, "Inmate Organization and Anomie in American Prisons and Soviet Labor Camps," *Social Problems*, 5 (Winter, 1957-58), 217-230.

17. Edwin H. Sutherland and Donald R. Cressey, *Principles of Criminology*, Sixth Edition, New York: Lippincott, 1960, 504-505.

18. Howard S. Becker and Blanche Geer, "Latent Culture: A Note on the Theory of Latent Social Roles," *Administrative Science Quarterly*, 5 (September, 1960), 305-306. See also Alvin W. Gouldner, "Cosmopolitans and Locals: Toward an Analysis of Latent Social Roles," *Administrative Science Quarterly*, 2, (1957), 281-306 and 2 (1958), 444-480.

19. Walter C. Reckless, *The Crime Problem*, Second Edition, New York: Appleton-Century-Crofts, 1945, 144-145, 148-150; Edwin H. Sutherland, *The Professional Thief*, Chicago: University of Chicago Press, 1937.

20. William Foote Whyte, "Corner Boys: A Study of Clique Behavior," *American Journal of Sociology*, 46 (March, 1941), 647-663.

21. Walter B. Miller, "Lower Class Culture as a Generating Milieu of Gang Delinquency," *Journal of Social Issues*, 14 (1958), 5-19.

22. Stanton Wheeler, "Role Conflict in Correctional Communities," Chapter 6 in Cressey, *op. cit.*, p. 235.

23. Compton Mackenzie, *Moral Courage*, London: Collins, 1962.

24. Miller, *op. cit.*, 12-13.

25. Richard H. McCleery, "The Governmental Process and Informal Social Control," Chapter 4 in Cressey, *op. cit.*, p. 179.

26. Clemmer, *op. cit.*, 116-133.

27. See Schrag, "Some Foundations for a Theory of Correction," *op. cit.*, p. 343.

28. See Donald R. Cressey, "Foreword," to Clemmer, *op. cit.*, vii-x.

29. "The Governmental Process and Informal Social Control," *op. cit.*, p. 154.

30. "But if latent culture can restrict the possibilities for the proliferation of the manifest culture, the opposite is also true. Manifest culture can restrict the operation of latent culture. The problems facing group members may be so pressing that, given the social context in which the group operates, the range of solutions that will be effective may be so limited as not to allow for influence of variations resulting from cultures associated with other identities." Becker and Geer, *op. cit.*, 308-309.

31. Stanton Wheeler, "Inmate Culture in Prisons," Mimeographed report of the Laboratory of Social Relations, Harvard University, 1962, 18, 20, 21.

32. Garrity, *op. cit.*, p. 377.

OBSERVATIONS ON GAMBLING
IN A LOWER-CLASS SETTING

IRVING KENNETH ZOLA

Introduction

Studies in gambling have often focused on matters of individual pathology[1] and yet, on a number of psychological dimensions, no significant differences have been found between gamblers and non-gamblers.[2] Part of the explanation for this lack of difference is the fact that so widespread an activity as gambling can be "many things to many people."[3] Another reason is that while recognized as one of our major social problems, gambling also constitutes a major American paradox, fluctuating as it does between tolerance and condemnation, with a very thin line drawn between legal and illegal forms.[4] It seems obvious that to exist in this state of limbo, gambling must serve important social and psychological functions. This report is an attempt to delineate some functions of one form of gambling as it occurs in a small lower-class residential community.

The Setting

East Side was a small working-class area within a large New England city. Successive waves of immigrants once flooded the

This report is part of a study entitled "Relocation and Mental Health: Adaptation Under Stress," conducted by the Center For Community Studies in the Department of Psychiatry of the Massachusetts General Hospital and the Harvard Medical School. The research is supported by the NIMH, Grant #3M 9137-C3. The author wishes to acknowledge Edward Ryan and Leonora K. Zola for their repeated readings and criticisms, and Frances Morrill, Stanton Wheeler, and George H. Wolkon for their valuable suggestions.

streets, but in recent years the population had become more stable, predominantly Italian with smaller segments of Eastern European Jews and Poles. As part of an anthropological field team, the observer spent several months in East Side, becoming an habitué of meeting places, bars, and taverns and participating actively with several sub-groups. His identity and role were, however, unknown to the community. Most of the observations on gambling were made at Hoff's Place, one of many taverns along the main street of East Side. It was a bar and grill frequented mostly by Italians and Poles who were either present or former residents of the immediate neighborhood. At Hoff's one type of gambling predominated: off-track betting where wagers are made with a "bookie" or "bookmaker." Though the men spent much of the day here, virtually all over thirty were married and relatively few were unemployed. Some were on vacation or on their day off. Some worked nearby, drove delivery trucks or taxis and dropped in and out while ostensibly working. Others worked on split shifts and visited between them. Still others had jobs which ended early in the day or started very late.

One of the first observations made of Hoff's was the dissociation of the bar from other spheres of the men's social life. Violent reactions often greeted any invasion or intrusion.

One wife became concerned when her husband did not return for supper and so she called and asked the bartender about his whereabouts. Although he knew, he gruffly denied any knowledge. Whereupon she burst into tears, pleading with him, "Please don't tell him I called, 'cause he would beat the shit out of me if he knew."

"One day my mother sent me after my father. It was gettin' late. When he came home was he mad! He kicked her all the way down Lawrence Street and back and said to her, 'Don't you never send anyone after me here. No buts, anything can wait till I get here.' And she never did it again."

A further distinction was made between gambling and other spheres of economic activity. A man was not expected to share his profits with his family and was thought a "damn fool" if he even told them of his winnings. The fact that most gambling activities take place in a context institutionally defined as "recreation" helps to emphasize this dissociation from ordinary utilitarian activities.[5]

A Group in Process

The men at Hoff's, however, did not constitute a group in the formal sense. Regardless of when in the day one entered, the men in the bar seemed only to be whiling away their time drinking, barely taking notice of one another. On any day the pattern would be quite similar.

In the first booth, Hal reads the *Morning Telegraph* while Sammy naps in a corner. Behind them Smiley studies the Star Racing Section and Silvio looks at Phil's Armstrong. Phil, the bookie, sits at the bar going over his slips. Beside him Nick stares blankly at the wall and not two stools away Johnnie and Joe sip beer without speaking. Further down the bar sits an unidentified man and next to him stands Al, the bartender, gazing aimlessly out the window as he washes glasses.

Ten minutes before the start of each race, however, this changed. Men who were outside came in and those previously silent began to talk.

"Do you think he's got a chance?"
"I don't like the jockey."
"He likes muddy tracks."
"He's long overdue."
"They've been keeping him for this one."

Some of the remarks were addressed to one's neighbor, some to no one in particular. The bookie began to take bets. Gradually, the conversation became more agitated.

"Get your bets in while you can," kids Phil. Silvio turns and hands him five dollars while Smiley shakes his head, "He'll never win." Sal laughs, "Here Phil, a bean on the nose, number seven, a 'sure thing.'" "I'm the one who's got that," roars Al, reaching into his pocket and taking out a twenty-dollar bill. "Twenty thousand on number one. C'mon Irv, stick with me." "Uh, uh," I answer, "You're bad news, I like Principio." Meanwhile Phil proceeds gingerly down the bar as others turn and bet, rise from their booths or motion him toward them.

Some last-minute bets or changes were made and then the race began. If the race was broadcast, a group formed near the radio. The cheering was restrained and muffled.

"See, look what's happening."
"Why is the jockey holding him back?"
"Just watch him finish with a spurt."

Regardless of whether the race was broadcast, the announcement of the winner always led to the same discussion. All attention focused on the winners.

"How did you figure it?"
"How come you picked her?"
"How did you know?"

And their answers. . . .

"I've noticed that jockey. . . ."
"Did you see the weight shift? Well. . . ."
"I figure they've been saving him. . . ."
"His last time out, he. . . ."

If no one picked the winning horse, the discussion was still the same, but more philosophical and not as prolonged. Within five minutes, however, it was quiet again.

Al is back washing glasses. Silvio and Smiley return each to a separate booth. Hal goes outside and Sammy goes back to sleep. Joe and Johnnie leave but Paul and Charlie replace them at the bar sipping beer without speaking. Nick studies the chart for the next race. Sal stands at the door looking at the sky and Phil, slips of paper in his hand, walks slowly toward the phone.

Once more they appeared to be strangers . . . until the next race.

Yet gambling is more than a mode of communication. It creates a bond between the men—a bond which defines insiders and outsiders. This function of gambling first became apparent when a newcomer arrived at Hoff's.

Joe did not live in East Side, though he was distantly related to one of the bookies. He worked on a nearby construction gang and gradually began to patronize Hoff's. At every opportunity, he would come in, order a drink, and sit at the bar or in one of the empty

booths. Although he was through work at 4:00 p.m., he often remained until 5:00 or 6:00. When he offered to buy someone a drink,
he was gently, but firmly, refused. All he gained was an occasional
nod, until, in an off-hand manner, he asked questions about the races,
horses, odds, and ways to bet. At first he bet the choices of others
and then finally his own. Only when he started betting did others
begin to interact with him, respond more than monosyllabically, and
"allow" him to join them as they sat at the bar or in the booths.

For the younger residents of East Side, gambling seemed
a way of preparing them for later adulthood. A number of
teenagers always hung around Hoff's, and, although they were
not allowed in the bar to drink, they were welcome to place bets.
It was during such times that they first initiated conversation
with the younger men (19-21)—a preliminary step in "anticipatory
socialization."

Thus, even though someone might appear at the same time
every day, or the same day every week, this was insufficient to
designate one a "member," a "regular," or an "insider." At
Hoff's, this was accomplished only by off-track betting—an activity
which served as the entrance fee, defining membership and initi-
ating newcomers.

The Preservation of Group Attachment

Three observations made by Devereux in his analysis of
gambling and the social structure are relevant here: (1) Although
the making of a wager polarizes the field and artificially creates
the gambler's bond of interest in the event, it does not follow that
winning money is the dominant motivational force; (2) many
gamblers go to great lengths to deny their emotional involvement
in specific events; (3) the importance and relevance of competition to gambling varies with the social context in which it occurs.[6]
Each of these observations was found to hold true for Hoff's,
but here in East Side they have yet a secondary function. In de-
emphasizing emotionality, monetary gain, and competition, not
only were several basic sources of hostility often emanating from
gambling eliminated but, at the same time, attachment to the
"group at Hoff's" was thereby reaffirmed.

While the excitement accompanying any sporting event was present, it was restrained. The extremes of overexcitement and depression were both negatively sanctioned. On more than one occasion, a person who went "over the line" when he won was called "nuts" or told to stop "acting like a jerk," or if one persisted in bemoaning his "hard luck," he too was reprimanded. Even overconcern during a race or contest was regarded with skepticism.

Donnie was disturbed about the ball game—he had bet $10 on the outcome. He would get up, pace back and forth, sit down again. Each time he asked questions about the ability of the players or the manager. "Do you think he knows what he's doing?" As he returned to his seat once more, Mario shook his head indicating Donnie. He commented on his nervousness, adding, "After all, it's only money."

While these men cared when they lost, such depression was remarkably short-lived, perhaps until post-time of the next race. Little systematic effort was made to retain one's winnings. These men never stopped while ahead, nor reduced or even maintained the size of their bets after having won. If a person was ahead at the end of the day, it was more likely because there were no more races than through any conscious effort to accumulate profits. At Hoff's, there was no prototype of the conservative gambler who quit while ahead. People who did were disliked, and not only by the bookies. Instead of admiring them, the regulars shook their heads and called them "cheap bastards." One would have to increase the bet continually in order to gain any substantial amount of money, and yet there is still the problem of a stopping or cutting-off point. The following legend is illustrative of this:

Bob was relating the experiences of an old East Sider. "I know a guy who won a $100,000. First here and then he wanted to gamble so badly he flew to New York and then back here and kept losing till he had nothing." "Yeah," added Spike, "it could happen. You lost twenty G's and figure you've still got eighty, so you take another shot, and finally you've got nothing."

Thus, if no limit, no matter how theoretical, exists then monetary gain *per se* becomes an indefinite goal and one impossible of attainment. Finally, individual competition was almost non-existent. Within the group itself, members were not explicitly compared with one another as being better or worse players. In part to salve the wounds of defeat, and to share the fruits of victory, there was the common practice of mutual treats where the winner paid for the drinks of his closer acquaintances.

Particularly striking was the shift of competition from within the group to "the system." There was continual talk of "beating the system," "cracking the system," "not letting the system beat you." While this ostensibly referred to the scheme or principle governing the results of races, the actual hostility was more often expressed against the agent of that system—the bookie. The group complained that "he can't be hit" or dubbed him "the undertaker," and alluded to how they would "like to bury him . . . in an avalanche of losses."

Joe told of one bookie. "Why, you know why that son-of-a-bitch makes more money than anyone else? It's because all the bettors hate his guts, so they make all bets with him, even 'hot tips' just in the hope they'll break him."

"Remember the time that 'Happy' bet 20-20-0 on a long shot and won. Do you remember Sam's face? I thought he would bust a gut."

"Well, I took care of that bookie. I bet $5 on the fifth and kept betting it all on each race. By the eighth, he had to close up shop."

In this situation, the bookie served a dual function. As the personification of the system they were trying to beat, he facilitated the shifting of competition from within the group to outside the group; and by serving as the target for their hostility, he also became an integrating force of the group—their scape-goat.

Thus the de-emphasis on thrill, money, and competition not only prevented the individual member from becoming too involved with his own personal success and failure; it also made him more dependent on the group and reinforced his attachment to it and the rewards which it alone can bestow—prestige and group recognition. To understand these rewards, it is necessary to examine their dispensation.

Systems of Betting and the Prestige Hierarchy

As depicted in the opening illustration, at Hoff's all available attention and admiration was focused on those men who had chosen winners. Everyone clustered about them, prodded them to reveal the basis of their choice, praised them on their good judgment, and regarded their subsequent opinions highly. Rewarding someone in this manner assumes that he has *done* something to merit such an action. Not all types of gambling warrant such behavior. In the "numbers" or "policy game" where full rein is given to hunches, omens, dreams, and where a person may have his own special number and play it day after day, year after year, no one is congratulated on his ability if he wins, nor asked to explain the rational basis for his choice; he is rather congratulated on his good fortune or luck. In short, methods of selection and the social rewards for winning reflect a conception of the numbers as a game of chance, whose outcome is beyond human control and comprehension, explainable only in terms of luck, fortune, or fate.[7]

The methods and social rewards of off-track betting reflect a different assumption, i.e., the existence of an underlying order, a principle which can be figured out and mastered by a skilled observer.[8] While segments of the larger society deny this in their educational and legal attempts to eliminate gambling, there is hardly a single major newspaper which does not publish the opinions of at least one professional racing expert. As a rule, the latter not only names his choices but gives his reasoning. This was similiar to the behavior of the bettors at Hoff's, who consulted with the winners or joined in a general discussion to explain the results, to figure out why it happened or what factors had not been sufficiently considered.

Not all criteria for making decisions were equally regarded. Basically, there were two positively valued modes, one subtype of these, and one devalued mode. Generally, an individual was characterized by his reliance on a particular mode, though it was possible that he might use more than one method on any given day. The four systems were differentiated not only by their basis of selection but also by the degree, amount, and quality of attention and recognition the group bestowed on the successful user of such methods.

Handicapping, the method which elicited the highest respect, was based on some pragmatic system of integration of available information such as past performances of horses and jockeys, weight shifts, post positions, track conditions, etc. Using any available factual data, there was an attempt to *figure out* one's choice. Calling an individual a "handicapper" was the highest compliment that could be paid. When someone wanted information about a particular horse or race, the "handicappers" were the ones to whom questions were directed. Moreover, their opinions were solicited even through their total losses might actually outweigh their gains.

At one time, I hit upon a system of betting a number of horses in combination. For three straight days, I won the daily double and in the next five days, at least one of my choices won while the other finished second or third. Each of these bets, however, was only for fifty cents and thus the net profit on each day was between five and ten dollars and after the first three days I lost. For this eight-day period I was operating at a loss, and yet for the next few weeks I was consulted by other bettors and kidded by the bookies as being "too good." One even joked about barring me.

Thus, it seems apparent that the "handicapper" gains and retains prestige not because of monetary profits or a preponderance of winners, but because he has demonstrated some technique or skill enabling him to select winners or at least come close.

The "hot tip" was the second positively valued mode. It was based on the use of "inside information," facts about the horses not published or known to the general public. Though the knowledge was supposedly secret, "hot tipsters" usually revealed its possession. For only in so doing could they be acknowledged by the group. While the method of selection is a rational one, the distinguishing feature is *access* to information and not the exercise of any particular skill. This fact was recognized by the men at Hoff's and though they would ask tipsters, "Got anything hot?" "Any inside dope?" their seeking of advice would not usually go beyond this. Nor were the personal choices of such men given undue weight or consideration unless they had also achieved some recognition as handicappers.

The "hedge" is more complex and seems to be a subtype of the above two methods. One or more of the following statements usually introduced the "hedge."

"You saw me give that to Spike and Angelo and the others and I told them it would win and then I go and bet on another. Whatta dope!"

"I couldn't decide which one of these would win so I didn't bet any."

"I had him [the winning horse] but I had to do an errand before I got here so I arrived too late to bet."

"Remember how I figured it out at home and picked number three to win but then I came here and saw the Armstrong so I bet the six. If only I hadn't seen 'the Arm.'"

The groundwork was usually laid before the race and the sequence was often as follows:

Before: "I like Ocean Rock but Principio is long overdue and that blasted Pilot's Express is always a threat with Hobbes aboard."
After: The fact that he bet Ocean Rock is ignored. "See, what did I tell you, that son-of-a-bitch Hobbes brought him in. I told you that would happen."

These remarks not only covered the bettor if his choice did not win, but also communicated to the group, "See, I also picked the winner, even though I didn't play it." For the most part, it succeeded. The group listened to the "hedgers," included them in the discussion of the results, and so allowed them to share to some extent the rewards of picking a winner. Considering their verbalization, it also seems likely that acceptance hinged on the presumption that the basis of their "unbet" choice was really handicapping or a "hot tip."

At the bottom of this prestige ladder was the hunch or random choice bet—lowest because it embodied a denial of the rationality which underlies the concept of "system" and hence "figuring out" of race results. Although "hunch betting" was chided as a "woman's bet," it was difficult to ignore if it produced a winner. Congratulations might be offered, but the reasoning behind the choice was never seriously solicited nor was future advice sought. The underlying attitude toward this technique was best shown when it produced a loser.

Jack bet on a dog called Cerullo because it was the name of a local hockey player. When it finished second, he was furious. "Damn it, that's what happens when you only have a bean [a dollar]—if I'd had more, I'd have bet him for second too." He barely uttered this when his friends began to tease him. "Say Mickey Mantle is running in the third and Williams in the ninth." They harped on the "why" of his bet. Jack fought back, shouting, "You wouldn't act that way if the shoe was on the other foot." But this only encouraged them. They continued berating him till he began to sulk and finally walked out.

Only in "hunch" betting and only when it lost did such hostility occur in the group.

The Functional Aspects and Satisfactions of Betting

A rational-cognitive dimension seems to pervade these methods of selection. Since the races were considered capable of human understanding, this emphasis on rationality reflected and manifested the idea of understanding. By using these methods, the players were "beating the system." The "system," which they frequently mentioned, referred to more than a principle underlying the races but rather to life or fate. Miller claims that many lower-class individuals feel that their lives are subject to a set of forces over which they have relatively little control and that furthermore this world view is associated with a conception of the ultimate futility of direct effort towards a goal.[9] Gambling can help deny this futility, as illustrated by the response of one "regular."

Joe continually talked about "hitting it big." Today was no exception as he spoke of just missing a $1000 double. I looked at him quizzically, "You know you always talk about your ship coming in. Do you ever think it will?" Startled, he raised his head and without looking at me, muttered, "No . . . but what else have I got besides this?" [betting on the races].

By "beating the system," outsmarting it by rational means, these men demonstrated they *can* exercise control and that for a brief moment they *can* control their fate. Off-track betting is thus a kind of escape. It denies the vagaries of life and gives these men a chance to regulate it. At Hoff's, there was an emphasis on rewards rather than punishments, on how much can be gained rather than lost. One was rewarded by increased attention and recognition when he won but never punished or ignored when he lost except when the very structure of the group was threatened. "Hunch" betting was just such a threat because it not only denied the concept of an underlying order but also was a way of admitting defeat, of granting that everything *was* beyond one's control.

Recognition was the supreme reward of the winner. By competing against the system rather than against themselves, however, recognition was no longer a scarce commodity, for theoretically there was no limit to the number of winners. Thus, wherever possible success and recognition were shared, whether by extending the definition of winners in the acceptance of "hedgers" or sharing the fruits of victory by "mutual treats." One regular revealed the meaning of being a winner when amid the talk and praise of his selection, he yelled, "What do you think I am, a nobody?" It was a statement so appealing that it was taken up as a byword and used over and over again by the group. In some ways, it was an insightful joke, for in picking the winner and becoming the center of attention, the winner leaves the realm of the nobody for the realm of the somebody.

Conclusion

Although betting doubtless serves many idiosyncratic needs, much of its structure, function, and persistence can be understood only by an examination of the social context in which it occurs. Gambling offers these men more than a means of recreation, just as Hoff's offers them more than a place to drink. Though such betting may produce neither recreation nor monetary gain, this does not necessarily mean that it is a sterile, non-productive, or even dysfunctional activity. As many observers have pointed out, these men are aware of the major goals and values of middle-class society but are either unwilling[10] or incapable of achieving them by the use of the ordinary methods.[11] However, as recent empirical[12] and theoretical[13] literature has demonstrated, deviance may be more than a symptom of dysfunctional structures. For these men, gambling may be a way of harnessing or channeling their otherwise destructive frustrations. Instead of lashing out at society, they lash out at "the system." In this sense, gambling may be an activity which helps reinforce and preserve some of the major values of the larger social system. At Hoff's they *can* "achieve" and *can* gain recognition for their accomplishments—by exercising skill or knowledge in the selection of horses.

Moreover, these goals of achievement and recognition can be aspired to with few of the conventional risks. In the society at large, one's success or failure alters and affects one's whole way of life while here it is completely incidental to it—a reflection of the isolation of gambling from other spheres of life. Here there is an emphasis on rewards rather than punishments, on gains rather than losses, on being a "somebody" and not a "nobody." For these men, gambling, or at least off-track betting, is not simply the flight, the withdrawal, or the escape as so often claimed. By making success and recognition possible, it allows the players to function in the larger society without suffering the consequences of the realization that they indeed have little else.

This paper is necessarily limited by the way the observations were made and thus depicts only one small but significant slice of the social context of gambling—the relation of bettors to one another. Unfortunately little was known of the lives of these men outside this particular setting, so no explanation is possible of how or why the groups at such places as Hoff's originated nor of the origins of gambling in general. As with so many other phenomena, the sources or causes have long faded into the background and may even be unimportant. This report is but a single case study—an attempt to delineate some of the possible reasons for the persistence of gambling and some of the functions it may presently serve. Whether similar observations hold for different settings[14] and for different types of gambling will have to be settled by further empirical and more systematic investigations.

1. Edmund Bergler, *The Psychology of Gambling*, New York: Hill and Wang, 1957; and "The Gambler—A Misunderstood Neurotic," *Journal of Criminal Psychopathology*, 4 (1943), 379-393.

2. James Hunter and Arthur Bruner, "Emotional Outlets of Gamblers," *Journal of Abnormal and Social Psychology*, 23 (1928), 38-39; and Robert P. Morris, "An Exploratory Study of Some Personality Characteristics of Gamblers," *Journal of Clinical Psychology*, 13 (1957), 191-193.

3. Edward C. Devereux, Jr., "Gambling and the Social Structure—A Sociological Study of Lotteries and Horse Racing in Contemporary America," unpublished doctoral dissertation, Harvard University, 1949.

4. Herbert A. Bloch, "The Sociology of Gambling," *American Journal of Sociology*, 57 (1951), 215-222; and "The Gambling Business: An American Paradox," *Crime and Delinquency*, 8 (1962), 355-364.

5. Devereux, *op. cit.*

6. Devereux, *op. cit.*

7. Gustav G. Carlson, "Number Gambling—A Study of a Culture Complex," unpublished doctoral dissertation, University of Michigan, 1939; and Devereux, *op. cit.*

8. Devereux, *op. cit.*

9. Walter B. Miller, "Lower Class Cultures as a Generating Milieu of Gang Delinquency," *Journal of Social Issues*, 14 (1958), 5-19.

10. *Ibid.*

11. Albert K. Cohen, *Delinquent Boys*, New York: The Free Press of Glencoe, 1955; and Robert K. Merton, *Social Theory and Social Structure*, Rev. and Enl. Ed., New York: The Free Press of Glencoe, 1957, Chaps. IV and V.

12. Robert A. Dentler and Kai T. Erikson, "The Functions of Deviance in Groups," *Social Problems*, 7 (1959), 98-107.

13. Lewis A. Coser, "Some Functions of Deviant Behavior and Normative Flexibility," *American Journal of Sociology*, 68 (1962), 172-181; and Kai T. Erikson, "Notes on the Sociology of Deviance," *Social Problems*, 9 (1962) 307-314.

14. Robert D. Herman, "Gambling Institutions: The Race Track," unpublished manuscript presented at the 1963 Meeting of The Pacific Sociological Association.

PHYSICIAN NARCOTIC ADDICTS

CHARLES WINICK

This study was undertaken in order to explore what would appear to be the anomaly of the substantial incidence of drug addiction among physicians. It is an anomaly because addiction is generally perceived as a degraded and visibly pathological form of deviant behavior which is associated with the lower socio-economic classes. In contrast, physicians are usually perceived as constituting one of the most prestigious and honored and wealthy occupations in our society.[1] A further anomaly is the extent to which the physician is clearly a person who early learns to defer gratifications during his very lengthy training. In contrast, the addict's orality and need for his drug frequently make it very difficult for him to defer gratifications.

The incidence of opiate addiction among physicians has been estimated by the U.S. Commissioner of Narcotics as being about one addict among every 100 physicians, in contrast to a rate of one in 3,000 in the general population.[2] According to official records of the Federal Bureau of Narcotics, 1,012 physicians were reported as addicts and 659 were found guilty of illegal narcotics sales or prescription activity from 1942 through 1956. One report identified the dean of a university medical school and other well-known physicians who became addicted.[3] The head of a leading state medical society became addicted and committed suicide. The number of physicians becoming addicted each year is roughly equivalent to the graduating class of a medical school. It is of course possible that there are physician addicts who are not known to the authorities, so that the incidence may be even higher.

A substantial incidence of addiction among physicians has

been reported from several other countries, suggesting that there may be something about the physician's role independent of his nationality which is related to his use of narcotics. England has reported that physicians are the occupational group most heavily represented among addicts, accounting for 17 per cent of the country's addicts.[4] One authority, summarizing United Nations reports on the subject, has said that in England one physician in every 550 and in Germany one physician in every 95 was an addict.[5] Another study reported that addiction in the 1930's among German physicians was 100 times more frequent than in the general population, and that the typical physician addict used more drugs than other addicts.[6]

There have been two statistical studies of physician addicts, both conducted at the U.S. Public Health Service hospitals. One study of 47 addict physicians conducted 20 years ago at the U.S. Public Health Service Hospital at Fort Worth reported that the typical addict physician was a native-born, 52-year-old, white male, engaged in general practice in a small town.[7] He began using morphine at the age of 39 for the relief of a painful condition, and came from comfortable economic circumstances. He had sought a voluntary cure in sanitaria on three occasions and been in jail once. He was married and had two children. He had approximately the same prospects for cure as the average addict. A study of 457 consecutive admissions to the U.S. Public Health Service Hospital at Lexington for meperidine ("Demerol") addiction reported that 32.7 per cent of these cases of primary addiction were physicians and osteopaths.[8]

Procedure

The purpose of this study was to explore the social and personality correlates of addiction in addict physicians. In order to explore these correlates, interviews were conducted in New York, Pennsylvania, Massachusetts, Rhode Island, New Jersey, and Connecticut, with 98 physicians who either were or had been opiate addicts. All the physicians had been addicts during a period of at least ten years prior to the interview, and some may have been addicts at the time of the interview. Access to the physicians was obtained through a variety of non-law-enforcement sources. The physicians had previously been asked by an intermediary if they would consent to be interviewed about their use of opiates, and all those interviewed had agreed to meet with the investigator who conducted the interviews.

The interviews were generally conducted in the office or home of the respondent and took an average of two hours. The format of the interview was simple: the respondent was asked to discuss his career, beginning with his first interest in medicine. If he did not mention his experience with opiates, he was asked to discuss it. Specific questions about the respondent's attitudes toward medicine and his early life were asked if he did not discuss these subjects in detail. He was asked about his youth, parents, career aspirations, health, and current family situation. The interviewer took notes on the physician's comments and these notes were content-analyzed into various content categories, which are summarized below.

Description of Interviewees

The physicians interviewed ranged in age from 28 to 78, with an average age of 44. There were 93 men and 5 women, 61 general practitioners and 37 specialists. All but one were married and 84 per cent had children.

The average age at which drug use began was 38. The average length of time since the addiction of the physicians interviewed had begun was six years. The range was one year to 22 years.

Of the physicians interviewed, 53 per cent had their practices in cities of over a million population, 33 per cent worked in communities of 250,000 to a million, and 12 per cent in communities of under 250,000. In contrast, 22 per cent were born in cities of over a million, 23 per cent in cities of 250,000 to a million, and 55 per cent were born in communities of under 250,000.

Every physician interviewed was in private practice and had some kind of hospital affiliations. None had been involved in any official or institutional research project on narcotics. The physicians interviewed ranged from a few who were less successful than the average in their professional careers to some who were extraordinarily successful national figures. The typical physician interviewed was more successful than the average, in terms of income, honorific and institutional affiliations, and general professional activity. Most were useful and effective members of their community. For example, one physician was brought to a private hospital for treatment by the public prosecutor in his community in order to avoid charges being preferred against him by the prosecutor.

Eighty per cent of the subjects were meperidine ("Demerol") addicts, 9 per cent took dilaudid, 7 per cent used morphine, and 4 per cent took codeine. Every subject interviewed was an addict and not a user, in terms of the traditional addiction criterion of daily use of an opiate. Some of the physicians took as much as 50 or 100 cc of meperidine daily, which is several times the amount given a hospital patient in considerable pain. Some physicians (2 per cent) turned themselves in for treatment because they were almost saturated with meperidine and it was having less and less effect. One man who was taking 50 cc a day said, "It's like drinking four or five gallons of water a day."

Most (74 per cent) of the respondents said that their wives had known of their addiction. Many (61 per cent) said that their nurses knew of their addiction, although there were no cases of contamination of the wife or nurse by the physician.

There appeared to be no significant socioeconomic differences between the respondent who was a minimal addict, taking a small dosage daily, and the heavy user who took a large dosage. It is possible to speculate that the minimal addict may be "more" addicted than the heavy user, because he is taking so little of the drug that he might be able to stop it altogether—yet he cannot do so.

In New York, meperidine is often called "the doctor's drug." Its label clearly states that its use should be discontinued if euphoria is noted. In spite of this caveat, the drug was selected by so many physicians for a number of reasons. They thought it less addicting and less toxic than other opiates. It is relatively available. The users thought its effects would be less visible than those of other narcotics. Its medical connotations made it more acceptable. There was a feeling that it was somehow easier for a physician to cure himself of meperidine addiction than of addiction to other drugs. Its being a synthetic opiate made it more attractive to some.

Law Enforcement and the Physician

Eight of the interviewees had had their license to practice revoked, 38 were on probation, 51 had completed probation, and one had not received any formal punitive action.

A small proportion of the physicians interviewed (4 per cent) sought help for their condition before they were apprehended or before some official or government functionary discussed their drug use with them. The rest (96 per cent) of those who were in trouble with the law did not seek help until they were apprehended or could tell that they were just about to be apprehended.

The physicians who had run afoul of the law enforcement agencies were treated relatively kindly by the law. One reason for this was probably that none had attempted to prescribe drugs for other addicts. Every physician who was taking drugs could have been charged with a crime. Only one, however, actually had been so charged, and only a few were arrested. The reason for the leniency afforded these physicians was perhaps not only the feeling that they would be punished enough by having their licenses to practice suspended for varying periods of time. It was probably also the assumption that they could be salvaged for the community and not lose their years of training and preparation for their careers.

Once a physician has begun taking drugs himself, he is likely to have difficulties in concealing his activities for any considerable length of time. The pharmacists and nurses or wives who observe their activities may report the physicians to state or federal authorities, who may have already observed unusual prescription activity on the part of a physician. None of the physicians interviewed was reported by either a colleague or a patient.

The physicians exhibited considerable ingenuity in obtaining drugs illegally. The most frequent method was to write prescriptions in a real or imaginary patient's name and use the drugs themselves. Others would give a patient a fraction of a dose and keep the rest for themselves. Some might order a standard 30 cc vial of meperidine for a patient in a hospital, give the patient a few cc, and keep the rest for themselves. Or they took what might be left from a hospital patient and withdrew it for "office use." Some might get drugs "in an emergency" from a friendly pharmacist without a prescription. Others might go to their hospital and feign having absent-mindedly left their prescription pads at their offices. All of these procedures, are, of course, illegal, and state and federal narcotics inspectors are on the alert for them.

A number of physicians (15 per cent) said that they were aware of the negative connotations of the way in which they got narcotics. "I've never done anything that has made me feel so degraded," said one respondent. "I went back to the hospital and told my nurse I had forgotten my prescription pad. She gave me some drugs and I took a shot. I knew it was wrong."

Federal or state narcotics law enforcement officials usually confront addict physicians with the evidence against them and turn them over to state licensing authorities who decide on the circumstances, if any, under which the physician will be able to practice. Some physicians were required to pay a fine and to demonstrate that they were not using drugs for a period of some years. Apprehended physicians are required to surrender their tax stamp which permits them to prescribe narcotics. The New York authorities have developed a procedure designed to protect the public against the addict physician while it assists the physician to rehabilitate himself. He usually has his license suspended and must demonstrate non-drug use for a year. He must agree to be treated by an approved physician and examined to check on his abstinence every three months for several years. A physician who has not demonstrated abstinence may have his license revoked.

Once confronted by state or federal authorities, the physicians usually said that they were relieved to be caught. They often said that they had been hoping someone would help them to stop drug use. No physician interviewed attempted to deny his use of narcotics once he had been caught.

Eighty-nine per cent of the physicians interviewed remained in the community in which they had been practicing, after being apprehended. There was practically no publicity about any of the cases. Where the physician had to leave his practice, he generally turned the practice over to a colleague and resumed it upon his return.

Physician Addicts and "Street" Addicts

The physician addicts interviewed differed in a number of ways from the typical "street" addict who buys drugs from a "pusher." The most obvious difference is that the age at which the physicians began to use drugs is just about the age that the typical addict stops using drugs, whether by "maturing out" or for other reasons. The "street" addict typically begins drug use in adolescence, while the physician begins when he is an established community and professional figure. The "street" addict takes heroin, while the typical physician addict took meperidine. The physician can get a pure quality of his drug, although it is not as strong as heroin. The "street" addict gets a diluted drug. He often starts with marijuana, although none of the physicians ever smoked marijuana.

The physician is usually discovered by the indirect evidence of a check of prescription records, while the "street" addict is usually arrested either because he has narcotics in his possession or has been observed making an illegal purchase. The physician is usually not arrested, while the typical "street" addict is arrested. Money to obtain drugs was not a problem for the physicians, as it usually is for the typical addict, who must steal in order to obtain money to buy drugs illegally. The physicians could use their professional access to narcotics to obtain drugs without much money. Even if they paid, the legal prices of narcotic drugs are very low.

Most non-physician addicts associate with other addicts. In contrast, the physicians interviewed almost never associated with other physician addicts, or did not do so knowingly. They did not have any occasion for doing so, either for the purpose of getting drugs or for passing time or for emotional support. They were solitary about their addiction. The "street" addict usually talks in a special jargon and often has a kind of wry insight into drug use, which stems from his extended discussions with his peers. The physicians did not talk in jargon and manifested very little insight into their drug use.

The typical "street" addict is not withdrawn in a medical setting. The physicians had almost all withdrawn in relatively comfortable medically supervised situations, so that there was little withdrawal distress. Seventy-four per cent had gone to a private hospital, usually under an assumed name; 11 per cent had gone to Lexington, and 15 per cent had made informal arrangements with friends and others.

"Street" addicts are likely to have been introduced to drugs by a contemporary. In contrast, none of the physicians interviewed had introduced anyone else to narcotic drugs or had "turned on" other physicians. It is possible to speculate that an addict physician, although he may not consciously wish to recruit addicts, may be unconsciously receptive to a patient who is especially eager for the physician to prescribe pain-killing drugs. He may identify with the patient's need and project his own need. Such a physician might possibly prescribe more drugs than the patient needs. It is possible, of course, that some addict physicians may be unusually sensitive to the possibility of patients becoming addicted and strive to prevent it. Twelve per cent of the respondents had come into contact with "street" addicts in hospitals. A typical reaction to such contact was, "I feel so degraded when I realize I'm like those people."

Factors Related to Drug Use

It took an average of two months of drug use for the physician to realize that he was addicted. The physician's professional knowledge of the qualities of opiates is certainly a factor in his using them himself, in terms of his knowledge of what effects they might have. His accessibility to drugs is not a complete explanation, because pharmacists are practically never addicted, even though they have much easier access to opiates than do physicians and can more easily manipulate their records.

It was possible to code several factors mentioned by the respondents as having been associated with their use of narcotics. In order of their incidence these themes could be categorized as overwork, physical ailments, self-concept, marital problems, level of aspiration, euphoric or depressing effect, liquor, insomnia, and age. A brief discussion of each theme follows, along with the proportion of respondents mentioning it. The total proportion of physicians interviewed who cited these themes came to 216 per cent, because many respondents mentioned more than one theme. Thus, the genesis of their drug use would appear to be multifactorial.

Overwork (41 per cent). Almost all of these respondents had come from lower class homes in communities of under 250,000, and practiced in big cities. These physicians usually mentioned their feeling low and depressed as a result of their overwork, and there appeared to be an association in their thinking between fatigue and depression. "Demerol builds up my resistance when I am working hard so quickly it is tremendous," said one respondent. "If I take some dilaudid, I might do eight perfect operations under pressure instead of two," said another who had said that he was overworked.

Overwork may mean different things to different physicians. Some of those interviewed were working so hard that, as one said, they might "end up as the richest doctor in the cemetery." Those who became addicted may have had some reasons either for working hard or for leading themselves to think that they were working hard, and for using their heavy schedules as the rationale for their drug use. Some seem to have almost created a situation of overwork so that they could use the overwork as an excuse for narcotics use. "Anyone who worked as hard as I did was entitled to a half of a grain of morphine each day," said one. Most of these physicians seem to have had an unrealistic notion of how long they could take drugs without becoming addicted.

Some of the respondents who talked of working very hard conveyed a feeling of resignation that medicine was so demanding, and some expressed negative feelings about having entered the profession. "I wonder why I ever got into medicine at all," or "This is not a field I'd recommend to anyone," were comments typical of these respondents. A number of these respondents mentioned that a parent, usually the mother, had wanted them to be physicians.

Physical Ailment (36 per cent). Five-sixths of the physical ailments reported by the physicians who said that their drug use was related to the ailment were gastrointestinal disorders, like ulcers and colitis. The others reported a variety of ailments. The ailments were all chronic conditions. All but one of the physicians who had reported physical complaints were treating the ailments by themselves, although a few had undergone surgery. The drugs they took usually alleviated both their pain and symptoms. It is curious that practically none of the physicians with ailments commented on the unusualness of opiates alleviating the symptoms of the relatively serious ailments which they had.

Although none of these physicians discussed their addiction with physician colleagues, some (27 per cent) said that when they discussed their physical ailments with colleagues they mentioned the narcotics they were taking for pain relief. "I told a friend I was taking Demerol for my stomach," said one respondent. This kind of disclosure to a physician may have been one way in which the addict physician justified his regular use of narcotics to himself.

Self-Concept (32 per cent). About a third of those interviewed said that they were surprised at becoming addicted. "I felt I could take a shot when a crisis arose," "I felt I could stop at any time," and "I thought I'd toy with it because I knew enough about it to inhibit its reaction and control its use," were typical comments made by this group. "I thought I was above getting addicted," said another physician. Their professional familiarity with the effects of drugs appears to have provided a rationale for their semi-magical belief that the drugs would somehow have a different effect on them than they had on non-physicians. Addicts other than physicians often believe that they can control the effects of drugs, or "take just one more shot," or reduce their intake. The physicians cited many of these rationalizations in clarifying their surprise at becoming addicted. The majority of these physicians believed that they were too smart to become "hooked."

Marital Problems (31 per cent). These physicians voiced a

wide range of marital difficulties. The largest proportion of these respondents said that their wives were to aggressive and driving. A number said that they should have gotten a divorce, and some expressed other kinds of dissatisfaction with their wives. None of these physicians had taken any action toward a divorce or separation. A number of these physicians were also among those who reported physical ailments.

Level of Aspiration (24 per cent). These physicians generally had a history of disaffection toward and disagreement with their profession, usually coupled with a record of considerable achievement within the profession. They often were officers of their college pre-medical society, and tended to be good students in both college and medical school. Their level of aspiration and competitive spirit tended to be high.

For the physicians in this group who developed physical symptoms, the illness appeared to have been perceived as a very threatening interference with their fantasies about their success. The pain associated with their illness may have occasioned almost a panic in the physicians, and one way in which they may have coped with the panic was to begin taking drugs. The drugs they took were usually effective in the physicians' attempts to cope with their pain. This diminution of pain may have provided the physicians with a variety of further rationalizations for drug use.

It is possible to speculate that the high level of aspiration and competitive spirit of these physicians was so integral a part of their personality that it may have been very difficult for them to express their disaffection toward medicine because their medical career was the embodiment of their level of aspiration. The aggressiveness and disaffection may have thus been partially drained off by drug use.

Euphoric or Depressing Effect (21 per cent). These physicians specifically mentioned the drug's effect on their mood. Most of these physicians said that the drugs made them feel good and improved their work. "I realized that here was something I'd been looking for all my life, and the last piece of the jigsaw puzzle fell into place," said one.

There were others who said that the drug lost its stimulus

effect after a while, and "I just took it to keep alive. It made me feel depressed and slow." These physicians tended to say that the continued use of opiates interfered with their work.

Liquor (17 per cent). These physicians said that they had been drinking fairly heavily before they began using drugs. Most of these respondents had been drinking by college and medical school days. Some began narcotics use because "You can't walk into an operation reking of liquor on your breath." Two had switched from alcohol to barbiturates before using opiates. Others began because "Alcohol makes you fumble," and they could function with opiates but not with alcohol. Some began opiate use, either self-prescribed or prescribed by others, as one way of coping with hangovers from liquor. Whatever needs were met by alcohol were apparently also met by narcotics, since none of these physicians continued drinking after beginning narcotics use. None of the physicians who had been heavy drinkers before their addiction had returned to liquor after stopping drug use. Few of those who drank also reported somatic complaints. A number of the drinkers generally had negative things to say about their profession.

Insomnia (11 per cent). The physicians who were insomniacs were among the most intelligent interviewed. They seemed to have special difficulties in talking about their feelings. They were likely to report marital difficulties and disaffection toward medicine. Some of the physicians who cited their overwork said that they began drug use because they fell asleep more easily after taking a shot, and thus saved time in falling asleep and thus had more time available for their practice.

Age (3 per cent). A small number of the physicians interviewed were older men, in their 60's and 70's, who became addicted during World War II. These men said that they had retired or semi-retired and were called back to practice, over their objections, because of the wartime shortage of physicians. Most of them were from non-urban areas, whose practices covered a fairly extended geographic area. They reported difficulties in meeting the increasing demands on them and in getting along with little sleep. They began taking a small dose of morphine in order to relieve fatigue and keep going. All of these physicians had ceased taking narcotics fairly soon after they returned to retirement, after the war.

Return to Drug Use

Over half the respondents had stopped drug use and then reverted, at least once. The circumstances of return to drug use varied. The physicians did not generally appear able to explain it. One said, "I got into a taxi to go to the hospital for an operation. Suddenly, as if it were another person inside me, I stopped the taxi at a pharmacy and got a shot." Another had gone to a ranch "cure" for three months, said he "felt great" there, and had taken some drugs within an hour after his return to his office. Some physicians returned to drug use after a period of abstinence while in the middle of an investigation by an official agency, which could not help but uncover their reversion. One physician had been withdrawn and spent a month at a hospital, and went to a movie in a nearby city one afternoon. When he returned to the hospital that evening, he said that he had actually gone to his private office for the purpose of getting a shot. One physician returned to drug use after 19 years of abstinence. As in the case of non-physician addicts, logic did not appear to be very influential in assisting many of these physicians in remaining off drugs.

Of the respondents who had been to the U.S. Public Health Service Hospital at Lexington, most had remained off drugs. One said of the hospital: "Lexington cured me forever. It made me acutely aware of how sick I was, and I decided never again. I was so shaken that I never even got another narcotic tax stamp." One of the few Lexington patients who reverted said, "The hospital helped me. I realized I could get a shot in my vein that would be better than one in my arm."

Prognosis

The prognosis for many of these physicians can only be regarded as guarded. A licensed physician who has to engage in subterfuge to get drugs and who is aware of the implications of drug use, and who only seeks help when crisis or the law threatens, may not be a good risk for abstinence. "You have to fudge so much to get your drugs," as one physician said, that an addict physician who has been so willing to "fudge" may have difficulties in giving up narcotics. He has to do so many things that are destructive in order to get drugs that his addiction may be relatively salient.

However, it has been estimated by one student that 85 per cent of addicted physicians return to their practice and to a drug-free life, with the other 15 per cent deteriorating or committing suicide.[9] This high recovery rate is attributed to a considerable extent to the physician's recollection of the agreeable way of life that he enjoyed before addiction.

A variety of methods of abstinence was mentioned by the physicians who had stayed off drugs successfully for a period of several years. Most had had several periods of relapse, with the periods of time between reversion becoming longer and longer. Many took "milder" drugs like paregoric to ease the transition. Some adjusted their external schedules in order to minimize temptation: "I made up my mind to handle only the amount of practice I could handle without fatigue." Those in pain decided to be uncomfortable and live with pain rather than take drugs. Others had a version of the Coue method: "Every morning I make up my mind that nothing will make me take drugs today." A very few of the physicians had sought psychiatric help. Wives and colleagues did not seem to have much of a role in assisting the physician to get off drugs.

Discussion

The established sociological theories of deviant behavior and of addiction do not completely explain the narcotics use of these physicians. The Mertonian theory of deviant behavior as a reflection of differences in the legitimate means of access to culturally prescribed goals does not appear to be relevant to these physicians, who had achieved such goals publicly and legitimately. The traditional explanation of addiction as the result of socialization in a particular kind of delinquent subculture does not appear to be immediately useful in explaining the addiction of these physicians. It was not possible to find even one addicted physician who was either Puerto Rican or Negro, the two subcultural groups most heavily represented in the general addict population.

In general, the social correlates of the physicians' addiction emerged less clearly than did the personality correlates.

There did appear to be some elements which a number of the physicians interviewed might have in common with other addicts. The physicians whose addiction appeared to have been related to their self-concept (32 per cent) and to their high level of aspiration (24 per cent) were essentially expressing fantasies of a kind common in other addicts. Opiate use enables the user to remove himself temporarily from the world of demanding external reality to a world in which his fantasies of achievement and power can be exercised.

The physicians who mentioned marital difficulties (31 per cent) were reflecting a common theme in the lives of many addicts. Although the typical addict is relatively unlikely to marry, when he does, he is often likely to marry the kind of aggressive wife described by these physicians.

Another dimension mentioned by the physicians was the actual euphoric or depressing effect of the drug (21 per cent), which is similar to what is reported by other addicts. Like other addicts, a number of respondents (11 per cent) reported insomnia. Addicts often have difficulties in falling asleep, possibly for the same reasons that they have difficulties in recalling dreams—perhaps because the free expression of feelings possible during sleep via dreams may be perceived as theatening.

There were a number of themes in the physicians' discussions of their addiction which are not usually found in other addicts. Most non-physician addicts do not complain of overwork, and are not even likely to have a regular job. Most addicts do not have an associated physical ailment. Since the addict often regards the alcoholic as an inferior "wino," drinking is not too frequently associated with addiction, although 17 per cent of the physicians were drinkers before they became drug users. There is probably also no analogue in the general addict population for the older physicians who began using narcotics during World War II.

These physicians do have some similarity to the addicted jazz musicians seen since 1957 at the Musicians' Clinic in New York. The musicians were all fairly successful in their profession and began to use heroin in their twenties as one way of coping with various reality problems, like those stemming from their work or marriage. The musicians also showed considerable interest in liquor. A number of them used drinking as one way of cushioning their leaving the use of drugs, whereas none of the physicians did this. The musicians had all sought psychiatric help at the Clinic, whereas practically none of the physicians had sought such help.

It is possible to speculate that there are probably several basic and different reasons for physicians' use of drugs, and that there is probably no one addict physician for whom all of the reasons are relevant. The factors that appear to be related to physicians' drug use, as reported by the physicians, are all problems that have confronted many other physicians. Yet only a small proportion of the physicians confronted by these problems became drug users. Perhaps there are some underlying threads that may run through a number of the external reasons for drug use cited by the respondents. We may speculate that there may be perhaps four such underlying threads: the addict physician's role strain, his passivity, his omnipotence, and the effects of the drug.

Role Strain. In the sample interviewed there were a number of respondents who had negative attitudes toward being physicians. Most of them are likely to have grown up in a small community and moved to a big city, to have been pushed into medicine by a parent, and to have moved up and out of the lower classes when they became physicians. They thus may have found themselves occupying a role which posed a variety of kinds of role strain. One way in which they could respond to such strain was by overwork, which may have provided less and less time to think about their dissatisfaction with their occupation. Another way of responding was by drinking. It is perhaps more than a coincidence that most of the drinkers had begun using liquor around college and medical school, at just about the time that their career commitment was made. Insomnia was another way of expressing role strain. The few older physicians who returned to practice during World War II clearly exhibited role strain.

If this hypothesis of role strain as an important underlying contributor to physician drug use is correct, it helps to explain some of the intermediate steps that seem to be related to narcotics use and that were identified by the respondents. About two-thirds of the physicians were following individualistic careers and one-third were following colleagues careers, in Hall's terminology.[10] Preoccupation with success, status, and income characterized the group interviewed, whereas there was not one example of Hall's person-centered friendly career. The struggle to get recognition professionally may have been so difficult and demanding that the physicians could barely experience their negative feelings about their profession while becoming established. By their late thirties, these respondents could confront the fruits of their hard work and of their status and role. Perhaps one effect of this kind of confrontation was related to their beginning drug use.

Passivity. It is well established that many narcotic addicts have an underlying passivity, which they reinforce by taking drugs. Physicians are so active and busy that it is difficult to see how they could be described as passive. The substantial number of physicians interviewed reporting physical ailments and marital difficulties suggests that their passivity may have manifested itself in significant but indirect ways.

The majority of the physicians with ailments had gastrointesinal disorders like ulcers or colitis. It has been fairly well established that these ailments are often methods by which certain conflicts are handled by some passive people. Ulcers seem to be related to a typical conflict situation involving a dependent person's seeking accomplishment and self-sufficiency, and colitis often first manifests itself when the individual faces a life situation which requires an outstanding accomplishment for which he feels unprepared.[11] Perhaps as one way of sustaining their illness, most of the respondents were treating themselves, in spite of the established medical principle that physicians ought not to treat their own illnesses. The physician's illness may thus have been a socially approved form of deviant behavior through which he could express the conflict between his passivity and the demanding and active role of the physician, until his use of narcotics provided him with another avenue for the expression of the conflict.

Passivity also manifested itself indirectly in the respondents who reported marital problems. These problems were generally related to their wives' being domineering. It is usually relatively passive men who marry domineering women. In spite of their complaints, none of these respondents had taken any action to improve their marriage situation, thus further underscoring their passivity.

Omnipotence. The self-concept of a number of the interviewees appeared to have been very high, and in some cases to have included fantasies of omnipotence. Such fantasies are common in other addicts. They may have been especially congenial to physicians because the physician's work makes it easy for him to have feelings of power over others and of grandiosity. It is perhaps an easy step from such feelings to believing that he can control the effect of an opiate.

The high level of aspiration of some of the respondents also may reflect feelings of omnipotence. Although they generally demonstrated considerable ability and achievement in their profession, their fantasies of what they might achieve left many dissatisfied. One physician, for example, dated his drug use from the day that he was told that he would not be getting attending privileges as a specialist at a particular hospital. He was so sure he would be granted these privileges that the disappointment of not doing so was directly related to his use of drugs.

It is possible that achievement was as much of a threat as non-achievement to some respondents. One said, "I was fighting to be top man for all those years, but when I reached the top, what did I have?" He began drug use because he felt that his victories were hollow, and there were no more conquests to make. No matter how successful such a man might be, his omnipotence would leave him restless. A number of these physicians began drug use when they had reached a stage in life at which they could begin to implement their omnipotence, and such implementation seemingly posed grave problems. Not one of the respondents reported any interest in drugs in the early stages of his career, even amidst the stress and demands of internship and the early stages of establishing a practice.

Effects of the drug. One ultimate dimension of drug use by physicians is the drug's effect on its users. The effect of the opiate appears to be mediated by the personality of the physician user. Some users feel better and other users feel worse after taking opiates. The relationships between either the euphoric or depressing effect of the opiate and other factors related to its use are not clear.

Some combination of these factors of role strain, passivity, omnipotence, and effects of the drug appear to underlie the narcotics use of the physicians interviewed. These factors may predispose physicians to addiction in a wide variety of external situations and environments. If these or similar factors are not present, the physician may not become addicted even in extremely taxing environments. No external situation, by itself, can be taxing enough to drive a physician to becoming addicted. Thus, there is not one recorded case of a Jewish physician who was in a Nazi concentration camp who became a drug addict during or after his incarceration. It would be difficult to imagine a more demanding situation than an experience in a concentration camp.

The external situations that faced the physician addicts interviewed, however, were perceived and experienced by the physicians themselves in a manner that gave rise to the deviant behavior of drug use. These physicians appear to have been addiction-prone through some combination of role strain, passivity, omnipotence, and effects of the drug. It is of course possible that the physicians interviewed are not typical of other addict physicians, or that they may be reflecting regional or other special factors.

1. National Opinion Research Corporation, "Jobs and Occupations: A Popular Evaluation," *Opinion News*, 9 (September 1, 1947), 3-13.

2. "Interview with Hon. Harry J. Anslinger," *Modern Medicine*, 25 (October 15, 1957), 170-191.

3. J. DeWitt Fox, "Narcotic Addiction Among Physicians," *Journal of the Michigan State Medical Society*, 56 (February, 1957), 214-217.

4. Her Majesty's Government, *Report to the United Nations on the Working of the International Treaties on Narcotic Drugs*, London, 1955.

5. Lawrence Kolb, "The Drug Addiction Muddle," *Police*, 1 (January-February, 1957), 57-62.

6. Alfred R. Lindesmith, *Opiate Addiction*, Evanston: Principia Press, 1947, p. 60.

7. Michael J. Pescor, "Physician Drug Addicts," *Diseases of the Nervous System*, 3 (June, 1942), 173-174.

8. Robert W. Rasor and H. James Crecraft, "Addiction to Meperidine," *Journal of the American Medical Association*, 157 (February 19, 1955), 654-657.

9. Edward R. Bloomquist, "The Doctor, The Nurse, and Narcotic Addicting," *GP*, 18 (November, 1958), 124-129.

10. Oswald Hall, "Types of Medical Careers," *American Journal of Sociology*, 55 (November, 1949), 243-253.

11. Franz Alexander, *Psychosomatic Medicine*, New York: W. W. Norton, 1950, 102-132.

CATS, KICKS, AND COLOR

HAROLD FINESTONE

Growing recognition that the most recent manifestation of the use of opiates in this country has been predominantly a young peoples' problem has resulted in some speculation as to the nature of this generation of drug users. Is it possible to form an accurate conception as to what "manner of man" is represented by the current species of young drug addict? Intensive interviews between 1951 and 1953 with over fifty male colored users of heroin in their late teens and early twenties selected from several of the areas of highest incidence of drug use in Chicago served to elicit from them the expression of many common attitudes, values, schemes of behavior, and general social orientation. Moreover, since there was every reason to believe that such similarities had preceded their introduction to heroin, it appeared that it was by virtue of such shared features that they had been unusually receptive to the spread of opiate use. Methodologically, their common patterns of behavior suggested the heuristic value of the construction of a social type. The task of this paper is to depict this social type, and to present a hypothetical formulation to account for the form it has taken.

No special justification appears to be necessary for concentrating in this paper on the social type of the young colored drug

This investigation was supported by research grant 3M 9030 from the National Institute of Mental Health, Public Health Service, and was carried on under the direction of Clifford R. Shaw and Solomon Kobrin. The writer acknowledges the generous assistance received in the clarification of the problems dealt with in this paper through discussion with Clifford R. Shaw, Henry D. McKay, and Solomon Kobrin, supervising sociologists at the Illinois Institute for Juvenile Research and the Chicago Area Project.

users. One of the distinctive properties of the distribution of drug use as a social problem, at least in Chicago, is its high degree of both spatial and racial concentration. In fact, it is a problem which in this city can be pinpointed with great accuracy as having its incidence preponderantly among the young male colored persons in a comparatively few local community areas. The following delineation of the generic characteristics of young colored drug users constitutes in many respects an ideal type. No single drug addict exemplified all of the traits to be depicted but all of them revealed several of them to a marked degree.

The young drug user was a creature of contrasts. Playing the role of the fugitive and pariah as he was inevitably forced to do, he turned up for interviews in a uniformly ragged and dirty condition. And yet he talked with an air of superiority derived from his identification with an elite group, the society of "cats." He came in wearing a non-functional tie clip attached to his sport shirt and an expensive hat as the only indications that he was concerned with his appearance and yet displayed in his conversation a highly developed sense of taste in men's clothing and a high valuation upon dressing well. He came from what were externally the drabbest, most overcrowded, and physically deteriorated sections of the city and yet discussed his pattern of living as though it were a consciously cultivated work of art.

Despite the location of his social world in the "asphalt jungle" of the "blackbelt," he strictly eschewed the use of force and violence as a technique for achieving his ends or for the settling of problematic situations. He achieved his goals by indirection, relying, rather, on persuasion and on a repertoire of manipulative techniques. To deal with a variety of challenging situations, such as those arising out of his contacts with the police, with his past or potential victims, and with jilted "chicks," etc., he used his wits and his conversational ability. To be able to confront such contingencies with adequacy and without resort to violence was to be "cool." His idea was to get what he wanted through persuasion and ingratiation; to use the other fellow by deliberately outwitting him. Indeed, he regarded himself as immeasurably superior to the "gorilla," a person who resorted to force.

The image of himself as "operator" was projected onto the

whole world about him and led to a complete scepticism as to other persons' motives. He could relate to people by outsmarting them, or through openhanded and often ruinous generosity, but his world seemed to preclude any relationship which was not part of a "scheme" or did not lend itself to an "angle." The most difficult puzzle for him to solve was the "square," the honest man. On the one hand the "square" was the hard-working plodder who lived by routine and who took honesty and the other virtues at their face value. As such he constituted the prize victim for the cat. On the other hand the cat harbored the sneaking suspicion that some squares were smarter than he, because they could enjoy all the forbidden pleasures which were his stock in trade and maintain a reputation for respectability in the bargain.

The cat had a large, colorful, and discriminating vocabulary which dealt with all phases of his experience with drugs. In addition, he never seemed to content himself with the conventional word for even the most commonplace objects. Thus he used "pad" for house, "pecks" for food, "flicks" for movies, "stick hall" for pool hall, "dig the scene" for observe, "box" for record player, "bread" for money, etc. In each instance the word he used was more concrete or earthier than the conventional word and such as to reveal an attitude of subtle ridicule toward the dignity and conventionality inherent in the common usage.

His soft convincing manner of speaking, the shocking earthiness and fancifulness of his vocabulary, together with the formidable gifts of charm and ingratiation which he deployed, all contributed to the dominant impression which the young drug user made as a person. Such traits would seem to have fitted naturally into a role which some cats had already played or aspired to play, that of the pimp. To be supported in idleness and luxury through the labors of one or more attractive "chicks" who shoplifted or engaged in prostitution or both and dutifully handed over the proceeds was one of his favorite fantasies. In contrast with the milieu of the white underworld, the pimp was not an object of opprobrium but of prestige.

The theme of the exploitation of the woman goes close to the heart of the cat's orientation to life, that is, his attitude toward work. Part of the cat's sense of superiority stems from his aristocratic disdain for work and for the subordination of self to superiors and to the repetitive daily routine entailed by work, which he regards as intolerable. The "square" is a person who toils for regular wages and who takes orders from his superiors without complaint.

In contrast with the "square," the cat gets by without working. Instead he keeps himself in "bread" by a set of ingenious variations on "begging, borrowing, or stealing." Each cat has his "hustle,"[1] and a "hustle" is any non-violent means of "making some bread" which does not require work. One of the legendary heroes of the cat is the man who is such a skillful con-man that he can sell "State Street" to his victim. Concretely, the cat is a petty thief, pickpocket, or pool shark, or is engaged in a variety of other illegal activities of the "conning" variety. A very few cats are actually living off the proceeds of their women "on the hustle."

The main purpose of life for the cat is to experience the "kick." Just as every cat takes pride in his "hustle," so every cat cultivates his "kick." A "kick" is any act tabooed by "squares" that heightens and intensifies the present moment of experience and differentiates it as much as possible from the humdrum routine of daily life. Sex in any of its conventional expressions is not a "kick" since this would not serve to distinguish the cat from the "square," but orgies of sex behavior and a dabbling in the various perversions and byways of sex pass muster as "kicks." Some "cats" are on an alcohol "kick," others on a marihuana "kick, and others on a heroin "kick." There is some interchangeability among these various "kicks" but the tendency is to select your "kick" and stay with it. Many of these young drug users, however, had progressed from the alcohol to the marihuana to the heroin "kick." Each "kick" has its own lore of appreciation and connoisseurship into which only its devotees are initiated.

In addition to his "kick" the cat sets great store on the enjoyment of music and on proper dress. To enjoy one's "kick" without a background of popular music is inconceivable. The cat's world of music has a distinct galaxy of stars, and the brightest luminaries in his firmament are performers such as "Yardbird" (the late Charlie Parker) and disc jockeys such as Al Benson. Almost every cat is a frustrated musician who hopes some day to get his "horn" out of pawn, take lessons, and earn fame and fortune in the field of "progressive music."

The cat places a great deal of emphasis upon clothing and exercises his sartorial talents upon a skeletal base of suit, sport shirt, and hat. The suit itself must be conservative in color. Gaiety is introduced through the selection of the sport shirt and the various accessories, all so chosen and harmonized as to reveal an exquisite sense of taste. When the cat was not talking about getting his clothes out of pawn, he talked about getting them out of the cleaners. With nonchalant pride one drug user insisted that the most expensive sport shirts and hats in the city of Chicago were sold in a certain haberdashery on the South Side. The ideal cat would always appear in public impeccably dressed and be able to sport a complete change of outfit several times a day.

The cat seeks through a harmonious combination of charm, ingratiating speech, dress, music, the proper dedication to his "kick," and unrestrained generosity to make of his day-to-day life itself a gracious work of art. Everything is to be pleasant and everything he does and values is to contribute to a cultivated aesthetic approach to living. The "cool cat" exemplifies all of these elements in proper balance. He demonstrates his ability to "play it cool" in his unruffled manner of dealing with outsiders such as the police, and in the self-assurance with which he confronts emergencies in the society of "cats." Moreover, the "cat" feels himself to be any man's equal. He is convinced that he can go anywhere and mingle easily with anyone. For example, he rejects the type of music designated "the blues" because for him it symbolizes attitudes of submission and resignation which are repugnant and alien to his customary frame of mind.

It can be seen now why heroin use should make such a powerful appeal to the cat. It was the ultimate "kick." No substance was more profoundly tabooed by conventional middle-class society. Regular heroin use provides a sense of maximal social differentiation from the "square." The cat was at last engaged, he felt, in an activity completely beyond the comprehension of the "square." No other "kick" offered such an instantaneous intensification of the immediate moment of experience and set it apart from everyday experience in such spectacular fashion. Any words used by the cat to apply to the "kick," the experience of "being high," he applied to heroin in the superlative. It was the "greatest kick of them all."

In the formulation now to be presented, the cat as a social type is viewed as a manifestation of a process of social change in which a new type of self-conception has been emerging among the adolescents of the lower socioeconomic levels of the colored population in large urban centers. It is a self-conception rooted in the types of accommodation to a subordinate status achieved historically by the colored race in this country, a self-conception which has become increasingly articulated as it responded to and selected various themes from the many available to it in the milieu of the modern metropolis. Blumer's classification of social movements into general, specific, or expressive appears to provide a useful framework for the analysis of the social type of the cat.[2]

In terms of these categories the cat as a social type is the personal counterpart of an expressive social movement. The context for such a movement must include the broader community, which, by its policies of social segregation and discrimination, has withheld from individuals of the colored population the opportunity to achieve or to identify with status positions in the larger society. The social type of the cat is an expression of one possible type of adaptation to such blocking and frustation, in which a segment of the population turns in upon itself and attempts to develop within itself criteria for the achievement of social status and the rudiments of a satisfactory social life. Within his own isolated social world the cat attempts to give form and purpose to dispositions derived from but denied an outlet within the dominant social order.

What are these dispositions and in what sense may they be said to be derived from the dominant social order? Among the various interrelated facets of the life of the cat two themes are central, those of the "hustle" and the "kick." It is to be noted that they are in direct antithesis to two of the central values of the dominant culture, the "hustle" versus the paramount importance of the occupation for the male in our society, and the "kick" versus the importance of regulating conduct in terms of its future consequences. Thus, there appears to be a relationship of conflict between the central themes of the social type of the cat and those of the dominant social order. As a form of expressive behavior, however, the social type of the cat represents an indirect rather than a direct attack against central conventional values.

It is interesting to speculate on the reasons why a type such as the cat should emerge rather than a social movement with the objective of changing the social order. The forces coercing the selective process among colored male adolescents in the direction of expressive social movements are probably to be traced to the long tradition of accommodation to a subordinate status on the part of the Negro as well as to the social climate since the Second World War, which does not seem to have been favorable to the formation of specific social movements.

The themes of the "hustle" and "kick" in the social orientation of the cat are facts which appear to be overdetermined. For example, to grasp the meaning of the "hustle" to the cat one must understand it as a rejection of the obligation of the adult male to work. When asked for the reasons underlying his rejection of work the cat did not refer to the uncongenial and relatively unskilled and low paid jobs which, in large part, were the sole types of employment available to him. He emphasized rather that the routine of a job and the demand that he should apply himself continuously to his work task were the features that made work intolerable for him. The self-constraint required by work was construed as an unwarranted damper upon his love of spontaneity. The other undesirable element from his point of view was the authoritarian setting of most types of work with which he was familiar.

There are undoubtedly many reasons for the cat's rejection of work, but the reasons he actually verbalized are particularly significant when interpreted as devices for sustaining his self-conception. The cat's feeling of superiority would be openly challenged were he to confront certain of the social realities of his situation, such as the discrimination exercised against colored persons looking for work and the fact that only the lowest status jobs are available to him. He avoided any mention of these factors which would have forced him to confront his true position in society and thus posed a threat to his carefully cherished sense of superiority.

In emphasizing as he does the importance of the "kick" the cat is attacking the value our society places upon planning for the future and the responsibility of the individual for such planning. Planning always requires some subordination and disciplining of present behavior in the interest of future rewards. The individual plans to go to college, plans for his career, plans for his family and children, etc. Such an orientation on the part of the individual is merely the personal and subjective counterpart of a stable social order and of stable social institutions, which not only permit but sanction an orderly progression of expectations with reference to others and to one's self. Where such stable institutions are absent or in the inchoate stages of development, there is little social sanction for such planning in the experience of the individual. Whatever studies are available strongly suggest that such are the conditions which tend to prevail in the lower socio-economic levels of the Negro urban community.[3] Stable family and community organization is lacking in those areas of the city where drug use is concentrated. A social milieu which does not encourage the subordination and disciplining of present conduct in the interests of future rewards tends by default to enhance the present. The "kick" appears to be a logical culmination of this emphasis.

Accepting the emergence of the self-conception of the cat as evidence of a developing expressive social movement, we may phrase the central theoretical problem as follows: What are the distinctive and generic features of the cat's social orientation? Taking a cue from the work of Huizinga as developed in *Homo Ludens*,[4] we propose that the generic characteristics of the social type of the cat are those of play. In what follows, Huizinga's conception of play as a distinctive type of human activity will be presented and then applied as a tool of analysis for rendering intelligible the various facets of the social orientation of the cat. It is believed that the concept of play indicates accurately the type of expressive social movement which receives its embodiment in the cat.

According to Huizinga the concept of play is a primary element of human experience and as such is not susceptible to exact definition.

"The *fun* of playing resists all analysis, all logical interpretation. . . . Nevertheless it is precisely this fun-element that characterizes the essence of play."[5] The common image of the young colored drug addict pictures him as a pitiful figure, a trapped unfortunate. There is a certain amount of truth in this image but it does not correspond to the conception which the young colored addict has of himself or to the impression that he tries to communicate to others. If it were entirely true it would be difficult to square with the fact that substantial numbers of young colored persons continue to become drug users. The cat experiences and manifests a certain zest in his mode of life which is far from self-pity. This fun element seemed to come particularly to the fore as the cat recounted his search for "kicks," the adventure of his life on the streets, and the intensity of his contest against the whole world to maintain his supply of drugs. Early in the cycle of heroin use itself there was invariably a "honeymoon" stage when the cat abandoned himself most completely to the experience of the drug. For some cats this "honeymoon" stage, in terms of their ecstatic preoccupation with the drug, was perpetual. For others it passed, but the exigencies of an insatiable habit never seemed to destroy completely the cat's sense of excitement in his way of life.

While Huizinga declines to define play, he does enumerate three characteristics which he considers to be proper to play. Each one of them when applied to the cat serves to indicate a generic feature of his social orientation.

(a) "First and foremost . . . all play is a voluntary activity."[6] "Here we have the first main characteristic of play: that it is free, is in fact freedom."[7] The concept of an expressive social movement assumes a social situation where existing social arrangements are frustrating and are no longer accepted as legitimate and yet where collective activity directed toward the modification of these limitations is not possible. The cat is "free" in the sense that he is a pre-eminent candidate for new forms of social organization and novel social practices. He is attempting to escape from certain features of the historical traditions of the Negro which he regards as humiliating. As an adolescent or young adult he is not fully assimilated into such social institutions as the family, school, church, or industry which may be available to him. Moreover, the social institutions which the Negroes brought with them when they migrated to the city have not as yet achieved stability or an adequate functioning relationship to the urban environment. As a Negro, and particularly as a Negro of low socioeconomic status, he is excluded from many socializing experiences which adolescents in more advantaged sectors of the society take for granted. He lives in communities where the capacity of the population for effective collective action is extremely limited, and consequently there are few effective controls on his conduct besides that exercised by his peer group itself. He is fascinated by the varied "scenes" which the big city spreads out before him. Granted this setting, the cat adopts an adventurous attitude to life and is free to give his allegiance to new forms of activity.

(b) . . . A second characteristic is closely connected with this (that is, the first characteristic of freedom), namely, that play is not "ordinary" or "real" life. It is rather a stepping out of "real" life into a temporary sphere of activity with a disposition all of its own. Every child knows perfectly well that he is "only pretending," or that it was "only for fun." . . . This "only pretending" quality of play betrays a consciousness of the inferiority of play compared with "seriousness," a feeling that seems to be something as primary as play itself. Nevertheless . . . the consciousness of play being "only a pretend" does not by any means prevent it from proceeding with the utmost seriousness, with an absorption, a devotion that passes into rapture and, temporarily at least, completely abolishes that troublesome "only" feeling.[8]

It is implicit in the notion of an expressive social movement that, since direct collective action to modify the sources of dissatisfaction and restlessness is not possible, all such movements should appear under one guise, as forms of "escape." Persons viewing the problem of addiction from the perspective of the established social structure have been prone to make this interpretation. It is a gross oversimplification, however, as considered from the perspective of the young drug addict himself. The emergence of the self-conception of the cat is an attempt to deal with the problems of status and identity in a situation where participation in the life of the broader community is denied, but where the colored adolescent is becoming increasingly sensitive to the values, the goals, and the notions of success which obtain in the dominant social order.

The caste pressures thus make it exceedingly difficult for an American Negro to preserve a true perspective of himself and his own group in relation to the larger white society. The increasing abstract knowledge of the world outside—of its opportunities, its rewards, its different norms of competition and cooperation—which results from the proceeding acculturation at the same time as there is increasing group isolation, only increases the tensions.[9]

Such conditions of group isolation would appear to be fairly uniform throughout the Negro group. Although this isolation may be experienced differently at different social levels of the Negro community, certain features of the adaptations arrived at in response to this problem will tend to reveal similarities. Since the struggle for status takes place on a stage where there is acute sensitivity to the values and status criteria of the dominant white group, but where access to the means through which such values may be achieved is prohibited, the status struggle turning in on itself will assume a variety of distorted forms. Exclusion from the "serious" concerns of the broader community will result in such adaptations manifesting a strong element of "play."

Frazier in *Black Bourgeoisie* discusses the social adaptation of the Negro middle class as "The World of Make-Believe."

The emphasis upon "social" life or "society" is one of the main props of the world of make-believe into which the black bourgeoisie has sought an escape from its inferiority and frustrations in American society. This world of make-believe, to be sure, is a reflection of the values of American society, but it lacks the economic basis that would give it roots in the world of reality.[10]

In the Negro lower classes the effects of frustrations deriving from subordination to the whites may not be experienced as personally or as directly as they are by the Negro middle class, but the massive effects of residential segregation and the lack of stable social institutions and community organization are such as to reinforce strong feelings of group isolation even at the lowest levels of the society.

It is here suggested that the function performed by the emergence of the social type of the cat among Negro lower class adolescents is analogous to that performed by "The World of Make-Believe" in the Negro middle class. The development of a social type such as that of the cat is only possible in a situation where there is isolation from the broader community but great sensitivity to its goals, where the peer group pressures are extremely powerful, where institutional structures are weak, where models of success in the illegitimate world have strong appeals, where specific social movements are not possible, and where novel forms of behavior have great prestige. To give significance to his experience, the young male addict has developed the conception of a heroic figure, the "ideal cat," a person who is completely adequate to all situations, who controls his "kick" rather than letting it control him, who has a lucrative "hustle," who has no illusions as to what makes the world "tick," who is any man's equal, who basks in the admiration of his brother cats and associated "chicks," who hob-nobs with "celebs" of the musical world, and who in time himself may become a celebrity.

The cat throws himself into his way of life with a great deal of intensity but he cannot escape completely from the perspective, the judgments, and the sanctions of the dominant social order. He has to make place in his scheme of life for police, lockups, jails, and penitentiaries, to say nothing of the agonies of withdrawal distress. He is forced eventually to confront the fact that his role as a cat with its associated attitudes is largely a pose, a form of fantasy with little basis in fact. With the realization that he is addicted he comes only too well to know that he is a "junky," and he is fully aware of the conventional attitudes toward addicts as well as of the counter-rationalizations provided by his peer group. It is possible that the cat's vacillation with regard to seeking a cure for his addiction is due to a conflict of perspectives, whether to view his habit from the cat's or the dominant social order's point of view.

(c) Play is distinct from "ordinary" life both as to locality and duration. This is the third main characteristic of play: its secludedness, its limitedness. It is "played out" within certain limits of time and place. It contains its own course and meaning."[11]

It is this limited, esoteric character of heroin use which gives to the cat the feeling of belonging to an elite. It is the restricted extent of the distribution of drug use, the scheming and intrigue associated with underground "connections" through which drugs are obtained, the secret lore of the appreciation of the drug's effects, which give the cat the exhilaration of participating in a conspiracy. Contrary to popular conception most drug users were not anxious to proselyte new users. Of course, spreading the habit would have the function of increasing the possible sources of supply. But an equally strong disposition was to keep the knowledge of drug use secret, to impress and dazzle the audience with one's knowledge of being "in the know." When proselyting did occur, as in jails or lockups, it was proselyting on the part of a devotee who condescended to share with the uninitiated a highly prized practice and set of attitudes.

As he elaborates his analysis of play, Huizinga brings to the fore additional aspects of the concept which also have their apt counterpart in the way of life of the cat. For instance, as was discussed earlier, the cat's appreciation of "progressive music" is an essential part of his social orientation. About this topic Huizinga remarks, "Music, as we have hinted before, is the highest and purest expression of the *facultas ludendi*."[12] The cat's attitude toward music has a sacred, almost mystical quality. "Progressive music" opens doors to a type of highly valued experience which for him can be had in no other way. It is more important to him than eating and is second only to the "kick." He may have to give up his hope of dressing according to his standards but he never gives up music.

Huizinga also observes, "Many and close are the links that connect play with beauty."[13] He refers to the "profoundly aesthetic quality of play."[14] The aesthetic emphasis which seems so central to the style of living of the cat is a subtle elusive accent permeating his whole outlook but coming to clearest expression in a constellation of interests, the "kick," clothing, and music. And it certainly reaches a level of awareness in their language. Language is utilized by the cat with a conscious relish, with many variations and individual turns of phrase indicating the value placed upon creative expression in this medium.

It is to be noted that much of the description of the cat's attributes did not deal exclusively with elements unique to him.

Many of the features mentioned are prevalent among adolescents in all reaches of the status scale. Dress, music, language, and the search for pleasure are all familiar themes of the adolescent world. For instance, in his description of the adolescent "youth culture" Talcott Parsons would appear to be presenting the generic traits of a "play-form" with particular reference to its expression in the middle class.

It is at the point of emergence into adolescence that there first begins to develop a set of patterns and behavior phenomena which involve a highly complex combination of age grading and sex role elements. These may be referred to together as the phenomena of the "youth culture." . . .

Perhaps the best single point of reference for characterizing the youth culture lies in its contrast with the dominant pattern of the adult male role. By contrast with the emphasis on responsibility in this role, the orientation of the youth culture is more or less specifically irresponsible. One of its dominant roles is "having a good time." . . . It is very definitely a rounded humanistic pattern rather than one of competence in the performance of specified functions.[15]

Such significant similarities between this description and the themes of the social type of the cat only tend to reinforce the notion that the recent spread of heroin use was a problem of adolescence. The cat is an adolescent sharing many of the interests of his age-mates everywhere but confronted by a special set of problems of color, tradition, and identity.

The social orientation of the cat, with its emphasis on non-violence, was quite in contrast to the orientation of the smaller group of young white drug users who were interviewed in the course of this study. The latter's type of adjustment placed a heavy stress upon violence. Their crimes tended to represent direct attacks against persons and property. The general disposition they manifested was one of "nerve" and brashness rather than one of "playing it cool." They did not cultivate the amenities of language, music, or dress to nearly the same extent as the cat. Their social orientation was expressed as a direct rather than an indirect attack on the dominant values of our society. This indicates that the "youth culture" despite its generic features may vary significantly in different social settings.

In his paper, "Some Jewish Types of Personality," Louis Wirth made the following suggestive comments about the relationship between the social type and its setting.

A detailed analysis of the crucial personality types in any given area or cultural group shows that they depend upon a set of habits and attitudes in the group for their existence and are the direct expressions of the values of the group. As the life of the group changes there appears a host of new social types, mainly outgrowths and transformations of previous patterns which have become fixed through experience.[16]

What are some of the sources of the various elements going to make up the social type of the cat which may be sought in his traditions? The following suggestions are offered as little more than speculation at the present time. The emphasis upon non-violence on the part of the cat, upon manipulative techniques rather than overt attack, is a stress upon the indirect rather than the direct way toward one's goal. May not the cat in this emphasis be betraying his debt to the "Uncle Tom" type of adjustment, despite his wish to dissociate himself from earlier patterns of accommodation to the dominant white society? May not the "kick" itself be a cultural lineal descendant of the ecstatic moment of religious possession so dear to revivalist and store-front religion? Similarly, may not the emphasis upon the exploitation of the woman have its origin in the traditionally greater economic stability of the colored woman?

W. I. Thomas in one of his references to the problems raised by the city environment stated, "Evidently the chief problem is the young American person."[17] In discussing the type of inquiry that would be desirable in this area he states that it should

lead to a more critical discrimination between that type of disorganization in the youth which is a real but frustrated tendency to organize on a higher plane, or one more correspondent with the moving environment, and that type of disorganization which is simply the abandonment of standards. It is also along this line . . . that we shall gain light on the relation of fantastic phantasying to realistic phantasying. . . .[18]

Posed in this way the problem becomes one of evaluating the social type of the cat in relation to the processes of social change. This social type is difficult to judge according to the criterion suggested by Thomas. Since many of the cat's interests are merely an extreme form of the adolescent "youth culture," in part the problem becomes one of determining how functional the period of adolescence is as preparation for subsequent adult status. However, the central phases of the social orientation of the cat, the "hustle" and the "kick," do represent a kind of disorganization which indicates the abandonment of conventional standards. The young addicted cat is "going nowhere." With advancing age he cannot shed his addiction the way he can many of the other trappings of adolescence. He faces only the bleak prospect, as time goes on, of increasing demoralization. Although the plight of the young colored addict is intimately tied to the conditions and fate of his racial group, his social orientation seems to represent a dead-end type of adjustment. Just as Handlin in *The Uprooted* suggests that the first generation of immigrant peoples to our society tends to be a sacrificed generation,[19] it may be that the unique problems of Negro migrants to our metropolitan areas will lead to a few or several sacrificed generations in the course of the tortuous process of urbanization.

The discussion of the social type of the cat leads inevitably to the issue of social control. Any attempt to intervene or modify the social processes producing the "cat" as a social type must have the objective of reducing his group isolation. For instance, because of such isolation and because of the cat's sensitivity to the gestures of his peers, the most significant role models of a given generation of cats tend to be the cats of the preceding age group. Where, in a period of rapid change, the schemes of behavior of the role models no longer correspond to the possibilities in the actual situation, it is possible for attitudes to be transmitted to a younger generation which evidence a kind of "cultural lag." Thus the condition of the labor market in Chicago is such as to suggest the existence of plentiful employment opportunities for the Negro in a variety of fields. But because such openings are not mediated to him through role models it is possible that the cat is unable to take advantage of these opportunities or the facilities available for training for such positions.

The social type of the cat is a product of social change. The type of social orientation which it has elaborated indicates an all too acute awareness of the values of the broader social order. In an open class society where upward mobility is positively sanctioned, an awareness and sensitivity to the dominant values is the first stage in their eventual assimilation. Insofar as the social type of the cat represents a reaction to a feeling of exclusion from access to the means toward the goals of our society, all measures such as improved educational opportunities which put these means within his grasp will hasten the extinction of this social type. Just as the "hoodlum" and "gangster" types tend to disappear as the various more recently arrived white ethnic groups tend to move up in the status scale of the community,[20] so it can confidently be expected that the cat as a social type will tend to disappear as such opportunities become more prevalent among the colored population.

1. Harold Finestone, "Narcotics and Criminality," *Law and Contemporary Problems*, 22 (Winter, 1957), 60-85.
2. Herbert Blumer, "Social Movements," in Robert E. Park, editor, *An Outline of the Principles of Sociology*, New York: Barnes & Noble, 1939, 255-278.
3. St. Clair Drake and Horace R. Clayton, "Lower Class: Sex and Family," in *Black Metropolis*, New York: Harcourt, Brace & World, 1945, 564-599.
4. Johan Huizinga, *Homo Ludens: A Study of the Play Element in Culture*, Boston: Beacon Press, 1955.
5. *Ibid.*, p. 3.
6. *Ibid.*, p. 7.
7. *Ibid.*, p. 8.
8. *Ibid.*, p. 8.
9. Gunnar Myrdal, *An American Dilemma*, New York: Harper & Row, 1944, p. 760.
10. E. Franklin Frazier, *Black Bourgeoisie*, New York: The Free Press of Glencoe, 1957, p. 237.
11. Huizinga, *op. cit.*, p. 9.
12. *Ibid.*, p. 187.
13. *Ibid.*, p. 7.
14. *Ibid.*, p. 2.
15. Talcott Parsons, "Age and Sex in the Social Structure of the United States," in *Essays in Sociological Theory*, New York: The Free Press of Glencoe, 1954, 91-92.
16. Louis Wirth, "Some Jewish Types of Personality," in Ernest W. Burgess, editor, *The Urban Community*, Chicago: University of Chicago Press, 1926, p. 112.
17. William I. Thomas, "The Problem of Personality in the Urban Environment," in Ernest W. Burgess, editor, *The Urban Community, op. cit.*, p. 46.
18. *Ibid.*, p. 47.
19. Oscar Handlin, *The Uprooted*, New York: Grosset & Dunlap, 1951, p. 243.
20. Daniel Bell, "Crime as an American Way of Life," *Antioch Review*, 13 (June, 1953), 141-154.